FLIGHT BY ELEPHANT

The Untold Story of World War Two's Most Daring Jungle Rescue

ANDREW MARTIN

LARGE PRINT

Oxford

Copyright © Andrew Martin, 2013

First published in Great Britain 2013
by
Fourth Estate
a Division of HarperCollins*Publishing*

Published in Large Print 2014 by ISIS Publishing Ltd.,
7 Centremead, Osney Mead, Oxford OX2 0ES
by arrangement with
HarperCollins*Publishing*

CIP data is available for this title from the British Library

ISBN 978–0–7531–5344–4 (hb)
ISBN 978–0–7531–5345–1 (pb)

Printed and bound in Great Britain by
T. J. International Ltd., Padstow, Cornwall

FLIGHT BY ELEPHANT

CONTENTS

N

CHAUKAN PASS

MARGHERITA •
• PUTAO
SHINGBIWYANG •
SUMPRABUM •
HUKAWNG VALLEY
DIMAPUR •
MYITKYINA •
IMPHAL •
CHINA
• TAMU
INDIA
LASHIO •
MANDALAY •
(SHAN
STATES)
INDO-
CHINA
BURMA
AKYAB •
PROME •
Bay of
Bengal
THAILAND
RANGOON •
Andaman
Sea
Gulf
of
Siam

ASSAM

BURMA 1942, SHOWING PRINCIPAL
EVACUATION ROUTES

-------- EVACUATION ROUTES

0   100   200 miles

0   100   200 300 km

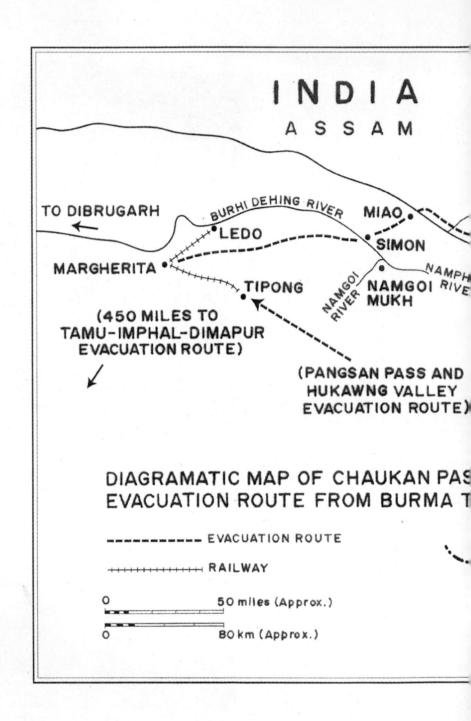

INDIA
ASSAM

TO DIBRUGARH

BURHI DEHING RIVER

MIAO

LEDO

SIMON

MARGHERITA

NAMGOI RIVER

TIPONG

NAMGOI MUKH

NAMPH... RIVE...

(450 MILES TO
TAMU-IMPHAL-DIMAPUR
EVACUATION ROUTE)

(PANGSAN PASS AND
HUKAWNG VALLEY
EVACUATION ROUTE)

DIAGRAMATIC MAP OF CHAUKAN PAS...
EVACUATION ROUTE FROM BURMA T...

- - - - - - - - - - - EVACUATION ROUTE

+++++++++++++ RAILWAY

0   50 miles (Approx.)

0   80 km (Approx.)

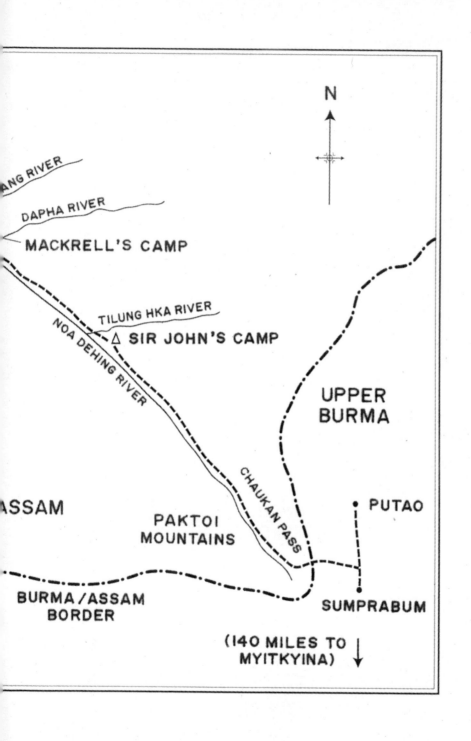

PRINCIPAL CHARACTERS

(In approximate order of appearance)

Guy Millar: a tea planter. Early in the war, he had been engaged on secret "government work", surveying the terrain of Upper Burma.

Goal Miri: an Assamese elephant tracker, and Millar's servant.

John Leyden: a colonial administrator in Upper Burma; owner of a pregnant spaniel bitch called Misa.

Sir Reginald Dorman-Smith: Governor of Burma, the elegant product of Harrow, Cambridge, Sandhurst.

George Rodger: British photographer and correspondent for the American magazine, *Life*.

In "The Railway Party" . . .
— Sir John Rowland: Chief Railway Commissioner of Burma (the top man on Burma Railways). In 1942, he was sixty years old, and working on "the Burma-China construction", a projected railway between Burma and China. He was the leader of the "railway party" of refugees, and he drove them on hard.

— Edward Lovell Manley: Chief Engineer of the Eastern Bengal Railway, he assisted Sir John on the Burma-China project. In the jungle, Sir John designated Manley his "number two". He was fifty-six years old.

— Eric Ivan Milne: District Traffic Superintendent of Burma State Railways; keen amateur cricketer and committed Christian.

— C. L. Kendall: railway surveyor on the Burma-China project.

— Captain A. O. Whitehouse: officer of the Royal Engineers.

— N. Moses: enigmatic Dutch railway surveyor, sometime magician and "international boy scout".

— E. Eadon: Anglo-Indian "anti-malarial inspector" on the Burma-China project.

— Dr Burgess-Barnett: medical doctor and Superintendent of Rangoon Zoological Gardens. In the jungle, Sir John designated him "PMO" (Principal Medical Officer).

In "Rossiter's Party" (sub-group of the above) . . .

— Edward Wrixon Rossiter: Colonial administrator of Upper Burma; member of the Anglo-Irish gentry, accomplished linguist and maverick.

— Nang Hmat: Rossiter's pregnant Burmese wife.

— John Rossiter: six-month-old baby son of Edward Rossiter and Nang Hmat.

Ronald Jardine: white-bearded devout Catholic; senior employee of Lever Brothers, soap manufacturers.

Frank Kingdon-Ward: botanist, explorer and loner. (He bore the nickname "Old Kingdom Come".)

Gyles Mackrell: fifty-three-year-old former fighter pilot, supervisor of tea plantations, elephant expert; the leader of the rescue.

Chaochali: Assamese; Mackrell's chief "elephant man".

"The Commandos" . . .
— Ritchie Gardiner: Scottish timber merchant and jungle wallah (a man adept at jungle-living). As one of the "last ditchers" he had helped blow up the infrastructure of Rangoon to keep it from the Japanese.
— Lieutenant Eric McCrindle: timber merchant and jungle wallah.
— Captain Ernest Boyt: as above. Very gung-ho; willing to march through uncharted jungle with "just biscuits and cheese".
— Second Lieutenant Bill Howe: rice trader (therefore not a jungle wallah); at thirty, he was the youngest of the Commandos, and the most ebullient.

A unit of the Special Operations network called The Oriental Mission, and a sub-group of the Commandos:
— Major Lindsay
— Captain Cumming
— Corporal Sawyer

Captain Fraser: escapee from Japanese captivity; he lost his glasses in the process.

Sergeant Pratt: escaped with the above, losing his boots in the process.

Captain Reg Wilson: tea planter, and officer in a special operations unit called V Force. A handsome, chain-smoking young Yorkshireman who "loved sport and loved action", Wilson was dispatched by the British authorities to replace Mackrell as head of the rescue.

Dr Bardoloi: Wilson's Principal Medical Officer.

Havildar Iman Sing: Gurkha sergeant and jungle wallah.

Wing Commander George Chater: RAF pilot, sometime dinner guest of Sir John Rowland.

Dispatched to attempt another rescue after Mackrell abandoned the Dapha camp:
— Mr Black: senior liaison officer with the Indian Tea Association relief effort.
— Captain Street: officer in the 2nd Rajputan Rifles.
— Webster: a policeman.

Havildar Dharramsing: Gurkha sergeant and jungle wallah; Mackrell's principal assistant in the later stages of the mission.

AUTHOR'S NOTE

This book is principally — and closely — based on the diaries of Guy Millar, Gyles Mackrell, Sir John Rowland, Captain Reg Wilson, Second Lieutenant Bill Howe and Ritchie Gardiner. Given the circumstances it is amazing that these diaries were written at all, but they are often sparse, and sometimes dwindle into telegraphese. Therefore, I have made some small embellishments. All quoted speech is as recorded in the diaries, but sometimes I have speculated as to a character's thoughts based on the preoccupations of the particular day and time as transcribed.

I have occasionally tried to evoke jungle scenes based on my having visited the jungles in question rather than because they are precisely so described in the diaries. And if, say, Gyles Mackrell mentions that it is raining on Thursday and Saturday, I might have concluded — given that he was in the middle of a monsoon — that it was raining on the Friday in between. I contend that it would be impossible to tell this story without such interventions, and it is a story that deserves to be told.

Andrew Martin

INTRODUCTION

In the monsoon season of 1942, deep in the jungles of the Indo-Burmese border, Captain Reg Wilson wrote of our principal, Gyles Mackrell, that he "knew what an E. could do". An "E" was an elephant.

Mackrell knew how to manage elephants as beasts of burden; he also knew how to kill an elephant with a single bullet if — and only if — it had gone rogue. He knew how to manage the elephant riders, or mahouts, who were known to be stroppy, a tendency exacerbated in many cases by a bad opium habit. If a cane and rope suspension bridge had been washed away by a swollen river, Mackrell knew whether it might be possible to cross that river on the back of an elephant; he knew which of any given herd of elephants might be best suited by strength and temperament to attempt the feat, and whether it might be best accomplished by the elephant swimming or wading. He would be perfectly willing to climb aboard the elephant himself rather than leave the job to the mahouts because he was a man who not only enjoyed a physical challenge, he also seemed to live for risk taking.

1

Gyles Mackrell went to the sort of minor English public school where the sinks had two cold taps, where a lecture on the Benin Massacre was classed as "entertainment", where visiting military men donated leopard skins and trophy animal heads for the adornment of the library rather than books, and where the pedagogical aim was to produce young men capable of assuming the white man's burden. It was not an intellectual environment and Mackrell was certainly no intellectual. In an age when "bottom of the class" was an official status (since the rankings were published every term) Mackrell repeatedly occupied that very position. Yet he had great practical intelligence, and the diaries disclose an elegant, spare writing style. He was not the all-purpose "hearty": he does not seem to have featured in any of the first, second, or even third elevens; his school did not make him one of those Edwardian boors with a caddish moustache and a racist turn of phrase, but in his late teens he did have a hankering after a life of adventure, and the British Empire was there to provide it. So Gyles Mackrell became a tea planter in Assam, India.

Unlike Australia or Canada, British India was not a colony in the literal sense. Its only settlers were the tea planters. In order to create their plantations they had to clear the jungle, but the jungle kept coming back. The tiger wandering through the living room of the bungalow was not an unknown sight to the Assamese planters and their wives, who wore galoshes in their flower gardens against snake bites. Elephants, when they were behaving, were the planters' allies in the animal kingdom, whether they were used for uprooting trees — which an elephant does by leaning casually on the tree — or for carrying cargo, or simply as a runabout: a means of getting the planter to his club for the six o'clock whisky and soda. A late nineteenth-century manual for aspirant tea planters describes the elephant as "the most useful brute in Asia".

Before the First World War, the planters' main enemy was Mother Nature. Their military involvement had been confined to membership of picturesque part-time cavalry regiments which, in between mess lunches and polo tournaments, mounted occasional expeditions against troublesome local tribes. The First World War did not touch the tea planters of Assam directly, although many of them volunteered to fight in Europe or the Middle East. Gyles Mackrell himself chose the almost suicidal option of becoming a fighter pilot on the Western Front with the Royal Flying Corps, a job carrying an average life expectancy shorter even than the six weeks an infantry officer could bargain for. Later in the war he was posted to conduct what were mainly surveillance operations against the rebellious Muslim tribes on the North-Western Frontier. In the flimsy death-trap planes of the time, Squadron Leader Mackrell, as he had now become, patrolled the skies over Waziristan in temperatures of 120 degrees Fahrenheit. At any one time more than half the flyers engaged on such missions were sick, which is not to say that the peril was not greater for the tribesmen beneath, who were sometimes bombed in their mud huts.

The volatile North-West Frontier was regarded as the Achilles heel of British India throughout the First World War, but, in the Second World War, the North-Eastern Frontier also became vulnerable as a result of the Japanese invasion of Burma. In the first half of 1942, the Japanese squeezed the British out of Burma like toothpaste from a tube, starting from the bottom. Tens of thousands of British soldiers, administrators and businessmen, and the million-strong retinue of Indian and Anglo-Indian servants and workers who had buttressed British rule in Burma, were harried into Upper Burma, from where they attempted to flee to the safety of Assam. They had no choice but to do so by walking through mountainous and malarial jungle in monsoon rain.

So the war came to the tea planters in the form of a tide of refugees. In response the planters mounted — their critics would say they were prevailed upon to mount — a relief effort. In conjunction with their wives, and their own Indian servants and workers, they deployed their logistical skills (the planters were great "organization men"), their medical supplies, their stores of food, their tractors, lorries, horses, ponies and elephants to assist what was called "the walkout". The planters built roads and established staging posts in the jungles for the refugees to be given medical treatment, food and, above all, tea. The first sign of these camps to the starving refugees staggering in from Burma was a stall in the jungle from which tea and biscuits were being dispensed; tea would be kept brewing throughout

4

their brief stay at these camps, one of which was officially called the "Tea Pot Pub".

Tea is the British panacea and cure-all, and it is fondly suggested that our response to any disaster is "put the kettle on". Here was the same reflex action on a huge scale, the disaster being the unprecedented collapse of a prop of the British Empire, triggering death by disease or starvation for hundreds of thousands.

What follows is the story of an episode within that epic disaster. It focuses on the most obscure and also the most treacherous of the evacuation routes from Burma. Before 1942 the number of Europeans who had followed that route could have been counted in single figures, and most of them were eccentrics with a taste for reckless action. None, however, were so mad as to attempt the feat in the monsoon season.

The hero of the story is probably the above-mentioned Mackrell. In 1942, he was fifty-three. In British India professional lives were foreshortened by the climate and the physical demands of the life. When a man reached his fifties, it was time to think of returning home, ideally to some coastal town — Eastbourne in Sussex was a popular choice — where bracing air would provide a corrective to years of stifling humidity. For Gyles Mackrell, fighter pilot, big game hunter, jungle wallah, the relief operation mounted by the Indian Tea Association provided a last chance to live life as he had grown addicted to living it: dangerously. The beauty of the situation to him was that, if he could take elephants and boats deeper "into the blue" than they had ever been taken before, he would have the reward of saving lives.

But the crisis brought out the best in other people as well, and the characters of the drama are presented as an ensemble cast. They are, in the main, middle-class British men, and they were often accompanied by Indian servants or received other assistance from the indigenous peoples, and to these two groups must go a great deal of the credit for such successes as the white men achieved, as Gyles Mackrell and most of the other principals pointed out. In particular Gurkha soldiers gave assistance, playing their habitual role of rescuing the British from messes of their own making. But it is the white men who kept the diaries, and they are therefore in the foreground of our story, which begins not with Mackrell and his elephants, but with two men for whom some elephants would have been very useful indeed.

Millar and Leyden:
The Men Without Elephants

On 19 May 1942 two Englishmen, Guy Millar and John Leyden, entered the Chaukan Pass in Upper Burma with the aim of reaching civilization in Assam, India. The pass — a vaguely defined groove through mountainous sub-tropical jungle, with fast-flowing rivers coming in from left and right — was either unmarked on most maps or dishearteningly stamped "unsurveyed".

Millar and Leyden did not want to be in the Chaukan Pass, but they had no choice.

John Leyden himself had been overheard describing the pass route as "suicidal" shortly before he set off along it. We know that Millar, who was keeping a diary as he entered the pass, was uneasily aware that very few Europeans had ever been through it before, and he seemed to recall that fatalities had usually been involved.

In the last decade of the nineteenth century, a few European parties had been through the Chaukan: Errol Gray, an elephant expert resident in Assam, had done

7

it, as had a certain Pritchard, whom nobody knows much about. Prince Henri of Orleans also traversed the pass in that decade, but then here was a man whose life seems marked by a determination to get himself killed. (Henri of Orleans discovered the source of the Irrawaddy river in 1893, earning himself a gold medal from the Royal Geographical Society in London, despite his being, as the *Encyclopaedia Britannica* of 1911 puts it, "a somewhat violent Anglophobe". In fact, he was somewhat violent full stop, and in 1897 he wounded, and was himself wounded by, the Comte de Turin in a duel.) All the above were accompanied by numerous elephants and porters.

In 1892, a quite well-known double act of English exploration, Woodthorpe and MacGregor — that is, Colonel R. G. Woodthorpe, a surveyor in the Royal Engineers, and Major C. R. MacGregor of the Gurkha Light Infantry — went from Assam to Burma *and back* through the Chaukan. But, then, they were accompanied by two fellow officer of the British Indian Army, forty-five Gurkhas, twenty-five men of the Indian Frontier Police "together with" — as Major MacGregor airily informed the Royal Geographical Society on his return — "the usual complement of native surveyors, coolies, & c". They also had with them a great builder of bamboo bridges and rafts (in the person of Colonel Woodthorpe himself), together with something called a "Berthon's collapsible boat" — the collapsing and uncollapsing of which caused wonderment among the tribes they encountered — and "some" elephants, the number of which MacGregor does not specify.

The rule of thumb in Upper Burma and Assam in 1942 was that a human porter carrying 50lbs of rice through the jungle must himself consume a minimum of 2lbs of that rice every day. An elephant, by contrast, can carry only 600lbs of food on its back and doesn't need to eat any of it, since it eats the jungle as it goes. Alternatively, an elephant can carry six large men on its back, together with its human assistant, the mahout (who is usually very small). An elephant's normal marching speed is six miles an hour, twice as fast as a man. With men on board, elephants can climb steep embankments — which they usually do on their knees. They can also carry men across fast-flowing rivers, and this is where the elephant really comes into its own on the Assam — Burma border: as a portable bridge. This is a territory where rivers are the problem and elephants are the answer.

But Millar and Leyden didn't have any elephants with them. Instead, they had an elephant *tracker*, a young Assamese man called Goal Miri (Miri denotes his tribe) who was skilled at finding and following the tracks that wild elephants made through the jungles, and was retained by Millar as his personal servant. They also had a dozen porters recruited from the Kachin, one of the Upper Burmese tribes more sympathetic to the British, and Leyden's spaniel bitch, Misa, who was pregnant.

Millar and Leyden had set off from Upper Burma on 17 May with enough rice, potatoes, onions, sugar, condensed milk and — being British — tea for fourteen days. They had to reach India before their supplies ran

9

out because the jungle could not be guaranteed to yield up any food, and the country along their route was uninhabited. They were aiming for the Dapha river. Only when they reached it would they know they were on target for the plain of Assam, but they also knew that when they did reach the Dapha they would have to cross it. This wasn't going to be easy. In 1892, Errol Gray had pronounced the Dapha "not fordable after early March" on account of the meltwaters of the Himalayas. On top of that, Millar and Leyden were approaching the Dapha in the monsoon season, the rains having started about a week before they entered the pass. All previous expeditions through the Chaukan had taken place in the cold weather season — in December and January — when the many rivers are singing but not roaring.

On the morning of that first day, 19 May, Millar and Leyden crossed a relatively small but meandering river called the Nam Yak. They then crossed it a further seventeen times, each encounter preceded by the depressing sound of its rising roar coming from beyond the trees. They would half wade, half swim over the river. The water was chest-high for Millar and Leyden, but higher for the Kachins, most of whom were about five feet tall — one of the pygmy tribes, as the early British settlers in Burma would have referred to them.

After three days, Millar and Leyden emerged from the Chaukan Pass, but the mountainous jungle continued. In fact, as Millar noted in his diary, "the going became still more difficult". They were descending only slowly from a height of about 8000 feet. They proceeded, slashing with their kukris (or large, curved knives) along the elephant tracks Goal Miri had identified, which at first, or even second, glance didn't look like tracks at all. Or they would follow the banks of the rivers. Hitherto, these had tended to go across their direction of travel, but when they came out of the pass, Millar and Leyden struck a river that was going their way — that is, west. It was called the Noa Dehing.

They couldn't cross the Noa Dehing, which was about 400 yards wide, and sunk in a deep, jungly gorge. They couldn't even *see* across it, steaming rain having reduced the visibility to almost nil. They were therefore stuck on the right-hand bank — and this confirmed their appointment with the Dapha, which was a tributary of the Noa Dehing shortly to come thundering in from the right. Meanwhile, it was usually better to follow the bank of the Noa Dehing than hack away at the jungle.

So Millar and Leyden walked along the stones at the water's edge — when there *was* an edge to the water — as opposed to a vertical wall of red mud. Some of these stones, Millar wrote, were about the size and shape of a cricket ball, and threatened to twist your ankle. Others were about the size and shape of a small house, so Millar and Leyden would climb up, across and down, often descending into deep pools, so that the leather of their boots began to rot. When the vertical mud wall was the only option, they proceeded monkey-like, holding onto the roots of trees or stout bamboos. It is unlikely that they talked much as they climbed. Their voices would have been drowned out by the crashing past of the river; and a malnourished man finds it hard to talk. It becomes a labour to formulate the thoughts and pronounce the words.

The rain made it hard to light the fires they needed at night to boil up their rice. They had to search the undergrowth for dry bamboo, which they cut into slivers to make kindling. This they then tried to ignite, but the Lion Safety Matches of India and Burma were considered by many of their users all *too* safe: the sulphur tended to drop off the end when they were struck, or they would break in half.

When bamboo does burn, it makes a mellow bubbling, popping sound. Every night after they'd eaten their rice, Millar and Leyden made tea: Assam leaves swirling in a brew tin full of river water. G. D. L. Millar was a tea planter from Assam — manager of the Kacharigaon Tea Company — and never let it be said of the British tea planters of India that they did not consume their own product.

On one those early evenings by the fire, Leyden took a photograph of Millar; it shows a tough forty-two-year-old, unshaven, standing in front of a bamboo fire. The porters crouch around him Burmese-style, like close fielders around a batsman; he wears loose fatigues and the manner in which he holds his cigarette is slightly rakish. Millar was christened Guy Daisy. In the Edwardian days of his birth, Daisy could be a boy's name; it might be further explained in Millar's case by the fact that he was born on a farm in Cornwall. Daisy means nothing more incriminating than "the day's eye" and you might think it would suit an outdoorsman. But Millar made that "D" stand for Denny.

He was on a three-month release from the Kacharigaon Tea Company in order to do "government work" in Upper Burma (and we shall come to the question of what that had involved) in the company of Goal Miri and a cranky sixty-four-year-old botanist called Frank Kingdon-Ward.

Before coming to Millar's companion, Leyden, a word about that cigarette of Millar's. How had he kept it dry when crossing all these rivers in monsoon rains? There will be a lot of cigarettes in this story, a lot of rivers and a lot of rain, so it is a question worth asking.

The cigarettes of the day usually came in cylindrical tins about two and a half inches in diameter. The tins were sealed below the lid. A small, levered blade was set into the lid; you pressed it down and rotated the lid in order to break the seal. Until then, the tin was entirely waterproof, and it was still *fairly* waterproof afterwards. The tins, which contained fifty cigarettes, were too big to put in a normal pocket, so most people decanted them into a slim cigarette case — but cigarette cases were for the drawing room, and in the jungle Millar smoked his straight from the tin.

Millar's travelling companion, John Leyden, was a civil servant of British Burma, a colonial administrator. He could be loosely referred to as a DC, or Deputy Commissioner. More correctly, he was a sub-divisional officer of the North Burmese district of Myitkyina where, according to *Thacker's Indian Directory*, the languages spoken included Burmese, Kachin, Hindustani,

Lisu, Gurkhali and Chinese. Myitkyina was the last decent-sized town in Burma; the railway ended there, but a dusty mule track snaked north from the town, through a mosquito-infested jungle and scrub unfrequented by Europeans apart from the odd orchid collector. The path winds towards a small settlement of green and red houses perched on top of a treeless green hill, like a place in a fairy story. This was Sumprabum, the centre of Leyden's particular sub-division. (And while we are in this remote vicinity, let us note an even narrower track winding down the hill and meandering still further north to an even smaller, even more malarial settlement called Putao.)

John Lamb Leyden was born into a distinguished Scottish family, and was a descendant of another orientalist, John Leyden (1775–1811), poet, physician and antiquary, who ran the Madras General Hospital and held various official posts in Calcutta. Ominously for John Lamb Leyden, his ancestor died of fever on an expedition to Java.

We have a photograph of John Lamb Leyden on his trek — probably taken by Millar after Leyden had taken *his*. It shows a cerebral looking man with swept-back, receding hair. At thirty-eight, Leyden was younger than Millar, but looked older. Next to him, a bamboo fire smoulders thickly. He and Millar would light these at every camp, hoping the smoke would attract the planes that periodically flew overhead, but as Millar wrote, ". . . on each occasion failure to observe us was apparent". They had no tents, so every evening they

14

spent a couple of hours building a hut of the type known locally as a basha.

How do you build a basha?

In a lecture entitled "Keeping Fit in the Jungle", given to the Bengal Club of Calcutta in early 1943, Captain Alastair Tainsh explained:

> The way to keep fit in the jungle is exactly the same as anywhere else. All one needs is sound sleep, clean water, a reasonable diet, and a liberal use of soap and water. But how is sound sleep to be obtained? Well, one must learn how to make oneself comfortable in the worst conditions. It is not being tough or clever to sit in the open all night . . . The easiest form of shelter to build is made by fixing two upright poles in the ground eight or nine feet apart. To the top of these is bound a long bamboo making a frame like goal posts. The roof is made by leaning a number of poles against the top bar forming an angle of about 45 degrees with the ground. A number of parallel bamboos are tied to the sloping poles and into this framework banana or junput leaves are thatched.

Then you had to build a chung, or sleeping platform, to keep the leeches off, and sometimes Millar and Leyden couldn't be bothered to do any of this, so they'd sleep in the crooks of trees. They always kept a fire burning in case a tiger should turn up, although as Millar wrote, about a week into their trek: ". . . this stretch of country is uninhabited for over a hundred miles. Not only is there not a trace of man, but mammal and even bird life is conspicuous by its absence; truly a forgotten world, where solitude reigns supreme."

Here, too, we can invoke the voice of reason himself, Captain Tainsh:

Nearly everyone is a little frightened when they hear they must work and live in the jungle. The word "jungle" conjures up in their minds a place literally swarming with lions, tigers, elephants and snakes. Nothing could be further from the truth, because wild animals and even snakes need food, and such wild animals as there are, live on the edge of cultivation, and are seldom seen in the thicker parts of the forest.

The larger animals are particularly scarce in the monsoon, when they retreat to the margins of the jungle, to avoid the leeches and mosquitoes that proliferate in the rains. Against these torments, Millar and Leyden slept with their heads wrapped in blankets but still Millar wrote, "Of the leeches, blister flies and sandflies I cannot give adequate description, sufficient it is to say that we were getting into a mess." For most of the nights, they didn't sleep at all, but just listened to the sound of rain drumming on palms or bamboo. In the morning, the rising heat of the day made clouds of steam rise up from the muddy jungle floor like smoke from a bonfire.

By 26 May, with nine of their fourteen days of food gone, there was no sign of the Dapha river, and Millar and Leyden were down to one cigarette tin of rice per man per day.

Why had these men entered the Chaukan Pass?

To escape something worse coming from behind.

The Languorous Dream

On the morning of 7 December 1941, the Imperial Japanese Navy attacked the American Pacific Fleet at Pearl Harbor and entered the Second World War. They wanted "Asia for the Asiatics", and for the Japanese especially. During the ensuing offensives — which have been called "the biggest land grab in history" — some Japanese soldiers carried a postcard to be filled out and sent home at a moment of leisure. It showed a cartoon of a Japanese soldier with a blank space where the face ought to have been. The sender inserted a photograph of himself, thus becoming the depicted soldier, who held two grinning children in his arms while a further two clung onto his knee-high puttees. The children — who waved the Japanese flag with their free hands — represented Malaya, the Pacific islands, China and the Dutch East Indies. Japan had appropriated eastern and central China in 1938. They would "liberate", as they liked to put it, the British colony of Malaya in March 1942. By the end of that month, New Guinea, largest of the Pacific islands, had been taken, and the Dutch East Indies had surrendered. No child represented the British colony of Burma, but that, too, was taken by the Japanese in early 1943.

That Burma did not have a child of its own shouldn't surprise us. It tended to be slighted in this way. Whereas Queen Victoria was, from 1877, the Empress of India, Burma was merely given to her as a "New Year's Gift" in 1886. She never went to Burma, but then she never went to India either. She didn't like "trips". The British had annexed Burma in 1886, following the third Anglo-Burmese War. There had been territorial disputes on the Burma — Assam border, and the British were concerned at French "interference" in the country. The British occupied Burma from the south and the west. They did not enter Burma from Assam, simply because there were no roads into Burma from Assam.

Prior to 1937 — when Burma was given a measure of self-government — Burma was by far the largest of the ten provinces of British India, but only two of those provinces had a smaller population. On the eve of the Second World War, seventeen million people inhabited a country as big as France and Belgium combined. To the British, it was like the field a householder buys to stop anyone building too near his own property, the property in this case being India.

The *Encyclopaedia of the British Empire: The First Encyclopaedic Record of the Greatest Empire in the History of the World*, Volume 2 (1924), is very pleased with the utility of Burma. The country

. . . forms the frontier with China, French Indo-China and Siam on the east, and the province of Assam in the north. Strategically, this province [Burma], which is often termed "Further India" is of considerable importance. It forms the east and north east coasts of the Bay of Bengal, and completes the semi-circle of British territory which encloses this great ocean highway to India. It was not conquered and annexed because of any premeditated plan of Imperial extension, but rather as a safeguard to India proper.

The passage continues to the effect that, with Burma up its sleeve, British India has no need to maintain a large fleet in the Bay of Bengal, or to keep large garrisons on the India-Burma border. The generals were thus able to concentrate on that more likely weak link of Indian defence, the North-West Frontier, while keeping Burma itself lightly garrisoned with just 6000 British and 3000 native troops. Tim Carew, author of *The Longest Retreat*, has a different perspective. The defence of Burma on the eve of the Second World War was, he writes, "ludicrously inadequate".

. . . Not least because Japan also wanted Burma as a buffer state: a 2000-mile-long protective wall to the west of its native islands. But Britain was insufficiently wary of the Japanese, who had been her allies (against Russia, the common bugbear) until 1921. To the British, the Japanese were small, dapper, decorous people, usually amusingly short-sighted, hence bespectacled. Emperor Hirohito seemed to fit the bill perfectly, as did the

Japanese consul in Rangoon (who, myopic or not, turned out to be running a network of spies drawn from the Japanese population of the city). For years after 1921, the Japanese enjoyed a good press, and they did not figure in the demonology set out by George Orwell in his famous essay of 1940 on boys' weekly comics. This ran:

Frenchman: Excitable. Wears beard, gesticulates wildly.
Spaniard, Mexican etc: Sinister, treacherous.
Arab, Afghan, etc: Sinister, treacherous.
Chinese: Sinister, treacherous. Wears pigtail.
Italian: Excitable. Grinds barrel-organ or carries stiletto.

The Japanese invasion of China in 1938 did cause a twinge of anxiety on Burma's behalf, and not only to Britain. In the first half of 1942, Burma was nominally defended by *three* Allied nations, but only half-heartedly in each case. To the British, Burma was a blind spot, as we have seen. Then there were the Chinese and the Americans, who defended Burma not for its own sake but because it was strategically significant in the battle of Chiang Kai-shek's Nationalist Chinese forces against the Japanese invader, which the Americans sought to assist. Both China and America saw Burma as a road: the Burma Road. That sounds like a major highway, but to European eyes it would have looked like not so much a minor road as a farm track. This lifeline for the Nationalist Chinese — since the eastern seaboard was under Japanese

21

occupation — had been opened in 1938: 600 miles of hairpin bends running through mountainous territory from Lashio, 500 miles north of Rangoon, into Kunming, China. America also added to the firepower within the Burmese borders, in the shape of the Flying Tigers, or the 1st American Volunteer Group of the Chinese Air Force. Its sixty or so planes — not enough — were decorated with the faces of sharks, and the flyers (paid such high wages by the Chinese that they have been characterized as mercenaries) were equally decorative, swaggering around Rangoon in their leather jackets.

But as far as the British were concerned, the role of the Flying Tigers was precautionary. After all, a Japanese invasion of Burma had been officially ruled out by Far Eastern Intelligence Bureau (an organization credited by Tim Carew with being "a mine of misinformation"). The Japanese couldn't possibly invade Burma. Proudly neutral Thailand was in the way ... unless Japan reached an accommodation with Thailand (which is just what happened, in October 1940).

It was as though the British in Burma, enervated by the climate, were sunk in a languorous dream: a world of white-turbaned servants bowing low in the clubs; of palms and jacaranda trees in the wide, white avenues of the city, with green parakeets skimming through the pale blue skies above; of pretty, pert Burmese women — unconfined by veil or purdah — sporting orchids in their piled-up hair, with golden bangles on their slender wrists. They would twirl their paper parasols while puffing coquettishly on outsize cheroots and generally presenting very good wife or (more likely) mistress material. Outside Rangoon, the flower-bedecked houses and shops ... the smiling villagers trundling by on slumberous bullock carts, through a shimmering countryside dotted with Christmas tree-like pagodas.

Burma offered a more leisurely life than India. Its branch of the Indian Civil Service was less competitive, and so attracted the more easy-going sahib. In *The Ruling Caste: Imperial Lives in the Victorian Raj*, David Gilmour writes that some members of the Indian Civil Service regarded Burma as "a place of banishment ... The climate was unhealthy and debilitating, especially in Upper Burma ... and the mosquitoes were so bad in some areas that even the cattle were put under nets at night." A vivid, if jaundiced, account of the life is given by George Orwell in his novel of 1934, *Burmese Days*, which is based on his experiences as a police officer in Upper Burma. The central character, Flory, works in the Forestry Department. In view of what would happen to the British in Burma, it is interesting that he seems half menaced by nature, half enraptured by it. He spends the cooler months in the jungle, the rest of the time in a bungalow on the edge of an Upper Burmese town. He describes Burma as "mostly jungle — a green, unpleasant land". In the garden of the town club, where the back numbers of *The Field* and the Edgar Wallace novels are mildewed by the humidity, some English flowers grow: phlox and larkspur, hollyhock and petunia. They will soon be "slain by the sun".

Meanwhile, they "rioted in vast size and richness". There is no English lawn, "but instead a shrubbery of native trees and bushes . . . mohur trees like vast umbrellas of blood-red bloom . . . purple bougainvillea, scarlet hibiscus . . . bilious green crotons . . . The clash of colours hurt one's eyes in the glare". Vultures hover in a dazzling sky; in early morning temperatures of 110 degrees Fahrenheit, the Englishmen of the club greet each other: "Bloody awful morning, what?"

The country grips him like a fever, and sometimes the effect is euphoric. When Flory meets Elizabeth Lackersteen, the love interest of the book (Flory's native mistress, Ma Hla May, cannot be so described), they bond over flowers. "Those zinnias are fine aren't they? — like painted flowers, with their wonderful dead colours. These are African marigolds. They're coarse things, weeds almost, but you can't help liking them . . . But I wish you'd come into the veranda and see the orchids."

Flory works some of the time "in the field", but even he gets lost on a short walk through the jungle with his own spaniel bitch, Flo. The box wallahs (office workers) of the British Secretariat would tend the flowers in the gardens of their bungalows at Maymyo, the hill station to which they repaired to escape the oven that was Rangoon in summer, just as their counterparts in Calcutta went to Darjeeling. They rode horses through the margins of the jungle, but they would not penetrate deeper, to encounter, say, the giant banana plants that might for all they knew be quite literally the biggest aspidistras in the world. The evening breeze might

24

bring the sound of a tiger's roar intermingled with the tinkling of the temple bells, but that tiger was safely confined in the Maymyo Zoo. The British were protected from the jungle by their punka-wallahs, their chowkeydars (nightwatchmen) on the veranda, by the elevation of their houses above the malarial ground, their quinine pills and the revolver in the study drawer.

The Governor of Burma, Sir Reginald Dorman-Smith (Harrow, Cambridge, Sandhurst), was a fitting leader for this decorous and unreal society. A very good-looking man — almost *too* good looking — with a fondness for fragrant pipe tobacco, Dorman-Smith had seen action briefly in the Great War, but his former tenure as Minister of Agriculture under Neville Chamberlain hinted at a bovine temperament. He was not the sort of man to notice that he sat atop a very rickety edifice.

Burma has been called an "anthropologist's paradise"; it might also have been called a colonialist's nightmare. Aside from a couple of battalions of British soldiers in Burma, the main defensive force was called the Burma Rifles, which had British officers and supposedly Burmese other ranks ... except that the soldiery of the Burma Rifles largely comprised ethnic minorities — the Shans of the east, Chins of the west, Kachins of the north, Karens of the south — because the loyalty of the indigenous Burmese could not be taken for granted.

The British in Burma were buttressed in their eminence by a million Indians. In Rangoon, they operated the infrastructure: drove the trams and trains, manned the docks, and they were hated by the Burmese, either for taking the jobs they themselves might have aspired to, or for abetting the imperial power. The Indians needed the social order to remain stable, otherwise they would be preyed upon by the Burmese dacoits, or criminal gangs, and the incidence of dacoity in Burma was high. The Burmese had rioted against the Indians in 1937, hence the granting of a measure of self-government, a reform that did not negate Burmese nationalism. In 1940, it had been necessary to arrest the first Burmese Premier to serve under the new dispensation, Baw Ma, on a charge of sedition. And with the coming of war, a Burmese Independence Army would at first fight alongside the Japanese invader before switching sides. Rising nationalism on the eve of the war had been manifested in an increasing intolerance of Europeans keeping their shoes on when visiting the pagodas. The ubiquitous sign "Footwearings not permitted" was ceasing to be a joke. But no alarm had been raised.

The Dapha River

May the twenty-sixth 1942, and it was still raining heavily in the jungle. With at best five days' food left, Millar and Leyden continued to follow the Noa Dehing, but had now moved to lower terrain. They were covered in sores, and their boots had fallen apart. At first, they had tried walking without boots, as the Kachin porters did, but that lacerated their feet. So they wound canes around their feet like bandages, and wore belts of reserve canes around their waists.

As they walked beneath the trees near the roaring river, they saw a tiger walking ahead on the same path. Even to "jungly" Englishmen — and Millar was more one of those than Leyden — the sight of a tiger would prompt an instinctive glance around for the cage from which it had escaped. The tiger walked on, and so did they "for some distance", not trying to catch it up, but not particularly lagging behind either. Millar *was* carrying his favourite single-action revolver; Leyden *was* carrying a rifle. In 1885, Major MacGregor had reported to the Royal Geographical Society: "A few tigers had also taken up their abode in the valley, a fact which came unpleasantly home to our coolies, two of whom, poor fellows, were carried out of camp at night by a man eater, who was, I am glad to say, eventually shot."

Millar and Leyden's tiger having veered off the path and jumped into the river, they came to a clearing where they saw a herd of sambhur, which are hairy deer. Sambhur don't look as if they belong in a jungle, or even a jungle clearing. They look as though they belong on a Highland moor in Scotland. The teeming rain added to the effect, even if the suffocating air detracted from it.

There were twenty-six sambhur. They had probably never seen a man before, and they continued to graze even as Goal Miri — who had requested the first shot — took Leyden's rifle and aimed. The porters ate their meat while it was still warm, and Millar and Leyden built a fire to cook theirs. The twenty-five surviving sambhur "just stood around in an interested sort of way, some lying down on the stones only sixty yards off".

When the tribes who live in the jungle clearings enter the jungle proper to hunt, they make obeisance to the spirits of the jungle, the nats. If something then goes wrong — say, a man is bitten by a snake — that shows permission had not been asked in the right way, or had been withheld or withdrawn, and the hunters leave the jungle. Of course, Millar and Leyden had not consulted the spirits before killing the sambhur, and they did not have the option of leaving.

They set off again reinvigorated. But an hour later, Leyden's spaniel was no longer behind them. Misa, at least, liked the jungle, and would frequently charge off into the undergrowth, but they called, and waited and . . . nothing. After a long search — reckless in the circumstances — they concluded that she must have fallen into the Noa Dehing gorge. Later still, when they were crossing a small river, Leyden was swirled off his feet, and cracked his head against a big rock. He said he was all right, but Millar kept a close eye on him from then on.

And the day still wasn't over.

When they lit the fire that night, Millar and Leyden discovered they had two days' less rice than they had thought. So they now only had enough to last them until 29 May. Then again, they calculated from the only two-inch map they possessed that had not been turned to pulp that the confluence of the Noa Dehing and the Dapha couldn't be more than six miles away. They ought to be there by the next day, the 27th.

That was, as Millar put it, "a dismal mistake".

On the 27th, it finally stopped raining, but their eternal companion, the Noa Dehing, chose that morning to present its steepest gorge yet, requiring from Millar and Leyden "the skills of trained climbers . . . Our fears for porters carrying loads were not without cause," Millar adds, without going into detail. The Dapha river did not appear that day, or the next; or the next.

On 31 May, their food had run out, "not a crumb of anything remained", and there was still no sign of the Dapha. To save strength, Millar and Leyden had jettisoned everything that was not essential: cooking

29

utensils, binoculars, cameras. On 31 May, Leyden stopped and sadly pitched his rifle into the gorge of the Noa Dehing river, then Millar did likewise with his "favourite single trigger gun". A gun is the most prized asset in the jungle, second only to a decent stash of opium and a few grains of quinine. But Millar did retain a *rifle*, a decision that would prove of the greatest importance.

The Noa Dehing still showed very heavy water, and remained uncrossable. They remained stuck on the right-hand side of it, with the Dapha surely looming. That river was like a prima donna, putting off its appearance to maximize the final effect. "I felt inwardly certain," wrote Millar, "that we could not ford it at this date."

At 2p.m. on 31 May, Millar and Leyden began to hear a louder river sound; it was the sound of *two* rivers, almost like the sound of a rough sea. At 3p.m., they came to what Millar described as "a delta" — the vast and foamy confluence of the Dapha and the Noa Dehing, and here was the moment of truth. Both rivers were hundreds of yards wide. Both carried leaping jungle debris in the form of whole 100-foot trees, complete with all branches and roots, to the intersection where they rotated in a giant, misty whirlpool. Looking at the confluence, Guy Millar felt sick.

The Red-Hot Buddhas

The bombing of Burma started on 11 December. The first raid on Rangoon itself came on 23 December at which point the residents would have recalled some elementary geography.

Rangoon was towards the south of a country bounded by sea and mountains to the west, and mountains and Japanese-occupied China to the east. If the docks and airstrip were taken out of commission, the only escape from an army entering Rangoon *from* the south would lie directly north, along the valleys of the Chindwin and Irrawaddy rivers, and towards India, that supposedly more secure bastion of the colonizing power. But India was 2000 miles from Rangoon, and protected by a barrier of the highest mountains and the densest jungles of all. Nevertheless, that first raid on Rangoon — which killed 2000 people — marked the start of what would come to be called "the walkout". Millar and Leyden were two of a million. The entire non-indigenous population of Burma would leave the country.

George Rodger, a thirty-four-year-old British photographer and correspondent with the American magazine *Life*, arrived in Rangoon in the third week of January 1942, a time when most sensible people were leaving. A practitioner of foreign correspondent sang-froid, Rodger touched down on the Irrawaddy in a BOAC flying boat as a Japanese air raid screamed overhead. It was impossible to get ashore, "so we sat in wicker chairs on a BOAC barge out in the river, drinking lemonade and waiting for the bombs to fall in the harbour". Rodger was — not very surprisingly — "the only passenger disembarking at Rangoon", and after the all-clear had sounded, he checked into the one hotel still open, the Minto Mansions. In his memoir, *Red Moon Rising* (1943), he writes, "There in the dingy hallway, trunks and packing cases were piled high. They were addressed in bold white paint to destinations in India and were the property of those who had decided to leave Rangoon before the raids became too heavy." As he sat down to dinner that evening, the air raid siren sounded again. "Immediately all lights were extinguished." Rodger wasn't going to be put off his soup by mere bombs. He determined to continue eating, albeit now in the dark, but after a few minutes he found himself completely alone in the restaurant, so he abandoned his dinner and wandered outside "with a few British officers to watch the progress of the raid from the garden". Rodger was intrigued to see most of the other guests lying down in slit trenches that had been dug in the garden between tall trees. Even here, botany obtrudes: "I noticed the smell of magnolia and sweet jasmine in the hot night air and huge bats were flying silently in silhouette against the light of the full moon." From one of the slit trenches someone insisted that Burmese fifth columnists were signalling to the enemy by means of red lights, assisting the raid. Rodger did not believe it, "but this is how rumours are born".

In mid-December 1941, the Japanese 15th Army entered south Burma from Thailand (which they had entered from Malaya) and began fighting their way towards Rangoon. Columns of Indian refugees were filing into the city from the south, and leaving again from the north, either for the town of Prome, 120 miles north, or for the Burmese second city, Mandalay, 250 miles north. Among them were the Indians essential to the running of Rangoon.

On 15 February, Singapore — the fortified island that supposedly guaranteed the security of Malaya and Burma — fell to the Japanese. In mid-February the English newspapers of Rangoon ceased publication.

Like Burnham Wood, the jungle was coming, and the trees themselves announced the fact. On 20 February, notices featuring the letter "E" were posted on the tree trunks of Rangoon. This did not mean "Evacuate", but the banks evacuated once the notices appeared nonetheless. In fact, E stood for "Essential": all vehicles were to be immobilized except those deemed — and marked — "Essential". On 28 February, "W" notices were put on the trees, and this was slightly less ambiguous. It meant "Warning", and it was the cue for all but non-essential workers to leave. Most had already done so.

European women and children were given priority on the ships leaving Rangoon for India. Sir Reginald Dorman-Smith later offered the rationale that Europeans would be worse treated by the invaders. In *The Story of Burma*, F. Tennyson Jesse writes,

> We made a mess of it at the beginning, as we always seem to make a mess of everything at the beginning. When we did begin to establish road convoys and air transport, there were not enough to go round, and in issuing passes for lorry or air transport we had to fix priorities; the more important the person the higher was his priority, and important persons were largely white; but even so the whites were few, for there were very few of them in Burma, and the coloured people secured the majority of the passes though not in proportion to their overwhelming numbers.

In her book *Evacuation Burma*, Felicity Goodall makes the point that this was the first time the British had been refugees, and they were not very good at it. In theory, a Defence Ordnance banned European men from fleeing the country. Indian men were not allowed to board the ships as deck passengers; that is, on cheap tickets. This was an attempt to retain the poorer Indian males who manned the docks. But thousands of Indians and Europeans continued to stream "up country" by road, rail or river steamer.

On 7 March the order was given — code "Red Elephant" — for the complete evacuation of Rangoon.

That evening, Royal Marines began heaving cases of whisky into the docks, having drunk as much as was reasonably possible themselves. (They knew the Japanese were partial to a glass of whisky.) The Reverend N. S. Metcalf, a chaplain with the 7th Armoured Brigade ("The Desert Rats"), ventured towards the Zoological Gardens:

> Fortified by a report that all animals of a dangerous nature had been destroyed, we made our entry [into the Gardens] only to discover that some were very much alive and outside their cages! There was a tense moment when it was discovered that a "tree trunk" was really a crocodile, and a "rope" hanging from a tree was a full-sized boa constrictor! There was also an orangutang loose in the town itself, handing out a nice line in assault and battery to anyone who crossed its path.

It was at about this time that George Rodger, once again going against the flow (this time he'd got hold of a jeep) and *returning* to Rangoon along the Prome Road after some adventures in Upper Burma, saw an armoured car with motorcycle outriders flashing past in the opposite direction. Inside sat Dorman-Smith. "Well, there goes the government," Rodger thought to himself. But, rather than fleeing the country, Dorman-Smith was hoping to re-establish his administration in Mandalay.

The Prome Road was periodically strafed by Japanese fighter planes. A little thing like that didn't bother George Rodger, and the Indians were as scared of the Burmese as they were of the Japanese. They were repeatedly stopped on their trek. Like the playground enemy who puts out his arm and demands "Password!", the Burmese, armed with swords and axes, had erected illicit tolls on the dusty roads. A length of bamboo would be slung across the Prome Road — not difficult since it was a dusty one-track affair — and the Indians were charged a fee of one rupee before they could continue.

George Rodger drove on, past the columns of refugees:

There must have been 50,000 to 60,000 of them. Dock labourers, coolies, and bearers plodded side by side with clerks and government servants, their womenfolk and children trailing beside them. In endless streams they came — women tired out and hobbling along by the aid of sticks; men carrying babies slung in panniers from their shoulders, others carrying small children on their backs. Some of the women carried bundles of dry wood on their heads for, with such a large party, it was not easy to find fuel for their fires wherever they stopped for the night, and it was not safe to forage in the jungle where Burmans might be lurking.

Others again carried more whimsical items: a tom-tom drum, a bicycle with the back wheel missing, a cross-cut saw. In the Chaukan Pass, Millar, as we have seen, did not have the strength to carry his favourite revolver. How much sooner would people abandon their harmoniums, oil paintings, photographic albums?

Prome was now a giant refugee camp infested with cholera and typhoid, where thousands of Indians waited for Irrawaddy steamers to carry them north — boats that never appeared. One option from here was to break out of Burma halfway up its western coast. This was a matter of crossing the Irrawaddy which lies immediately west of Prome — in Burma, there is always a river in the way and this was a wide one — then traversing the jungles of the Arakan Mountains by means of the Taungup Pass, aiming all the while for the small port of Akyab in the Bay of Bengal, from where it might be possible to take a boat for Chittagong, India. This was the first of two or three routes to be known, more or less officially, as "Valleys of Death", and refugees were on it even as it was being surveyed — and found to be a hopeless prospect — by British officials. Among the difficulties likely to be encountered were Burmese dacoits, Japanese bombers, lack of food and water, cholera, typhoid and malaria. But it is estimated that between a hundred and two hundred thousand Indians escaped via the Taungup Pass.

On 9 March, meanwhile, Japanese forces had entered Rangoon, which had been set ablaze and partly demolished by a team of British officials and soldiers called "the last ditchers". Oddly, some of them were accountants. When they'd finished their work, the cranes in the docks stood at crazy angles; the Irrawaddy river paddle steamers had been scuttled, a thousand trucks burnt out . . . and so the great theme of the flight from Burma — the theme of pedestrianism — was underlined. Two thousand Burmese criminals and lunatics roamed the streets. The doors of the prison, the lunatic asylum *and* the leper hospital had been thrown open. There seemed no alternative, the staff having all departed, but the official responsible, Judicial Secretary Mr Fielding Hall, was so disturbed by the action he had performed that he took his own life.

This was just the kind of setting that George Rodger liked, and he went on a sight-seeing tour, revolver in hand. He observed twenty brass Buddhas glowing red hot above a temple wall. They were thrown into relief by the black cloud that hung over Rangoon, caused by the burning of the 150 million gallons of oil in the tank farm of the Burmah Oil Company's refinery just outside the city. This had been blown by 700 charges of gelignite laid by a captain of the Royal Engineers called Walter Scott. He was only twenty-three, but already a demolition veteran, having blown up much of the infrastructure of northern France prior to the evacuation of Dunkirk. The refinery would burn for six weeks.

In the second city, Mandalay, things were going the same way, except that here it was hotter (120 degrees Fahrenheit in the shade), Mandalay being in the burning desert plain of central Burma. Many of the refugees had arrived here by train, only to step directly into another giant refugee camp in which cholera had broken out. In Mandalay, as in Rangoon, the prisoners had been let out of the jail. Here, too, Dorman-Smith said the city would be held, and people ought to stay put, at least until suitable evacuation routes had been prepared. Here, too, the Burmese rioted against the Indians (resulting in 600 dead), and here also a single Japanese bombing raid — on the night of 3 April — killed 2000 civilians.

Mandalay had never been as beautiful as its name: Kipling romanticized it in his poem "The Road to Mandalay", but he'd never been there. It was a shanty-town of wooden houses; a Wild West-looking place. The tallest structures on the dusty streets were the telegraph poles. Most of these were skewed after the bombing, and it is said the vultures of Mandalay had become so fat on the corpses in the streets that when they perched on the wires, the poles would collapse entirely. It was only a small comeuppance for the vultures, and in any case the telegraph station was out of action.

The predominant drift from Mandalay — for both refugees and the Burma Army — was to the north-west, over the Irrawaddy river by boat or by the Ava Bridge. The latter was supposedly closed to refugees, but there were reports of British soldiers charging them to cross, and pocketing the proceeds. The Japanese, approaching up the Irrawaddy, were kept back from the bridge retreat by 48th Gurkha Brigade. One thousand seven hundred Gurkhas faced 4000 Japanese and killed 500 of them. The bridge — a graceful iron pontoon (there being so many rivers, the British in Burma had become great bridge builders) — was blown up by the British on 30 April. To Field Marshal Sir William "Bill" Slim, commander of the Allied forces in Burma, the collapse of the bridge symbolized the collapse of British power in Burma, and the military now joined the civilians in the evacuation to India.

The north-westerly drift led towards the border town of Tamu, which became the start of the main evacuation route from northern Burma. The first leg of the route ran from Tamu to Imphal, capital — and only town — of the nominally independent Indian state of Manipur. From Imphal, the route led to Dimapur in Assam, a pretty Victorian town with a railway station and pine trees, but it was very malarial and the spring rains of 1942 had brought out the notorious Dimapur mosquito. About 200,000 would go this way, contending with — besides the mosquitoes, cholera and malnutrition — dust and burning scrub giving way to mud and monsoon.

Other evacuees, including the Governor, Dorman-Smith, headed 200 miles north of Mandalay, going along the railway to Myitkyina, and into a cul-de-sac.

The Man in the River

Millar and Leyden had retreated behind a boulder, so as to be screened from the horrible sight, if not the sound, of the Dapha river. One of the Kachin porters volunteered to go a little further north along the Dapha to see whether he could find a crossable point. The quicker he came back, the better the news was likely to be. Millar and Leyden waited, and Millar smoked. When half an hour had passed, they knew it was unlikely to be good news. It was now raining again. More than an hour had passed by the time the Kachin re-emerged from the jungle. My life depends on this man's answer, thought Millar, and he, Leyden and Goal Miri stepped out from behind the rock to greet the man, who indicated that they should walk through the trees with him, a little way towards the red-earth bank of the Dapha.

The river fumed below them, and the Kachin pointed to where it disappeared into violet-coloured hills intersecting neatly, as in a children's story. The Kachin believed that if they walked five or six miles along the riverbank in that direction, they might come to a crossable point. But Millar knew that, in their present condition, it would take two and a half days to cover that much dense jungle and then, the river having been crossed, they would have to spend the same time heading back south along the other side in order to be on track for civilization. It was no go; they could not afford another five days without food.

Millar looked at Leyden; Goal Miri was looking at the waters of the Dapha. Suddenly, he shouted, "Look, a man is being washed down the river!" One of the Kachins was in the middle of the Dapha. Just his head and shoulders were showing, and he was going down stream at what Millar called "an unpleasant pace".

But the man was *not* being washed down the river. He was crossing the river, in that his feet were — albeit intermittently — on the bottom: he was moving at a rapid diagonal. For every step he took towards the opposite bank, he seemed to be swept two paces downstream, towards fast rapids. If he hit those he'd be straight into the confluence whirlpool, from which he would eventually shoot out, and be borne along the Noa Dehing to its intersection with the mighty Brahmaputra, that creator of the Assam plain, and there he would arrive at civilization, most likely as a drowned corpse.

But the Kachin reached the opposite bank. He staggered out, turned, then waded in again, and came directly back. He had proved it could be done. "That man will live in my memory forever," wrote Millar. Unfortunately, he will not live in the memory of history forever because we do not know his name. Why had he risked his life in that way? It is not enough to say he was

42

being well paid. The Kachins had been retained by Millar and Leyden in return for silver rupees (paper money was too flimsy for jungle dwellers; it tended to rot, get burnt, or be turned to pulp by the rains, or eaten by termites), and far more of them than they could earn from selling the superfluous produce of their agriculture. But the Kachins were not being paid enough to justify risking their lives, and they all knew they were doing precisely that. Millar and Leyden had told them the food was going to run out; they had been offered the chance to turn back on more than one occasion and the offer had been rejected. It was a matter of honour. Some of the porters told Millar and Leyden that their brothers served in the Burma Rifles, so they were loyal to the British (in the shape of Millar and Leyden) because their brothers were loyal to the British.

A conference was held on the original bank. The Kachins tied the party's diminished packs onto the tops of their heads. On the rocky river beach the party formed a human chain, each man holding the other's wrists, and the chain walked slowly into the water. Every man was thus anchored by all the other men; on the other hand, if one man was swept into the rapids, they all would be. They would move a little way, then brace, then move again, Millar — who was at the front, holding his rifle above his head — shouting "Go!" every time.

They reached the opposite bank, and climbed out exhausted. There was no possibility of any further walking that day. They moved into the trees, so as to escape the worst of the rain, and the Kachins set down the loads. Every man looked at every other man, and every man grinned. Millar was thinking of the enigmatic Errol Gray, of Woodthorpe and MacGregor and their collapsible boat, of swaggering Henri of Orleans. He had, in a sense, beaten all of them. He wrote, "We felt extraordinary mental elation — at least I did — at having crossed this river after heavy rain three months later than the last date it was thought to be fordable."

They made a rough canopy of bamboos, lit their fire and continued to gaze at each other, too tired to speak, let alone move on. And then a new thought came to Millar. Would anybody ever know they'd crossed the Dapha?

What use was mental elation without food? Also, Leyden was now running a fever. What this amounted to we don't know. Park Street Cemetery in Calcutta is full of young British men and women who died of unspecified "fever". In Leyden's case, the possibilities were all too numerous. The most obvious is malaria. It's true that mosquitoes thin out above 2000 feet, so there had not been too many of them in the Chaukan Pass itself, but now Leyden was lower down. In any case sandflies, which the British in Burma called polaungs, *increase* above 2000 feet, and these transmit leishmanaisis, with its own accompanying fever. Or their bites can turn septic, as can leech bites, or any other cut, and monsoon rain turns the skin wrinkly — as when one has spent too long in the bath — and liable to splitting. Or the fever might have been

44

dysentery, typhoid or cholera — the embarrassing symptoms of these perhaps being thought unmentionable by Millar.

All these possibilities would have been encouraged by exhaustion and malnutrition.

Going back to the sambhur in that jungle clearing ... why didn't Millar and Leyden shoot more than one? The true jungle wallah might also demand to know why they didn't preserve the hacked meat by wrapping it in a wide leaf — a bamboo leaf would have done perfectly well — and smoking it in the embers of a fire so that it would last for many days. And then again, surely there are edible plants in the jungle?

There are, but even Captain Tainsh couldn't list many in the Bengal Club of Calcutta, and he was a man obsessed with emergency nutrition, to the point where his autobiography is entitled *Fungi in Peace and War, 1917–47*.

The fact is that Millar and Leyden did not have time to be smoking meat or nibbling plants to see whether they were poisonous. Instead they were in a great hurry, because they formed an advance guard, a breakaway from a party of British and Indian evacuees whose ability to proceed through the mountainous jungles of the Chaukan Pass and beyond was considered less than that of Millar and Leyden. In short, if Millar and Leyden did not get through, many people behind them would die.

Beyond Mandalay

In coming to Myitkyina, the British had reached the end of the line — literally, in that it was the last stop on the sparse Burmese railway network. It was also a dead end. Mountainous jungle lay to the north and west, occupied China to the east, Japanese soldiers to the south. The only way out short of entering those jungles was by air, and there *was* an airfield outside the town. It was just a clearing in the trees with a bamboo hut, like a cricket pavilion. Evacuation flights — to Dinjan, Assam — had been shifted there as airfields to the south were successively abandoned to the Japanese.

Life correspondent George Rodger had stopped off at Myitkyina airfield before he himself walked out of Burma. He took a photograph and sent it to *The Times* where, to the annoyance of the British government, it was published on 15 April 1942. The caption ran: "Ready for Evacuation — The RAF has evacuated hundreds of women and children from the fighting areas in Burma. Some are seen sheltering from the sun under the wing of an aeroplane before leaving." Sunglasses, smiles and sola topees are the order of the day, and the subjects look very unharassed, like tourists rather than refugees. The half-dozen women, five children and one man look to be British or Anglo-Indian at the darkest. There are no Indians among their number, even though Indians constituted the great majority of the refugees.

In *The Story of Burma*, F. Tennyson Jesse attempts a corrective:

> The following figures may be of interest to those who accuse us of furthering the interests of the whites, for they show what the RAF, the US Air Corps, and the Chinese National Airways Co did to evacuate people from Myitkyina to India in May 1942: 8616 persons were evacuated, of whom about 6000 were civilians and 2000 were army casualties. Of the 6000 civilians, 3500 were Eurasians and Burmese, 2200 were Indian, and 300 were English.

By "May" she means "early May" because the flights would not continue throughout that month.

Every morning, would-be passengers trekked through jungle scrub from the nearby refugee camp, suitcases in hand, to wait for the two Douglas Transports — lumbering mules of planes that landed each day from Assam. With each successive day, they appeared later and later out of the thick white cloud in which the monsoon was brewing. From mid-April, these clouds had been threatening to halt the flights altogether; by 6 May they had blotted out the mountains to the north-west over which the refugees hoped to be carried.

47

The cloud also made each day more suffocating, yet the women and children — they mainly *were* women and children — who waited for the planes seemed to have been at the dressing-up basket: the women might be wearing two hats, or two dresses, or they might be wearing coats in 110 degrees Fahrenheit. These were the clothes they could not fit into their suitcases.

On 6 May the first Transport landed, and those with passes for it boarded by means of the usual regulated scramble. When the doors of the aircraft were closed, a small girl stood screaming repeatedly beside it. Her mother was on the plane and she was not. This minor tragedy (nothing much by the standards of the evacuation) was about to be overtaken by a bigger one. As the Douglas Transport prepared to take off, the sound of another plane was heard coming from within the cloud. It was not the second Douglas Transport; that was not due, and this unseen aircraft had a thinner engine note. A Japanese fighter — one of those nihilistically called a Zero — came out of the clouds and the refugees who'd been unlucky a minute ago, being unable to board the plane, were lucky now, because they could race into the jungle. As they ran, the first Zero circulated the airfield three times with a red flag sticking from the cockpit window. It was later surmised that this had been a warning pass, and the door of the plane on the ground did open, and three or four people did jump out; but, by then, another three Zeros had come out of the cloud, and they machine-gunned the Douglas Transport. They circled away, came back, machine-gunned it again. At least thirty-five people were killed, and many more injured.

Just as Rangoon and Mandalay had been abandoned after a Japanese air raid, so now was Myitkyina airfield, and two days later, the Japanese took the town. It is estimated that 40,000 refugees were scattered into the surrounding countryside by the fall of Myitkyina, and they were the ones who'd been banking on the airlift, and who were all geared up for it, with their cotton frocks, high-heeled shoes and children in tow. They were not dressed for long-distance walking.

The Governor, Sir Reginald Dorman-Smith, had himself boarded one of the last flights. He would establish a Burma government-in-exile from the hill station of Simla, India, where he would write an elegant, rueful report on the evacuation, characterizing the main theme as *sauve qui peut*, possibly because it sounds better than "every man for himself". The military word was "fluid". The situation had become fluid. This was especially the mindset post-Myitkyina. Army officers (always British) lost their men (usually Indian), and vice versa. Senior British police officers found that all their Burmese and Indian policemen had melted away. Telegraphic and telephonic communication did not exist. There was a shortage of wireless sets, which in any case didn't work well in the mountainous terrain towards which everybody was heading. All civil and military authority collapsed.

Given that survival now depended on a person's ability to walk into India, some maps would have been useful. But one of the sub-divisional officers in

Myitkyina had rounded up a cache of maps and burnt them, to keep them from the Japanese. Some decided to stay in the villages to the north. But most refugees felt it better to try a "Valley of Death" than wait in Myitkyina, so a route to Assam began to be talked of. It had been "opened" since March; it lay through the Paktoi Hills, and ran along something called the Hukawng Valley.

The route began at a village called Shinbiwyang, which stood at the beginning of the Daru Pass, which in turn became the Hukawng Valley. Shinbiwyang was about 120 food-free miles west of Myitkyina, and the Kumon Range of mountains was in the way. Another option was to duck south of the Kumon Range, and go along a rough road considered motorable for the first thirty of its 130 miles; indeed, a "bus" — that is, a dusty lorry with a tarpaulin over the back — travelled along this stretch as often as two or three times a year. The road became unmotorable at a spot called Pakhenbum where one track branched left towards a district of jungle scrub, friable red earth, dried-up river beds, jade mines and mosquitoes. Beyond the mines lay Tamu and the start of the aforementioned main thoroughfare for evacuees, the Tamu-Imphal-Dimapur route. The other, rightward pointing, track headed towards Shinbiwyang, the Hukawng Valley, and *its* mosquitoes. At this junction of Pakhenbum a rough wooden notice was put up in April indicating the latter track, and reading: "This route is a death trap for women and children. Women and children should turn left." (That is, towards Tamu-Imphal-Dimapur.) In other words, the Hukawng Valley was officially disapproved of as a route for refugees. But the alternative, the track leading leftwards, also led *southwards*, and the Japanese were to the south.

In his Evacuation Report, Dorman-Smith wrote, "Little evidence is available of the treatment of those who stayed received at the hands of the enemy", so he makes one august example stand for many: ". . . it is known that the Ven. W. H. S. Higginbotham, Archdeacon of Rangoon, while trying to prevent looting, was cut down by a Japanese officer." On the other hand, one of the refugee administrators would write in 1942, "I have kept a careful watch for stories of Jap atrocities towards refugees. I have heard of none in the Shan States or the Northern Districts of Burma. In fact, the reverse is true. There are instances of refugees who fell behind Jap lines actually being given lifts in Jap lorries." The whole purpose of their invasion, after all, had been to get the British out of the country.

But from the late 1930s, the Japanese had been rapidly reassessed by the British; they had graduated to the demonology. After Pearl Harbor, cartoonists were as likely to depict them as giants as midgets. Here was the Yellow Peril incarnate and the British refugees who had read the fictions of Sax Rohmer might — on a subconscious level — have been fleeing the clawlike hands of Dr Fu Manchu.

Japan had been opened up to the world — and tied into one-sided trade treaties — by the gunboat diplomacy of Commodore Perry in 1853. Industrialization and Westernization had followed, and, at the end of the First World War, Japan was one of the big five economic powers. But the transformation was accompanied by a feeling of guilt, a nostalgia for the Togukawa period of the seventeenth century, when Japan turned its back on the Christianizing West. Japan had been seduced, violated. The Western powers had made of her an inferior version of themselves; she felt patronized, and encircled by Western imperial possessions. This triggered a militarization of society, and the doctrine of "line of advantage", Japan's own version of Lebensraum, which in turn prompted the invasion of China. The economic sanctions this brought down on her confirmed the Japanese view that international law was a conspiracy to preserve the hegemony of America and Britain, and out of this persecution complex came what John W. Dower calls in *Japan in War and Peace* (1993) a desire for "racial revenge".

Whereas the Japanese were dwarves (when they weren't giants) in British newspapers, there was no generic image of the enemy in the Japanese mind. In the same book, Dower writes, "In Japanese war films produced between 1937 and 1945 . . . the enemy was rarely depicted. Frequently it was not even made clear who the antagonist was." The enemy was beneath notice. The Japanese had signed, but had not ratified, the Geneva Convention of 1929. They did not agree with the protocols concerning prisoners of war; the Emperor had banned the use of the term. Japanese soldiers would never allow themselves to be taken as prisoners — the officers would disembowel themselves whereas the privates would do the job communally, huddling around a grenade while one of them pulled the pin — so they did not see why they in turn should be hospitable to a defeated enemy. And it appeared little distinction would be made between enemy soldiers and enemy civilians.

The Nanking Massacre of December of 1937, in which perhaps a quarter of a million Chinese civilians were murdered, many having been raped, was reported in Britain. Then the Japanese nastiness came closer to home. During their invasion of Hong Kong, Japanese soldiers had killed patients on hospital operating tables, and raped and killed civilian women. On 11 March 1942, *The Times* reported,

> Rarely has any Minister of the Crown had to make to the House of Commons a statement more terrible than that made by Mr Eden yesterday regarding the treatment of prisoners of war and civilians by the Japanese after the capitulation of Hong Kong, when the Japanese forces were permitted and indeed encouraged to commit atrocities seldom rivalled and never surpassed in the history of international war during the last century.

Mr Eden said, "The military code of the Samurai did in fact have some influence upon Japanese military practice in the Russo-Japanese War [just as well, since we were allies at that point] . . . but the new Japan has

53

no regard for the virtues of self-restraint, incorrupt-ibility, courtesy towards honourable enemies which that code prescribed."

Japanese soldiers felt entitled to their racial revenge by their own racial purity, a notion underpinned by the divinity of their emperor — all of this inculcated by the "spiritual training" of the Japanese soldier. In his apparent unstoppability, there was something of the automaton about the Japanese soldier. In *Quartered Safe Out Here*, the novelist George MacDonald Fraser, who fought in the jungles of Burma, described Japanese soldiers circling a burning tank as looking like "clockwork dolls". The Japanese soldier's smallness was deemed to fuel his rage. In 1944, the American general Douglas MacArthur, who was five foot nine, would write, "Some observers claim there would have been no Pearl Harbor had the Japanese been three inches taller." Smallness was a particular asset in the jungle. It made the Japanese soldier nimble and silent; he required less food and drink than a big man. He was super-fit; he carried a light pack, didn't care too much about doing up his tunic buttons, or shaving; he wore his cap at an angle that might have been called — were he *not* a Japanese soldier — jaunty. He would creep up and kill you before you'd even seen him, although you might be alerted to his presence when it was too late by his gratuitously alarming scream of "Banzai!". There was something uncanny about his sudden manifesta-tions; he was like a goblin or a wood sprite, or a jungle nat in human form.

The jungle might have loomed in the colonial mind as being the dark side of the country, the murky subconscious, but it was not thought of as an arena of conflict. That would be to dignify the jungle in a way it did not deserve. In *The Longest Retreat*, Tim Carew writes "in the summer of 1941 the jungle was not mentioned in polite military circles". The Japanese could have the jungle if they wanted it, and, in early 1942, *Punch* magazine depicted Japanese soldiers as monkeys swinging through the trees. The Japanese had established their own jungle warfare school as early as 1934, in their colony of Formosa, where they practised on live Formosans.

When, in 1941, the inadequate British garrison in Burma was supplemented by the arrival at Fort Dufferin in Mandalay of three battalions of the Indian Infantry Brigade, the men immediately set about training for *desert warfare*. The main threat to India would surely come from the Middle East. It is true that, before Pearl Harbor, the British had established a so-called Bush Warfare School in the Burmese summer retreat of Maymyo; but as Colonel "Mad" Mike Calvert, Chief Instructor at the School, would write in his autobiography, *Fighting Mad* (1964), "The name Bush Warfare School was in itself a deception. We were not preparing to fight in the Burma jungle; our task was to train officers and N.C.O.s to lead guerrillas in the plains of China, a very different type of warfare." Given what was to come in Burma, it would have been better if the school had actually been called the Plains Warfare

55

School, in order to disguise the fact that it was in reality a *Jungle* Warfare School.

The danger of meeting the Japanese trumped the consideration that getting from Shinbiwyang, at the start of the Hukawng Valley, to the supposed safety of the route's terminal point, Margherita, in Assam, was a matter of walking 140 miles over eight jungle ridges, each about 4000 feet high, and crossing seven or eight fast-flowing rivers and numerous streams. British officials in Burma had only ever ventured into the Hukawng Valley in well-equipped and well-armed parties. The last hundred miles were uncharted, and almost uninhabited. *Almost.* The territory was in fact the home of the Naga tribesmen, known to the British for their great charm and their even greater violence. In particular, they were head-hunters — but *Christian* head-hunters, since many had been converted by the American Baptist missionaries who, with British encouragement, had been busy on the Indo-Burmese border at the turn of the century.

Ever since the British first arrived on the border, they had been alternately fighting against and cooperating with the Nagas, who held a romantic appeal to a certain kind of British official/anthropologist as being nobler than the Burmese or the Bengalis, both considered effete and evasive. The British took steps to protect the hill tribes of the Indo-Burmese border, requiring visitors to have a special permit, and these efforts would be increased as Indian independence, and the prospect of homogenization on the sub-continent, loomed after the war. (In *Nagaland*, Jonathan Glancey writes, "We fool ourselves if we think that just because a keen young man staring out from an old photograph in khaki and a sola topee looks like a parody of a bumptious British officer of nearly a century ago, he must have been aloof and narrow minded.")

At the time of the *First* World War, some Naga tribes had been getting on sufficiently well with the British for a unit of Nagas to have fought for the Allies on the Western Front where, it is said, they hunted the heads of German soldiers, who complained to their commanding officers at having to fight "savages". The aim of the head-hunter was to capture the spirit of the deceased, and the skull of a foreigner is ideal, because the spirit does not know the lie of the land, so is less likely to escape having been captured. And any head counts: there is no taboo against taking the heads of women or children.

In the 1920s, the British criminalized head-hunting. British officials would visit Naga villages where, emboldened by a sense of moral superiority — and fifty supporting rifles — they would opine that the dozen desiccated heads dangling from the head tree in the centre of the village were really nothing to be proud of. But head-hunting by the Nagas — mainly of other Nagas' heads — continued to the extent that an anti-head-hunting expedition was mounted in 1937. It didn't work, and the British were still fighting the Nagas about head-hunting and territorial questions in 1939. They were the most notorious of the hill tribes, and British and Indians undertaking the Hukawng route might have wondered whether the murderous or hospitable tendency would be uppermost.

The other big question was when the monsoon would start. In early May, the atmosphere was oppressive enough to suggest it might be soon, but humidity was better than the things the monsoon would bring, so with luck it would hold off until most of the refugees had completed most of their treks. It did not do so. Whereas the monsoon of 1941 had started on 21 May, that of 1942 started in mid-May. *Nobody* (apart from the Nagas, who were already there) went into the Hukawng Valley in the monsoon.

But in 1942 normality was suspended, and those who did undertake the Hukawng trek were assisted by teams of volunteers placed along the route, all of whom worked in the same profession: the same one as that from which the volunteers who staffed the Tamu-Imphal-Dimapur route had come. They were tea planters, and their Indian labourers. We will describe their work in more detail shortly, but let us say for now that the Hukawng Valley would become the second main evacuation route from Upper Burma after Tamu-Imphal-Dimapur. It is estimated that 20,000 went through (soldiers and civilians), of whom 5000 died.

One other route had been talked of in Myitkyina.

On 3 May, before the bombing of the airfield, a group of Burmese officials had flown to Dinjan to suggest this route. Its main — and only — attractive feature was that it lay about as far to the north as you could go in Burma, so was well away from the Japanese advance. But officials in Assam had ruled it out because they knew the terrain to be impassable on the Assamese side. It was decided therefore to send radio messages to Myitkyina warning against this route and urging use of the Hukawng Valley instead. But the receiving station at Myitkyina had closed down. Therefore letters were sent by plane conveying the same warning to the Deputy Commissioner of Myitkyina, but it seems these were never delivered. That Deputy Commissioner was a man called McGuire. He was the immediate superior of John Leyden, and the frowned-upon route in question was the Chaukan Pass.

The Railway Party

Exhausted after crossing the Dapha river on the evening of 31 May, John Leyden finds that his head reels every time he stands up. Night is descending rapidly. Despite having a wife and young children (all safely evacuated from Burma at an earlier date), Leyden tells Millar — a single man — that he must save himself and go on without him. He also urges Millar to do this on behalf of the people they are trying to save.

Who were these people?

They were a party of government officials and engineers; they were mainly British, but their number also included Indians, Anglo-Indians and a pregnant Burmese woman and her six-month-old mixed-race baby. Their *de facto* leader was Sir John Edward Maurice Rowland. In the summer of 1942, Sir John was sixty years old. He was an engineer, and the top man on Burma Railways: the Chief Railway Commissioner no less. In the Warrant of Precedence, the formal social hierarchy of the country, he stood at number sixteen, on a par with army officers of the rank of general, and he had been knighted in 1941. So he would be very indignant at finding himself starving to death in the jungle.

Sir John was not only head of the ordinary Burma Railways; he also ran a side project, which he called "The Burma China Construction". This was a railway meant to run parallel to the Burma Road, and for the same purpose: to keep China supplied in its battle against the Japanese. The railway would run from Lashio, a hundred or so miles north of Mandalay, to Kunming in China, through some of the most disease-ridden country in the world, so it would have been as much a medical as an engineering feat . . . if it had ever been built. There is something strained about the future tense used in an article on the line that appeared in the *San Francisco Chronicle* on 27 November 1941: "As the Panama canal's construction was a triumph of medical strategists, so will the completion of the Yunnan-Burma railroad be a victory of malaria, and the potential of plague and cholera." The author stated that 250,000 coolies would build the line, which ought to be finished in fifteen months' time "if all goes to schedule". Just as the Burma Road would be closed by the Japanese invader, so the Burma-China railway would be stopped. It has gone down as one of the great ghost railways of the world, like the plan for a railway under the English Channel in the 1880s, or the early twentieth-century German pipe dream of the Berlin-Baghdad railway.

Having been distracted by this futile endeavour, Sir John found the ordinary railways of Burma to be in what he frankly called "a damnable mess" at the time of the invasion. He used the phrase in a letter. We know from the same letter that he asked for and obtained from the man he called "HE" — His Excellency, the Governor — "dictator powers" to facilitate evacuation north by rail.

Sir John began, as he put it, "hare'ing all over" north Burma from his base at Maymyo, the hill station and hot-weather resort, from where he was ousted by the enemy on 27 April. "The Army had legged it a day and a half before. I had been promised 72 hours notice to evacuate [railway] personnel . . ." As it turned out, Sir John was given twelve hours' notice, and he underlined the word "twelve" in his letter. The railway employees — mainly Indians or Anglo-Indians — would be pitched into "sauve qui peut", for which Sir John blamed "the cracking up of the 5th and 6th Chinese armies" (which had been dispatched by Chiang Kai-shek to protect the Burmese infrastructure). The reader is now perhaps beginning to get the hang of Sir John. He was not a man lacking in confidence, or opinions, and he had a paternalistic concern for "his people", the "railway folk".

By the end of April he had shifted 4000 of these to Myitkyina, where he attempted to shift them further — by the above-mentioned airlifts to Assam. But the airlift was so very "meagre" that "we had to send thousands of men and women trekking on foot out of Burma". It had been observed at the Myitkyina airfield that, while some young and able-bodied men were putting their wives and children on the planes before themselves returning to duty or starting the dangerous walk to

Assam, others had been boarding the aeroplanes along *with* their wives and children. On 22 April, permission was given for all men over forty-five to fly out. Being sixty, and a very senior man in the administration, Sir John — whose wife had already been evacuated — could have taken advantage of this, but, as he wrote in his letter, "I had a seat on a plane which I refused, my remark being, 'Having brought all these women and children to Myitkyina, and as they are forced to walk out, so will I.'" The phrase "my remark being" is very typical of Sir John, who continued, "Having brought them here, many of them to die, I would lose all self respect and would never be able to look a woman in the face again if I escaped by plane leaving them to their fate."

By early May, a party had crystallized around Sir John, and it comprised the following:

Edward Lovell Manley. As a captain of the Royal Engineers, he had worked on the railways built by the British in Mesopotamia from 1917. After demob, had risen to become the Chief Engineer of the Eastern Bengal Railway, whose motto was *Ex Fumo Dare Lucem* ("From Smoke Let Light Break Out"), and whose crest depicted elephants and palm trees, but that didn't mean Manley was used to living in their midst. In 1942, he was fifty-six years old, and on secondment to the Burma-China construction. He had been living with Sir John, and Sir John's wife, in Rangoon. He had been Sir John's guest, in other words, and Sir John felt a particular duty to get him safe out of Burma. As they entered the Chaukan Pass, Sir John would designate Manley his number two.

Eric Ivan Milne. He was another senior railway official, aged forty-three in 1942, and the District Traffic Superintendent of Burma State Railways. He was a keen amateur cricketer who, in his final game before the Japanese invasion — railwaymen against an RAF team — had scored seventy-six not out.

(Both Manley and Milne were married men, and their wives and children had already left Burma.)

C. L. Kendall. A surveyor on the Burma-China construction.

Captain A. O. Whitehouse of the Royal Engineers. We do not have his age. A photograph shows a mild looking man of about thirty in horn-rimmed glasses and pork pie hat.

E. Eadon. An Anglo-Indian "anti-malarial inspector" on the Burma-China construction. (His wife and three children — with the very Anglo-Indian names of Fred, George and Isabelle — had already left Burma.)

N. Moses. He was a railway surveyor (among other things), rather rudely referred to by Sir John as "Dutch Jew". But then Moses carried the stigma of having directed Sir John and his party into the Chaukan Pass, as we will see.

There were also three Indian railwaymen, who had all been based at Lashio, and we know at least how they described themselves:

C. V. Venkataraman, "store clerk of the Burma-China Railway".

R. V. Venkatachalam, "office superintendent of the Burma-China Railway".

S. T. Rajan, "divisional accountant of the Burma-China Railway".

All the above three were in their fifties or sixties, and another diary of the Chaukan would describe them as "elderly railway servants".

There was also Dr Burgess-Barnett, a medical doctor, but also Superintendent of the above-mentioned Zoological Gardens in Rangoon since 1938, the place from which the boa constrictor had escaped. He had been a house physician at St Bart's in London, and an honorary captain of the Royal Army Medical Corps. He had been the curator of reptiles at London Zoo from 1932 to 1937, and the author, in 1940, of a pamphlet on *The Treatment of Snake Bites*. A good man to have in the jungle, then, except for his age (he was fifty-four), and Sir John would designate the doctor his MO, or medical officer, on the Chaukan trek.

This, then, was "the railway party". It also included two Indian porters and five Indian servants, none of whom belonged to Sir John, who wrote in his letter: "I brought no servants. They had all gone previously. The cook, his wife and family to India. Poor Sam, my butler, found his wife and three children had fled from Maymyo when we arrived there; his brother killed by a bomb and his sister injured by another, so he went into the wilds to seek his family. I never saw him again." We have the name of only one of the servants: Applaswamy, butler to Manley.

The railway party managed to commandeer some "vanettes" at Myitkyina, and in these they drove along the track (now strewn with abandoned cars) towards the town on the hill, Sumprabum. Another diarist has left a terse description of the "road" to Sumprabum at this time: "Everything was burning." It was mainly cars that were burning — torched to keep them from the Japanese. As they neared Sumprabum, Sir John and his men abandoned their vanettes and rolled them into a gulley. They knew they wouldn't be any use beyond Sumprabum. They then walked into the town of that name, and there, on 10 May, as rain fell on the tin roofs of the red houses, Sir John mustered rice rations, recruited some Kachin porters and retained two elephants and their mahouts.

The route leading to the Chaukan Pass branched off to the left from the track leading from Sumprabum to the most northerly settlement, Putao. On 11 May, at a village along this track referred to by Sir John as Hkam Ho (it does not exist on any modern map), the railway party joined forces with what we will call Rossiter's party.

This was led by Edward Wrixon Rossiter, who was a colleague of one of our opening pair, John Lamb Leyden, even if he did work eight days' travel north of him. Rossiter, like Leyden, was a sub-divisional officer of the Myitkyina District. Rossiter's particular sub-division was Putao. In other words, he administered the most northerly and remote territory in Burma. He was also a Superintendent of the Frontier Service, the body that dealt with the outlying minorities of Burma, particularly the Shans of the north and east, with whom the British were on reasonably good terms. (Britain had never conquered the Shans, but just inherited them when she conquered the Burmese, whom the Shans did not like. They were tenants, so to speak, who had found themselves with a new and slightly more congenial landlord.)

Edward Wrixon Rossiter's job called for an independent-minded man, and he seems to have fitted the bill. Rossiter is the wild card of our pack, and this may have been genetically determined.

He had been born in 1904, into the Anglo-Irish gentry. His father was a buccaneering character called Walter Wrixon de Rossiter, who had found the "Wrixon" insufficiently distinctive, hence the "de". As a teenager he'd left Ireland to join the Canadian Mounted Police. He also fought in the Boer War, after which he returned to Ireland and married an heiress called Catherine Frances Wright. They had five children. The first was called Edward, and died in infancy; the second, born a year later, was also called Edward and he is our Edward Wrixon Rossiter. Even though he was by now living in Frankfort Castle, which sounds roomy enough, Walter felt constricted by domesticity, and in 1910 he moved back to Canada, without his family. He became a lawman in the distinctly ungenteel environment of Moose Jaw, Saskatchewan, where he may or may not have started another family entirely. At the start of the First World War, he lied about his age — he said he was younger than he was — to get into the 42nd Royal Highlanders in Montreal. The battalion went to France in October 1915, and Walter Wrixon de Rossiter was killed at Passchendaele, aged fifty.

It will be worth keeping in mind the life of the father, as we learn more about the life of the son. Let us say for now that Edward Wrixon Rossiter sailed for Rangoon in 1927, after graduating from Trinity College Dublin, and that in 1942 he had recently married and fathered a child with a young Shan woman called Nang Hmat — two children, in fact, because, in May 1942, Nang Hmat would enter the Chaukan Pass three months pregnant, while also carrying her six-month-old baby son, John, in a sling.

Since 7 April, Rossiter hadn't had a clue what was going on in Burma, because his government radio had been commandeered and his personal radio was on the blink. All he knew was that the Japanese were coming, and he'd better get out. In early May, he had received a visit from the other of our original pair, Guy Millar, who was accompanied by his elephant tracker, Goal Miri, and Frank Kingdon-Ward.

Frank Kingdon-Ward, botanist, explorer and thorough-going eccentric, was the author of books such as *On the Road to Tibet, Land of the Blue Poppy, In Furthest Burma* and *Assam Adventure*. In 1942, he was fifty-seven years old, and he bore the nickname "Old Kingdom Come". He was a depressive who could easily go for a whole day without saying a word to his travelling companions, one of whom noted that his real happiness was to be "utterly alone", which in the context of the British-in-Burma actually meant

68

". . . with nothing but coolies, a cook, and a couple of servants to make his bed". He was one of the few men who knew the topography of the Burmese-Indian border, and, early in the war, he had been given the special — and odd — military number of 00100. Reviving his First World War rank of captain, but operating as plain Mr Ward, he was dispatched to South Asia. In October 1941, he had checked into the Strand Hotel, Rangoon, from where he wrote to his sister, Winifred, that he was "off on an expedition plant hunting", plausible enough given that, aside from the above-mentioned books, he was also the author of *Plant Hunting on the Edge of the World, Plant Hunting in the Wilds* and *Plant Hunter's Paradise*, but he had underlined "plant hunting" in red, a likely indication that this time he was, for once, *not* going plant hunting, but was engaged in work for one of those martial agencies that proliferated in Burma, under the auspices of which any old jungle wallah might immediately become an army officer: the Military Survey Service. Certainly by March 1942, Kingdon-Ward was in Upper Burma, and helping to facilitate the civilian evacuation, and it seems that Guy Millar had assisted him in this endeavour, which he refers to in his diary simply as "government work".

Kingdon-Ward, Millar, Goal Miri and Rossiter discussed their options. Rossiter was all for heading east, to China. He knew of a couple of airfields there from which a flight to Assam might be secured. He knew that all evacuees had been ordered to stay out of China, an enemy-occupied country, but as an independent-minded man with a small baby and a pregnant wife, he was willing to defy this diktat. Kingdon-Ward, too, thought China a reasonable idea. He also suggested simply hanging around until the Japanese came, his consideration being that a Japanese prisoner-of-war camp would be easy to escape from. In the end, Kingdon-Ward went off on his own, as he tended to do, walking into Assam via the shakily independent mountainous state of Tibet ("the Roof of the World"), where the flora were particularly varied and fascinating.

The "Chaukan Club" Sets Off

On 9 May a Kachin runner or messenger arrived at Rossiter's bungalow. He had been sent along the track from Sumprabum by Rossiter's colleague, Leyden. He handed Rossiter a chit (or note), written by Leyden. It said Myitkyina had been entered by the Japanese. All the officials had been cleared away "by another route". Leyden himself had been ordered to leave, and he had been destroying important papers prior to doing so. The Chaukan Pass had been recommended to Leyden. He admitted that he had heard bad things about the Chaukan, but he had reason to believe a rescue party would be sent into it from the Assam side, a theory apparently based on radio messages, or rumours of radio messages. In fact, at about the time Leyden was writing this chit, RAF planes sent from Assam were dropping messages in the vicinity of Sumprabum specifically *forbidding* entry into the Chaukan Pass, it being considered impassable. But these messages were never picked up, just as letters and radio messages giving the same warning were never received.

Rossiter, too, had heard bad things about the Chaukan Pass, but it seemed that Leyden's message convinced him, or half convinced him. He mustered his own party, with supplies of food but no elephants. The party consisted of Rossiter, his Shan wife and child, Millar, Goal Miri and twenty Indian "subordinates and servants", plus an unspecified number of porters. On 11 May, as mentioned, they teamed up with Sir John and the railway party at the spot called Hkam Ho, fifty miles short of the Chaukan Pass. On 13 May, they were joined by Leyden, who brought some porters of his own, and a man called Ronald Jardine, who was forty-five but, being white-bearded and already haggard, looked older. He was an employee in Rangoon of Lever Brothers, the soap manufacturers, and, although not currently very fragrant, he had married into Coty, the French perfume dynasty. (Jardine's wife, too, had already been evacuated.)

On 14 May, by which point they had progressed about fifteen miles towards the pass from Hkam Ho, trudging along a rocky mule track winding through fine soil — dust, really — and dried scrub, Sir John's two elephant men refused to go any further "as the road is so bad and there is no fodder for animals". Sir John paid them off, and they and their elephants turned back to Hkam Ho.

On 17 May, the monsoon proper started, and Sir John was getting into his rhetorical stride: "The day's march was a most loathsome one, carried out under the most disgusting weather conditions along a jungle track which went up hill and down dale with slopes as steep as 1-in-1 in some places, the track itself being in many places a stream of liquid mud inches thick." It brought them to a village of bamboo houses, called by Sir John Hpaungmaka: "This camp is full of winged insects of every description, sandflies and blood blister flies, abounding in myriads, were a pest to everyone."

The going had become next to impossible, and they weren't even at the pass yet. It was therefore decided to dispatch three of the younger, fitter men as an advance guard, together with porters. So it was that Millar, Leyden and Goal Miri set off with their dozen porters, with the idea, as Sir John fate-provokingly put it, ". . . of doing double marches per day, get to Assam as quickly as possible and to send a relief force to us with rations and medical stores at whichever point we might have reached on the route".

The Footprint

It was cold at dawn in the jungle on 1 June, and still raining. Leyden was definitely not at all well, and he kept insisting that Millar go on without him. "I was unsympathetic," Guy Millar wrote, "and even uncouth, I'm afraid."

With the rising sun came heavier rain. There was no food for breakfast, so Millar lit a cigarette and he made a decision: he and the young elephant tracker, Goal Miri, would make a last dash for a village, while Leyden and the Kachin porters would come through at their own pace.

The two set off, marching all day "at a hard pace" through thick jungle, and making tree cuts — incisions in the bark — on the way so that Leyden and the Kachins might follow. Eventually they came to what Millar called "a small river, the Debawng". But the Debawng, or Debang, river is small only by the standards of upper Assam. It occupies a gorge about 200 yards wide. In the dry season, a few shallow streams — each as wide as an ordinary English river — meander through the white rubble of the river bed. In the monsoon, things are different: Millar and Leyden were staring at white rapids. It was probably shallow enough to wade through, but there was the question of tree cuts. How would the following Kachins and Leyden know where they resumed on the opposite bank? At four o'clock, the rain stopped. In two hours, it would be pitch dark. Millar contemplated the river, then he looked at the red mud of the riverbank, and he saw a footprint.

At first, he didn't point it out to Goal. He just sat and stared at it: ". . . the first signs of man for nineteen days over a journey of a hundred miles."

It was not a boot print, but a *footprint*. It pointed left, in the direction of the bigger river towards which the Debang was flowing, in other words the Noa Dehing, the river that Millar and Leyden had been shadowing all along, and whose tributaries they had been crossing, and falling into. Millar pointed out the footprint to Goal Miri; they lit a bamboo fire as the light faded.

A fire ought to go with food, but there was none. After an hour or so, they heard the sound of twigs snapping in the jungle. That meant people. Animals did not break twigs as they walked. The beam of an electric torch shone through the trees: Leyden and the porters had arrived. Leyden could hardly walk, and seeing Millar by the river he lay down immediately. Millar wrote, "The pangs of hunger were now acute. The [porters] sat around glaring at each other, thinking, I suppose, the end was in sight." Nobody seemed very impressed by the footprint. After a while, the Kachins made flares of burning grass. They took these to the water's edge in order to hunt for crabs — which they did not find. When they had left his immediate vicinity, Millar realized he could still see the footprint quite clearly. Moonlight. *The moon was full* — they did not need to wait for dawn to follow the track indicated by the print.

They followed the prints, Leyden being supported by two of the Kachins, and after a while these were joined by two other sets of prints, indicating three men going towards the Noa Dehing river. Satisfied that this was the direction, Millar and Goal Miri returned to Leyden. They explained that they must all follow the tracks, but it was obvious that Leyden could not stand up again, let alone walk. His feet were bleeding, swollen and infected; they looked as if boiling water had been poured over them, and his temperature was higher than it had been the day before. Again, he insisted that everyone else go on and leave him, but Millar and the Kachins cut down bamboos to make a stretcher. Leyden would be carried. It took them an hour to make the stretcher. At four o'clock in the morning, they set off in the direction of the footprints.

At nine o'clock in the morning they arrived at the place towards which the makers of the footprints had been heading: two bamboo and palm huts in a red-mud clearing, the Noa Dehing singing beyond the trees, otherwise all quite silent and deserted. And then things were not silent. Leyden, lying on his stretcher, opened his eyes. A plane was approaching. It came over fairly low; then another came, equally low and loud. Millar did not believe they were Japanese planes; they had come from the west, from central Assam, and civilization. Surely they were rescue planes. They might come back; a signal must be sent. The sun was now shining, and while the ground in the clearing might be muddy, the huts were dry. Millar struck a Lion Safety Match and put it in the palm-leaf roof of the first hut. The hut began to smoke, then to burn furiously, sending up a thick column of black smoke . . . just as the sound of the aeroplane engines faded from earshot entirely.

They pushed on, and looked down at the Noa Dehing river. It was wider here: 600 yards of water racing west. As they watched, an entire tree came rotating past them and other, smaller parts of trees, as the Noa Dehing raced to merge with the five-mile-wide Brahmaputra, which cuts laterally through the middle of Assam. Millar and Leyden needed to go west as well — not as far as the Noa Dehing's confluence with the Brahmaputra, but about thirty miles in that general direction where habitation began. Thirty miles, two days' march, might bring them to a proper village, with not only food, but shops — or at least a government rice dump — and the possibility of medical assistance. They watched the trees go swirling past; the river's edge was strewn with further broken trees. What was a canoe but a hollowed-out tree? Millar suggested to Goal Miri that, since everything else had failed, they might push a log into the river, keep hold of it and see what happened. "It would wash us down to civilization quicker than we could ever hope to walk." But "Goal pointed to two rapids pouring down on either side of an island in the river — there were probably other rapids all the way down at intervals."

Millar moved closer to the river's edge for a better look at the rapids, and he saw a tree cut. It was new, and it indicated a path along the river's edge, just inside the trees. They began following the path, which curved around to a wooded bulge in the riverbank. Here was another clearing, and this time only a single hut, smaller than the others had been. Millar called out in Assamese, asking, "Who made the tree cut?" No reply. Only the river's roar; the heat of the day bearing down on Millar. He smelt smoke; he looked about, and he saw, on the margin of the trees, a smouldering bamboo fire. Millar advanced. The bamboo door of the shack was closed; he pushed at it. Three men crouched inside — members of the Mishmi tribe. They stood upright and stepped into the clearing, where they faced Millar, who had now been joined by Goal Miri. Each of the Mishmis carried a long knife. Millar and Goal Miri bowed towards the Mishmis; the Mishmis bowed back, but Millar was watching their knives. They made Millar understand that they had seen him burn the two huts in the other clearing, and they took this to be an "expedition" — that is, a British revenge raid. Revenge for what? In this case, they didn't know, but the British were certainly not above burning the huts of the Mishmis, or of any of the thirty or so major tribes of Assam. The burning of huts — empty huts, the occupants having been ejected at gunpoint (and occasionally shot into the bargain) — was a standard tactic in any dispute. Fortunately for Millar, these particular Mishmis had not been abused in that way; in fact, he was the first white man they had ever seen close up, and they were now having a very good look.

Millar risked another glance over to the fire, which the Mishmis had tried to damp down. But why had they lit it in the first place? Breakfast. On top of the fire were many parcels made of banana leaves; inside them, fish were being smoked. Bowing again at the Mishmis, Millar — who was "ravenous" — began inching towards the fire. The Mishmis, who had settlements along the Debang river, were known to be expert fishermen. They would divert the water on the margins of a river by building stone dams; a small pool would be created at the termination of these, and after a while there would be fish in that pool.

"To cut a long story short," wrote Millar, "we made great friends — not by words but by signs." The rest of the party were brought into the enclosure, including Leyden on his stretcher. A breakfast of smoked fish was eaten — and fast. A deal was then made with the Mishmis, who had been very interested in Millar's .450 rifle when it had been glimpsed protruding from one of the packs carried by a Kachin. The tribes of Assam could make most things they needed from jungle materials, but they couldn't make guns, and who could deny the usefulness of this particular one? It had saved the life of the party when they'd come upon the herd of sambhur, and it would now save their lives again. Millar offered his rifle to the Mishmis if they would assist in the trek west. The Mishmis agreed, and so further parcels of dried fish were loaded into the packs and they set off. "What a joy," wrote Millar, "our whole party intact and saved — except for little Misa."

In the late morning of that day — 2 June — they crossed the Noa Dehing in its lower reaches, Millar does not say how, but probably by boat, since they were now into inhabited territory. Thirty miles after leaving the Dapha confluence, they came to the mainly Buddhist village of Miao, which sat on the river's left bank. They walked on, skirting the deep puddles of a rocky track. The jungle continued on either side, but it was sparser now, and flat, which was just as well since Leyden was still being carried on the stretcher. Looking left in gaps between the trees, they could see the misty outline of hills bristling with trees, through which the bigger evacuation route, the Hukawng Valley, ran. In the fading light of late afternoon on 4 June, they came to the tiny settlement known to the British — and only to the British — as Simon. (The locals called it Sangmo.) Here a small camp, and rice dump, had been established as a north-easterly outpost of the Hukawng Valley refugee relief effort, and, when they arrived here, Millar and Leyden finally knew they were safe.

They were met — and "given a great welcome" — by a man called J. A. Masson, a tea planter who had volunteered to work on the refugee relief effort. If they were given the meal that usually met the British Burma refugees then they would have had sausages, fried potatoes and sweet milky tea — none of that foreign muck, in short — but the meal is not recorded.

Masson had heard rumours that people were trying to come through the Chaukan, and he told Millar and

Leyden — which they already knew — that planes had been flying over to look for the Chaukan trekkers. Millar and Leyden told Masson of Sir John's railway party, and the Rossiter party, of which two they were the advanced guard. Millar and Leyden said that a rescue effort had to be mounted immediately. Masson quite agreed, and what was more he knew just the man for the job.

His name was Gyles Mackrell.

Guy Millar knew Mackrell, too. He insisted that a runner be sent immediately to him.

The Man With Elephants

Gyles Mackrell — the man whose name had caused such an upwelling of hope in Guy Millar — was working on the relief effort directed towards that major escape route, the Hukawng Valley, but he was rather out on a limb. He was at a spot called Namgoi Mukh, about eight miles south of the camp at Simon where Millar and Leyden had been greeted with sausages and tea. If Simon was obscure, Namgoi Mukh was more so, and the map at the front of this book is one of the few on which it has ever appeared. Before Mackrell had arrived there in early May there'd been nothing but a couple of broken bamboo houses built amid the trees. On arrival, he had written a letter to a friend, beginning, "I don't know quite where 'here' is, as we have no maps, but here I am anyway!"

Actually, Namgoi Mukh would have been a logical place for a village, because it stood at the confluence of two rivers. The first ran south from Simon, and its name fluctuates exasperatingly depending on who's referring to it, but let's call it the Namphuk. The other river, branching off to the south-west from the Namphuk, was called — by some — the Namgoi. If, in early June 1942, you'd taken a boat fifteen miles from the place called Namgoi Mukh along the Namgoi river, you would have arrived at a refugee relief camp called Nampong, which lay more or less in the middle of the Hukawng Valley evacuation route. But you would have been going against a strong current, since the river flowed north, which is why Gyles Mackrell was sending most of the supplies he was dispatching to the Nampong camp by porter or by elephant.

At Namgoi Mukh, Mackrell inhabited a humid, watery world, living amid the roar of the rain and the additional roar of the two rivers. The supplies — "rice, dall, potatoes, blankets etc" — came in by boat from the camp at Simon. Mackrell paid the boatmen their fee of eight silver rupees per boatload, from government money labelled the Burma Refugee Fund. He then loaded the stuff onto elephants, for which he tended to use the Hindi word "hathis" or "haths", and of which he had thirty-one at his disposal. He spent all day unloading and loading, and slept on a camp bed in a basha, next to the main, tin-roofed godown, or warehouse, on a riverbank that was at all times a foot deep in reddish mud.

He was probably enjoying himself greatly, the only reservation being that he was not in the thick of the action. He was fifty-three, and it bothered him that this might preclude him from a more central role. Mackrell was a former fighter pilot turned supervisor of tea plantations and big-game hunter. He lived in a big house in Shillong, the capital of Assam, but was hardly ever there. He was a burly, kindly, avuncular looking man — bald, but you wouldn't know it because he always wore (for reasons of practicality, not vanity) either a sola topee or a bush hat. He also always wore long shorts, and below these, and above his long socks, his large knees had the touching appearance of being on the wrong way round. He was somewhat elephantine, in fact, and he certainly had an affinity with elephants.

He had turned up at the Ledo camp in late April, volunteering for any work at all in the relief operations, whereupon he was given the nebulous title Indian Tea Association Liaison Officer. As he wrote in that letter to a friend, "It all seems most casual ... Even now, I don't know who or what I am." On 17 May, he reported for duty at Simon camp with, according to an official document, "four and a half elephants" in tow — that is, four adults and one baby elephant. (A female elephant which has lately given birth will continue to work, but only if she has her baby by her side.) He was immediately dispatched to Namgoi Mukh, where a man called Bathgate was in charge. But Mackrell noticed that when he arrived with his four and a half elephants, Bathgate barely looked at them. You don't look a gift *horse* in the mouth, but it seems you should do with an elephant. But Bathgate was depressed. He'd been a timber merchant in Burma and had lost his entire business; the rain and mud and general obscurity of Namgoi Mukh wouldn't have helped. Bathgate wasn't an elephant expert, and he couldn't speak Assamese, the language of the mahouts. Mahouts had the reputation of being difficult. They not only rode the elephants, they had also captured and trained them — very difficult and dangerous work. They combined the independence of all taxi drivers with the unionized bolshiness of some train drivers. They also had a certain priestly status. Elephants are revered to some degree in most Eastern religions, and the mahouts held the key to their mysteries.

At Namgoi Mukh, Mackrell quickly accumulated eighty-four elephants. They were what Mackrell called "Kampti elephants", native to the border of Burma and Assam, and schooled by the Buddhist Kampti people of eastern Assam — who originated in north-west Burma and had in fact migrated into India via the Chaukan Pass in the early nineteenth century. But Mackrell inhabited a very multicultural world, and although he designated his chief elephant man at Namgoi Mukh a "Kampti Raja", the man was in fact a member of the Naga tribe. He habitually wore a turban, a light waistcoat and what looks like a long tartan skirt, and his name was Chaochali. The porters Mackrell worked with were from the Abor tribe: wiry men with long black hair and crosses tattooed on foreheads.

The runner from Simon reached Mackrell at five in the evening. He was working in the rain, unloading rations. On a normal evening, he would have knocked off work at about six, when pitch darkness rapidly descended on Namgoi Mukh. He would have had a hot soak in his portable canvas bath, then had dinner (tinned sausages, rice and dall). At 7.30, he and Chaochali, the Kampti Raja, would have listened to the news on Mackrell's portable HMV radio; they would then have had a couple of glasses of whisky — Mackrell made a point of having "a peg" every night no matter where he was — and talked shikar, that is, hunting, in either English or Assamese. Mackrell would then have gone to bed at 8.30p.m., ready for a prompt start at dawn.

Having read the chit, however, Mackrell got into a boat "as quickly as possible".

The boat was a canoe about twenty foot long and was punted with the current — and through the rain — by one of the Abors. Mackrell sat in the boat in his rain cape; he had an unopened bottle of whisky beside him. That was for Millar and Leyden. He would have recognized the name of Guy Millar, whose brother was a colleague of Mackrell's in the tea business. As the banks of the Namphuk slid by — sodden paddy fields and jungle alternating in the gloom — Mackrell lit his pipe.

At Simon, Mackrell handed over the whisky to Millar and Leyden — "that did them good", he noted in his diary, presumably unaware that his volunteer colleagues on the Hukawng Valley route had concluded "Alcohol could mean instant death in starvation cases". He then settled down to hear Millar and Leyden's story. We might picture the three — plus Goal Miri and Masson, the tea planter — in a bamboo hut, the rain falling all around (and trickling down the wall at one corner); a kerosene lamp on the collapsible table of the kind used for jumble sales in English village halls; Leyden wrapped in a blanket . . . the whisky going round. (Leyden was already on the mend, but as his health improved he became increasingly miserable about his dog.)

They discussed routes. There were known tracks, and Millar and Leyden had been somewhat assisted by a party of explorers not so far mentioned. These were Chinese, and they had hacked their way along the mule tracks between the riverside village of Miao and the Chaukan Pass in the cold weather season of late 1941, marking the route with tree cuts, the aim being to see if the Chaukan could form a communications lifeline for China. (It could not.)

Mackrell was amazed at the story of the Dapha crossing by means of human chain. He knew it to be so far "up" at that time of year that a crossing even by elephant would be risky. It was obvious to all — as they listened to the teeming rain — that if the river had been "up" when Millar and Leyden crossed over, it would be a lot further up by now, and Leyden made the point very firmly that Sir John Rowland and his party, groping their way through the jungle towards it, would most likely be starving already. Goal Miri said that, in view of the size of Sir John's party, and their likely condition, twenty elephants would be needed.

Mackrell said he would leave for the Chaukan the following morning. Millar wanted to accompany him, but Mackrell and Leyden wouldn't hear of it. Millar was in no condition for a Sunday stroll let alone another visit to the Chaukan Pass. Millar would write, "As one of our party was required to show Mackrell the way we had come, my brave little tracker, Goal Miri, volunteered to accompany the rescue party back,

despite the fact that his condition was none too good."
This offer was accepted, and it was agreed Goal Miri
would be paid 200 rupees for his trouble. As a measure
of this, a tea plantation labourer of the time earned
perhaps five rupees a week. Later, Millar, Leyden and
Goal Miri went off to slightly more comfortable
quarters, while Mackrell wrapped himself in a blanket
and slept on the floor of the hut.

It continued to rain all night.

The Boy Who Took *Acidalia trigeminata*

Guy Millar slept well on that night of 4 June, in spite of the roaring rain. After all, he had accomplished his mission. He wrote, "I knew that if anyone would succeed, Mackrell would, and my relief at his presence there that night cannot be adequately expressed."

Who was this man who had inspired such hope?

You might say that, as a grown man, Gyles Mackrell lived a *Boy's Own* fantasy — compensation, perhaps, for an actual boyhood played out in a very minor key.

He was born on 9 October 1888 in Marylebone, London, second son of Doctor Alfred Sextus Mackrell and his wife, Mary. From 1898 to 1905, he boarded at the school commonly known as Epsom College, which had been opened in 1855 as the Royal Medical Benevolent College. As such it had been in effect an orphanage for the sons of dead doctors, a profession with a lower status then than now.

By the time Mackrell went there, Epsom College was an English public school of the heartier sort, catering especially to the sons of medical men, although it continued to take in orphaned or disadvantaged sons of doctors as well. The boys in this latter category were said to be "on the foundation" — they did not pay fees. Gyles Mackrell was not "on the foundation", and nor was his older brother and only sibling, Ashton Mackrell, who also attended the school, this even though the boys' father, Alfred, had died in 1891, when Gyles was three. It was more common in those days for a parent to die at an early age, but the acknowledged psychological effect has presumably remained constant: the loss of a guiding authority makes the bereaved child more than averagely determined to impose his own pattern on the world. It would take Gyles Mackrell a while to get round to this, however.

Epsom College preached *mens sana in corpore sano*, and, having medical associations, it was in the vanguard of this movement. It was Victorian Gothic, high-ceilinged, and would have been draughty even if it hadn't been set high on the South Downs, well away from the possibility of contagion by Epsom itself. The location of the school chapel, 500 yards from the main building, gave the opportunity for a bracing walk every morning at 6.30, after a night in a Spartan dormitory under a single blanket. In 1862, Epsom College had become the first school in Britain to have its own swimming pool — not a heated swimming pool, mind you — and a benefactor of the school in the early 1870s was Dr Erasmus Wilson, who had founded the first Chair of Dermatology at London University, and who popularized the idea of the daily (cold) bath.

Back in the 1870s the school had been not so much hearty as wild. External inspections uncovered bad teaching, poor morale, bullying and theft among the boys, and the nature of the school in Mackrell's time was determined by the occurrence in 1882 of a mutiny — *The* Mutiny, as the records have it, of 1882. Trouble had been brewing for a while that summer. As an Old Boy, memoirist John Gimlette recalled that the pupils had mounted an expedition to beat up their long-standing class enemies "the stable boys in the stables at Burgh Heath near Tattenham Corner ... Nearly the whole school set out with cricket stumps and sticks to give them a hiding, consequently nearly everybody was absent from roll call." For this, as for most other transgressions, they would be beaten.

Soon afterwards, "A French boy was sent down for setting the gorse on fire, and then Lloyd, the captain of the school, was caught with a betting book and, to our great indignation and astonishment, expelled." Lloyd was supposed to go back home to the Isle of Wight, but he did not, and we can imagine the masters swallowing hard as he loomed up the next morning on the back playground. Lloyd was popular. He'd been the captain of the First XI and the First XV, and an elite bodyguard made up of members of those teams formed around him. There would be no roll calls and no classes that day. The shout went up, "To the Downs!" They would go and beat up the stable boys at Tattenham Corner! ... But no, they'd already done that, so they went to the dining hall instead, where, coming upon a school waiter known as

"Red Herring", they pushed him down the serving lift. "But he was not much hurt," according to Gimlette. The headmaster, Dr West, "supported by two sergeants", entered the dining hall. "Boys," he cried, "desist!" — at which every loose object in the place was picked up and hurled at him. Dr West cancelled term prematurely, and all the boys were sent home. The school had suffered a sort of nervous breakdown. The Reverend Dr West was replaced by The Reverend W. Cecil Wood; better qualified teachers were appointed, and, after the school had been repaired, it was refurbished. Muscular Christianity was determinedly brought about. Games were made compulsory, the chapel was extended; discipline was tightened up. According to Alan Scadding, historian of the school, Epsom College was "not a happy school in the 1890s", but it was a more efficient one.

A word that comes up in connection with Gyles Mackrell, as he seemed to others in his later years, is "shy" and — perhaps made reticent by the death of his father — he obviously did not put himself forward as a schoolboy. A browse through the school magazines of the time reveals that he was not in any First XV or First XI, or indeed any Second XV or Second XI. Neither his batting average nor his bowling analysis is deemed worthy of mention. He is not listed as winner of the Carr Divinity Prize, the Sherry Divinity Prize, the Engledue Latin Verse Prize, or even the Wilson Prize for Carpentry . . . or any prize at all — "And there were a lot of prizes at the school," says Alan Scadding. "They were an attempt to encourage the boys after the mutiny." Fittingly enough, given the amount of time he would spend in the jungle, Mackrell did join the Natural History Society, but even here he was low-key.

He did not participate in what appears to have been the main activity of the Natural History Society: measuring the amount of rain falling on Epsom. He did not log the number of times he saw or heard a song thrush. Mackrell may or may not have been one of the boys sitting close to the camera when a photograph was taken of the Society on a picnic on the Downs. More likely, his would be one of the indistinct faces at the far end of the long tablecloth stretched over the grass, on which a few bits of cake are sparsely dotted.

But in July 1901, he did briefly approach centre stage. A report of the recent doings of the Natural History Society states, "On a field trip to Oakshott, Mackrell took *Acidalia trigeminata*, an insect new to our lists." It is otherwise known as the Treble Brown Spot Moth, and in his beautiful book of 1869, *Illustrated Natural History of British Moths*, Edward Newman writes, "The moth appears on the wing in July, and has occurred in Devonshire, Hampshire, Sussex, Berkshire, Suffolk, Gloucestershire, and Worcestershire." It was pretty rare. Most natural history societies — and there were a lot in Edwardian Britain — would have thought it worth recording.

Epsom College was a cockpit of empire builders; most English public schools of the time could be so described. This was the heyday of the New Imperialism, a systematic promotion of empire in the face of international competition; the magnanimous shouldering of "the white man's burden". The Boys' Empire League, founded in 1900, set out its stall as follows: "Every member promises to treat all foreigners with Christian Courtesy and, in the spirit of noblesse oblige, to try to do nothing that would lower his country in their eyes."

A photograph of the school library at Epsom College shows a chilly looking room, rather sparsely furnished with books themselves, but with crossed rifles on the wall along with what look like African tribal shields. In 1899, Lord Rosebery, that great Imperial advocate, became President of the School. On Wednesday 22 November of that year, the Debating Society held a literary evening: "Before a poor audience, the following read selections from Rudyard Kipling's works: A. H. Platt: *Gunga Din*, from *Barrack Room Ballads*; G. Neligan: *Fuzzy-Wuzzy*, from *Barrack Room Ballads*." The latter begins, "We've fought with many men acrost the seas,/An' some of 'em was brave and some was not:/The Paythan an' the Zulu an' Burmese;/But the Fuzzy was the finest o' the lot."

Gyles Mackrell was "on the classical side", which is perhaps why his war diary of the monsoon season of 1942 is so casually elegant. His rankings show him in the middle of the forms in his early years, but sinking. In the lower fourth, he was fifth from bottom out of twenty-two. In the lower fifth, he ended by striking, for once, a resounding note: plum bottom out of twenty. By now, he would have been considering his future. What with being bottom of the class, university was out. He would have been reading in the school magazine of the choices made by Old Boys. Many trained as doctors, mainly at London University, but there was another persistent theme: "The Reverend Canon F. E. Carter, of Canterbury, has been appointed to the Deanery of Grahamstown." "Captain C. S. Spong, Royal Army Medical Corps, and G. D. Hunter, have been awarded the Distinguished Service Order" in recognition of their services during the Sudan Expedition. "R. M. Carter has passed into the Indian Medical Service." And then there was his own brother, who, being perhaps even more unacademic than Gyles (Scadding suspects so, having trawled the records of both), was listed in 1901 as follows: "A. Mackrell has been appointed to the Indian Staff Corps and has left England for his station in India."

Here was a route indicated to a perhaps under-confident young man. "Going out east" was a standard option for "younger sons", and *both* the Mackrells were younger sons in that they would have to earn their keep. If you proposed going to India without the top-drawer academic ability required by the Indian Civil Service, then the army was the easiest way, not least because half the British population of India was in the army. There was another option for the less bookish sort of boy: tea growing in Assam. According to Alan Scadding, "a number of boys at the school had done very well at that".

In the event, Gyles Mackrell would do both, as we shall see, and as a result he would step right into the pages of the adventure books in the school library. The reserved and undistinguished schoolboy would find in India a playground far more suited to his nature than the sports fields of Epsom College.

Sir John Meets the Commandos

We last saw Sir John Rowland on 17 May. He was being rained upon and besieged by insects in the jungle village he identified as Hpaungmaka. He had just dispatched Millar and Leyden. Shortly afterwards, he also sent some of the porters retained by himself and Rossiter back to Hkam Ho for more rice. The porters returned with the rice on 21 May, but while away they had decided to threaten a strike, since Sir John was keeping three days' wages in hand. Sir John had an argument with them about this, which he lost. "Eventually agreed to pay them daily which is a bad arrangement — however there was no alternative."

On 22 May, the railway and Rossiter parties set off at a slow pace, together with about thirty porters: enough men carrying enough rice for what Sir John envisaged as a 300-mile trek. "During the day's march," he wrote, "we followed the Paungma River which we had to cross thirty-six times for some extraordinary reason." (The reason would be that the river meandered.) All the time they were climbing towards the Chaukan Pass, and all the time it was pouring with rain. Conversation did not take the form of pleasant chit-chat: Sir John wrote:

"True, as a leader, I almost — and indeed did — hammer some people and lashed everyone with my tongue when they were for giving up and so drove them along . . ."

On 24 May, the parties had reached a river called the Nam Yak. It was raining and the river was in heavy flood. Eric Ivan Milne, the forty-three-year-old official of Burma State Railways, was running a temperature. They camped on the "wrong" side of the river, the east side. They had yet to cross it. Their camp involved some tents, some strung tarpaulins and some bamboo and palm-leaf bashas. They lit a fire, and flew a bed sheet from a tall bamboo, in the hope of attracting aeroplanes.

Here, at noon on the 24th, the railway and Rossiter parties were joined by a third lot: seven amiable jungle wallahs-cum-soldiers who had been rapidly co-opted into the effort against the Japanese.

At the time of the invasion, any young British male in Burma became an army officer more or less overnight, the default options being either the above-mentioned Burma Rifles or in the paramilitary Burma Frontier Force. This body (British officers, largely Gurkha soldiery) had been created to do for Burma what the Assam Rifles did for Assam — keep the minorities in line — but it became a more generalized defensive force on the eve of the invasion, before disintegrating under the pressure of events. All of the following four men were in either of these two forces, and their *de facto* leader was the oldest of their number, a thirty-nine-year-old Scotsman called Ritchie Gardiner.

Ritchie Gardiner — and you don't end up being called Ritchie unless you're a likeable man — had taken a degree in mining at the Royal Technical College in Glasgow. A requirement of the course was that students spend a year working in a coal mine, and the experience helped develop in Gardiner a social conscience and an interest in politics. In Burma, he rose to become a "senior forest man" with the timber merchants MacGregor's. As such, he was based in Rangoon, but spent eight months of the year "on tour" in the jungles, which he somehow managed to combine with having a seat on Rangoon City Council. As a responsible and respected citizen of Rangoon, Gardiner had been one of those entrusted with the task of wrecking the city in the face of the Japanese advance — the "last ditchers". Job done, he escaped Burma in a boat from Rangoon, but he then *came back* "to see if he could be any use" against the Japanese. He would keep a diary of his second attempt to escape the country.

He was accompanied by his colleague at MacGregor's timber merchants, a Lieutenant Eric McCrindle. There was also Captain Noel Ernest Boyt. He, too, was a forestry man, but in his case with the firm of Steel Brothers. Boyt was wiry, capable, pipe-smoking. In his diary, Gardiner presents him as amusingly gung-ho. Uniquely among the Chaukan refugees, he had no reservations about the pass, and was willing to march into it "with just biscuits and cheese".

Then there was Second Lieutenant William Arthur "Bill" Howe, at thirty the youngest of the four. He had been an employee "up country" (in north Burma) of the Anglo-Burma Rice Company. He was not therefore a forestry man; he was, as Ritchie Gardiner noted, without any disparagement, a "non-jungle wallah".

Like Gardiner, Bill Howe kept a diary, a very ebullient one in the circumstances. (On the apocalyptic Sumprabum road, he had found on the back seat of one of the abandoned cars a manual called *Sexual Improvement by Exercise*; it had flicker pages at the back to show what might happen if you followed the book's advice. "Odd situation," he wrote, "everything burning, the Japs presumably coming up the road, and us having a giggle.")

Whatever their regiments, it seems that Gardiner, McCrindle, Boyt and Howe were also attached to something called the Oriental Mission. It sounds like one of the American evangelical churches that brought Christianity to Upper Burma, but was in fact something rather more glamorous: a network of small Special Operations units whose job was to foment resistance to the Japanese. But so far it hadn't done much fomenting, just "a lot of marching about in the jungle", according to young Howe. Along with Gardiner, McCrindle, Boyt and Howe at this early stage, but forming a separate team or bond of friendship, there was also a Major Lindsay, a Captain Steve Cumming and Corporal Sawyer, a radio operator. These three had actually been functioning as a unit of the Oriental Mission, as opposed to just training, but there were no diarists among them, so they are doomed to a shadowy role in this story. We will call all these seven "the Commandos", and Sir John called them "a dashed stout crowd".

The Commandos had set off from Sumprabum on 13 May in good heart. They were carrying two wireless sets, and they had just made contact with "Calcutta", who replied that arrangements would be made to meet them coming through the Chaukan Pass, together with essential rations, medical stores and guides. The Commandos were accompanied by their own thirty Kachin porters, with whom they were on good terms. They paid them in silver rupees — "at a rate," Ritchie Gardiner wrote, "which would be considered fantastic in normal times" — and opium. ("No opium," wrote Gardiner, "no coolies. It is perhaps a shock to those unacquainted with local customs to learn of this.") After their first two days' march, Gardiner wrote, "My only fears now are malaria and knees". (He had weak knees.) He was "Taking ten grains of quinine every other day for former and trusting God for the latter!"

But soon the word "heavy" begins to recur in the diary: "very heavy going", "heavy mud", "heavy evergreen jungle . . . and LEECHES, in numbers I have never seen before." Each Commando would at some point find a leech up his urethra, and Ritchie Gardiner woke up one night after dreaming of eating a succulent bit of steak, to find a leech attached to the roof of his mouth.

When, on that 24 May, the Commandos met up with Sir John, they told him of the expected relief party, which he pronounced "very cheering news". He now

101

had two irons in the fire, the first being Millar and Leyden.

Ritchie Gardiner declared Sir John's camp on the Nam Yak in a plantation of young poplars a "topping site". From it, the Chaukan Pass could be seen: a gap in the treeline disappearing into clouds. Gardiner wrote, "It cheered me as a timber man to see our first pines — a group of 5 trees with fine clean stems of 70–80 feet, and 7–8 foot girth at breast height." Edward Wrixon Rossiter appreciated them, too; he identified them as *Pinus excelsa*. This Trinity College Dublin intellectual then cooked everyone a curry, perhaps from a recipe taught him by his Shan wife, and he managed to serve cake and coffee afterwards. But Eric Ivan Milne, railwayman, stayed in his tent when dinner was served around the fire. Dr Burgess-Barnett confirmed that Milne's temperature had risen to 105. He was in no state to resume the trek.

On 25 May, Rossiter, mindful of his pregnant wife, was for pushing on. He did not think it necessary that *everyone* should wait for Milne. He and his party and the Commandos set off, but Sir John and the railway party remained behind with Milne, who couldn't stand up. On 26 May, the railway party finally did set off, wading the Nam Yak and carrying Milne on a stretcher made from a ground sheet and two tree branches. That morning, an aeroplane passed overhead but ignored them. It was Sir John's fate to be regularly ignored by passing aeroplanes. The planes in question were probably ferrying supplies from Assam to Chiang Kai-shek's forces in occupied China, flying over what the pilots — mainly Americans — called the Hump, the eastern end of the Himalayas. These flights were in default of a road link to China, the Japanese having cut the Burma Road in April. In response, a new road, the Ledo Road, would be built, work getting properly underway in December 1942, this one approaching China across Upper Burma, and beginning from Ledo in Assam.

The railway party entered what they took to be the Chaukan Pass at 11.20a.m. on 28 May. Here they caught up with the Rossiters and the Commandos, and Sir John wanted to know where this famous relief party might have got to, since rations were "dangerously low ... rice and a few tins of cheese and meat and practically nothing else". Dashed stout crowd as they might be, the Commandos didn't know.

The Wizard's Domain

What was this place they were in? They were on the border of India and Assam. They were at a height of 7000 feet above sea level. The trees had become more like the trees at home, but also less like anything on earth. There were what might have been chestnut trees, except they were improbably big, and there were rhododendron *trees*, not bushes. It was rather cool, raining in such a way that it was difficult to imagine it ever *stopping* raining, and there was no other sound. Sir John described the setting as "a weird, eerie forest which resembled the Wizard of Oz's domain". By coincidence, the Commando diarist Ritchie Gardiner said the same: the trees "are gnarled and look very old. They are frequently hollow at their base and the trunks and branches heavily festooned with moss, which gives them an unearthly and depressing appearance, reminiscent of the forest in 'The Wizard of Oz'."

You can see why *The Wizard of Oz* (released in 1938) might have been on their minds. What does Dorothy say after the tornado? "I've a feeling we're not in Kansas anymore." And "People keep disappearing around here." The strange, rain-filled, melancholic light of her enchanted forest, the ferns of incredibly bright green, the trees of enormous girth . . . these all might have seemed familiar to our Chaukan wanderers. (But, in the film, you don't see the tops of those trees.) There were poppies in Dorothy's forest, and opium was everywhere in eastern Assam. Our evacuees were trying to follow a red-mud rather than a yellow brick road, and their destination wasn't the Emerald City . . . but it was verdant enough: the vast acreage of dark green tea bushes in Assam. Like the film, our story has featured a little dog that goes missing, and it will feature a potentially malicious monkey. On a more grandiose level, we could ask who or what corresponds to the Wicked Witch of the West, and the Wicked Witch of the East? And as for the Munchkins . . . better not to speculate, perhaps.

Gardiner thought the pass beautiful as well as frightening, and he picked five orchids that he did not think had been taken before, including an unearthly copper-coloured one. Since "there was nothing in their weight" he put them in his pack.

The forest was all around, rising steeply on both sides, and there was no clear forward path to be seen. This country was in fact suspiciously unpass-like. There might be a very simple explanation for that, said Sir John, who liked simple explanations. Perhaps they were not in the Chaukan Pass at all. On the way up, Sir John had seen another saddle on a mountain to the south, and he'd been thinking for a while that that seemed a better route. It could hardly be a worse one.

And at this point, his frowning gaze turned towards Moses the Dutch Jew. He claimed to have been through the pass before, in December 1940. He had recommended the route to John Leyden at Sumprabum, which is probably why John Leyden had recommended it to his colleague Edward Rossiter by means of the dispatch runner. Moses had also sold the idea of the pass to Sir John. But now he was telling them he didn't recognize the scenery. Chaukan means "leaning rock" in Burmese, and nobody had seen a leaning rock.

In his diary, Ritchie Gardiner attempted — and failed — to clarify the situation regarding Moses:

Moses name will occur from time to time in this Diary and it is perhaps as well to say a little about him. Of Dutch nationality, I had met him about two years previously whilst he was on a hiking-cum-conjuring tour in the Shan states. He was apparently an International Boy Scout amongst other things, and stated that he had been in Tibet, and I think Northern Siam. At the period we are dealing with he was employed by the Burma China Railways as a Surveyor and apparently it was his story of having crossed [the pass] in 10 marching days . . . that had influenced Sir John to take this route. The various discrepancies between his description of the route and the route as ultimately found are hardly explicable but there is little doubt Sir John made a bad bargain when he was influenced by Moses' tale.

Sir John would describe his entry into the pass as a "mistake"; it was "the worst of all routes to India". The Kachin porters evidently thought the same, because once they'd had a good look at the pass they decided to turn round and go home. They had been peeling away for a few days, and the Commandos had been forced to abandon their two wireless transmitters in order to carry more rice.

Sir John wrote, "All the Kachin porters refused to go one step further as they were afraid of being caught by the heavy monsoon and so not being able to cross the numerous rivers on the return journey. No amount of cajoling or money would induce them to go on and so they all cleared out, back to Putao district." The porters took some of the supplies with them, and other supplies had to be left behind, since it was impossible to carry them. "The immediate result of the desertion of the porters," Sir John continued, "was that one month's food had to be made to last three months . . ." He would later add, "The major hindrance to our progress, irrespective of other conditions, was the fact that all the Kachin porters deserted us at the Chaukan Pass, that is when we still had some 200 miles to reach Margherita. If these porters, as they had promised, had taken us to the Dapha-Noa Dehing confluence all would have been well . . ."

Thirty-year-old Commando Bill Howe viewed the departure more sentimentally: "Coolies fixed up our camp and then after their food said their goodbyes and left us. I thinking they were as sorry to leave us as we were to see them go. Said a special goodbye to Ah

Pong, Jap Naw and the headman . . . How I hate this running away and leaving these damn fine people."

On 29 May nothing happened. The parties stayed put at the entrance to the pass, hoping for the promised rescue party to turn up. Here are the meals eaten by Ritchie Gardiner on that day:

7 o'clock — one cup very weak tea with no milk or sugar
11 o'clock — rice and bamboo shoots
3 o'clock — one cup very weak tea as above
7 o'clock — rice and bamboo shoots with a few potatoes and onions.

On 30 May two newcomers stumbled into the camp. They looked haggard even by the standards of the Chaukan Pass; they were Captain John Fraser of the Burma Frontier Force and Sergeant Pratt of the Seventh Hussars. Young Bill Howe was delighted to see Fraser, a friend of his. (More or less everyone knew more or less everyone in British Burma.) They had been delayed for some reason in Myitkyina, and had then "run into some Japs". They were taken to a Japanese officers' mess, which had been set up in a chummery — a base for forest workers — outside the town. Fraser and Pratt had been paraded before some Japanese officers; things had then happened as they do in films.

Fraser and Pratt were tied hand and foot, and put into the walled garden to the rear of the house. Their guards took Pratt's boots and Fraser's glasses, which seems lax of them. (Why not, for example, take Fraser's boots as well?) Furthermore, one of the guards, seeing that Fraser and Pratt's wrists and ankles were becoming swollen, considerately loosened the bonds before going back into the house. While wriggling about the garden that night, Fraser and Pratt found a cigarette tin, and the prised-away lid was sharp. They managed to scrape it against the ropes at their wrist and so freed themselves. They then "beat it", although Fraser had lost his spectacles, and was practically blind without them, and Pratt had to walk in his stockinged feet.

They found the track to Sumprabum, and the wrecked cars, one of which had been wrecked by Fraser himself — which was his right, since it was his own car. Most of its contents had been purloined, but inside the glove box he found his prescription sunglasses, and so John Fraser would go through the mist, rain and jungle-gloom of the Chaukan route wearing a pair of round wire-rimmed sunglasses. As for Sergeant Pratt, he did manage to find some boots.

On their trek towards the Chaukan, Fraser and Pratt had fallen in with 102 Indian soldiers, from those two martial peoples of British India the Gurkhas and Sikhs, mainly the former. These men were pouring into the Chaukan camp even as Fraser and Pratt told the story of their escape from the Japanese. There seems to have been a fleeting attempt by Sir John to offer them money in return for their services as porters, but the men wanted to push on. They were all other ranks, officerless. In Myitkyina, a British officer they'd never seen before had ordered them to evacuate via the

Chaukan, a route about which they had heard bad things. They knew that the longer it rained, the more impassable would be the tributaries of the Noa Dehing. They had their own supplies of rice. They stayed one night in the camp, and on the morning of 31 May they continued on.

Later that same day, four of the Commandos — the four friends, Gardiner, McCrindle, Boyt and Howe — together with the lately escaped Fraser and Pratt, also left the camp. They would try to contact the elusive rescue party and send it back to the railway and Rossiter parties. The enigmatic surveyor Moses left with the Commandos, possibly to escape the reproachful stares of Sir John. Mr Jardine of Lever Brothers also went with them, in spite of being forty-five, and looking more like seventy with his white beard.

And so, after Millar and Leyden, a second advance guard was being sent on.

Sir John and Edward Wrixon Rossiter had been reconciled to staying put in the Chaukan Pass and waiting for assistance, a tricky strategy with so little food, and one that went against the grain for Sir John, a man of action. The trouble had been a lack of porters, but, on 1 June, a party of about sixty soldiers turned up outside Sir John's tent. As with the 102 "other ranks" who'd come in with the two escapees from the Japanese, Fraser and Pratt, the majority of these were Gurkhas, and more typical of the breed in that they were inclined to be helpful to a Briton in distress.

Any British history of the Raj will feature encomium to the Gurkhas, "our faithful allies in India since 1813". Gurkhas are from Nepal, a state lying between India and Tibet. It is sometimes mentioned in those encomia that the British had been fighting the Gurkhas before 1813, but this was regarded by the British as a good clean war (no doubt because they won), in which the enemy showed himself a formidable fighter. A deal was struck: Nepal was allowed independence from British rule in India. In return, the rulers of Nepal allowed their martial tribes (and the word Gurkhas encompasses many tribes and castes) to fight for the British. So it might be said that the Gurkhas ensured the independence of their homeland by curtailing that of other peoples who came up against the British in India.

Much sentimentality, and some mythology, surrounds the Gurkhas. In his memoir, *Bugles and a Tiger*, John Masters tells the story of a Gurkha regiment whose British officers called for volunteer parachutists. It was explained that this would involve jumping out of planes at about 1000 feet. "The officers were surprised and pained to find that only seventy men volunteered", while others looked sceptical. It was later discovered that the volunteers had not appreciated the significance of the parachute. As far as they were concerned they were volunteering simply to jump out of a plane at 1000 feet, hence the slight reluctance. Masters also tells the story of the Gurkha who walked out of Burma after the Japanese invasion. He navigated

111

alone from Rangoon to Assam using what turned out to be a street map of London.

The point of the story is to illustrate the mystical kinship between the Gurkha and the mother country that had adopted him. The typical Gurkha, with his direct gaze, satirical humour, intolerance of bullshit — all backed up by his trademark razor-edged kukri, or curved knife — would have done very well in the East End. Yes, he might be a Hindu, but not the picky kind. He liked a gamble, a smoke and a drink, and he was certainly not a vegetarian. (It is said that, in the First World War, Gurkha officers would even, *in extremis*, permit their men to eat bully beef, albeit with the labels removed from the tins, and on condition it was presented to the men as corned mutton.) And like many an East End hard man the Gurkha was only five foot tall and wore a wide-brimmed felt hat.

On 1 June, Sir John struck a deal with his Gurkhas, who had some food of their own: in exchange for payment, they would act as porters to the railway party and the Rossiters, and on 2 June they all set off: "The track was an exceedingly difficult one up and down hills and mountain sides. Some of the gradients were as steep as 1 in 1 . . ." On 4 June, Sir John noted, it "Poured with rain from mid-night and continued all day . . . The weather and road were vile." 5 June: "Another vile pathway." 6 June: "Another vile pathway."

A Bad Start for Mackrell

When he woke from his sleep on the floor of the basha early in the morning of 5 June, Gyles Mackrell was confronted with a familiar problem: river trouble. It was still raining and the Namphuk was flowing fast, and — as far as he was concerned — in the wrong direction. Progress upstream in the canoe was slow, and it wasn't until late morning that he reached his camp at Namgoi Mukh, where he found that "all the best elephants" of his eighty-four had been loaded up by Chaochali and sent off towards the Hukawng Valley, and its starving refugees.

Other good elephants were "dispersed in the jungle". It should be explained that tame elephants at work in the jungle are kept on a "free-range" principle. They are left to forage in the vicinity of the camp, perhaps lightly hobbled with ropes tied around the two front feet, but in any case trained not to wander too far. Even so, the elephant man in the jungle is resigned to spending the first hour of his day rounding up his charges. The only alternative would be to bring the jungle to them, which would involve a lot of chopping down of leafy branches and scything grass.

Mackrell did not have the time to spare, so he began loading up twenty *reasonably* good elephants. The first thing a tame elephant carries on its back is a soft pad to protect its spine. The luggage is secured on top of that. What did Mackrell and Chaochali load onto those elephants? Firstly, food: the rice, dall, tea and so on that had been accumulating at his camp for dispatch to the Hukawng Valley route. Besides such basics, Mackrell took tinned sausages, tinned cheese (cheese generally came tinned in Assam in 1942) and jars of Marmite, which was popular with the British in India: it was easily transportable, and it didn't go off. Marmite also symbolized home, even though it was named after a French cooking pot (*marmite*), and it was a German scientist, Justus von Lieberg, who first bottled brewer's yeast as a savoury — and very salty — food. Whether Mackrell loved or hated Marmite — and the mythology is that no intermediate position is possible — he knew that it was considered a good prophylactic against the Vitamin B deficiency that causes beriberi, and its pungency was such that a small amount of it could flavour a lot of mouldy rice. He also took Bovril, which could change the taste of boiled water should anybody be so heretical as to become bored with tea. When Mackrell himself wanted to move on from tea, he tended to drink whisky or rum, and he took bottles of those, too. With his evening peg — and at other times — he liked to smoke cigarettes or, for preference, his pipe. So he took tins of cigarettes and tobacco. (The most popular brand of pipe tobacco in India in 1942 was called Barney's, and it was advertised in magazines with a testimonial — allegedly unsolicited — from a man who had supposedly knocked about a good deal with the Norwegian whaling fleets. In the advertisements he told of how one night, while iced in somewhere close to the Arctic, he was offered £2 for his tin of Barney's, which normally retailed at a shilling. He turned it down.)

Mackrell also took a wooden box full of medical supplies; some bed sheets, blankets and a collapsible camp bed for himself. He took some tents (unlike Millar and Leyden, he would have the benefit of these); some tarpaulins; some tins of kerosene; his portable HMV radio (which actually wasn't all that portable); a fishing rod (but not necessarily for fishing, as we will see), at least two fishing nets, nail scissors (but not for cutting his nails, as we will also see), a quantity of dabs (sharp swords) and kukris, some rifles or shotguns, a Bren gun (a light machine gun); a gun-like lamp (switched on with the press of a trigger) for sending Morse signals to aeroplanes, together with a battery pack for same; two lengths of white oilcloth rolled around steel poles, on which three-letter Morse codes could be written out, with stones or jungle mud, to be read by passing aeroplanes. He took a number of umbrellas; a quantity of silver rupees; rope for tethering elephants; some tobacco tins containing raw opium wrapped in silver foil; pens, paper and envelopes bundled in a leather stationery folder with an oilcloth cover (for the writing of diary and chits); a collapsible canvas bath (an article commonly employed in India, and always sold with the proviso "For outdoor use only;

some leakage is inevitable"). And he took at least one 16mm cine camera and film in canisters, because he was a keen amateur film-maker.

Mackrell packed in a hurry. Not only was he trying to save starving people, but if he delayed his departure he might be ordered not to go. He knew the Chaukan route was considered by military and civilian authorities alike to be unsurvivable in the monsoon; a rescue mission would be deemed too dangerous, a waste of manpower and elephants. Millar and Leyden had survived it, but only just, and they were relatively young and fit and had the good luck of meeting the Mishmis. Also, the route was becoming more difficult with each successive day's rain.

Mackrell set off at dawn on Saturday 6 June. He had left instructions for Chaochali to muster another team of elephants, and to follow him into the Chaukan as soon as he could hand over the original relief operation from Namgoi Mukh — serving the Hukawng Valley — to others.

At 4p.m. on the 6th, Mackrell and his elephants arrived at Miao, the village on the south bank of the Noa Dehing that Millar and Leyden had come to about thirty miles after crossing the Dapha. Miao is pronounced — by the British — like the noise a cat makes. It was, and still is, a pretty spot: a tight cluster of tin-roofed shops and bamboo houses overlooking the wide river, fields of grazing cattle and the soaring blue hills beyond.

Mackrell would have to cross to the north side of the Noa Dehing because any Chaukan refugees would be progressing along this side. Millar and Leyden had probably been rowed across it by a Miao ferryman, but it was higher and faster now, and Mackrell wanted to get his elephants over. Besides, the ferrymen of that Buddhist village — and every other resident — were attending a funeral. Life in Assamese villages is communal. If a house is built, everyone chips in with a material or physical contribution. Similarly, everyone attends a funeral: the sacrifice, the prayers, the interment, the feasting. The headman of the village, a man called Mat Ley, told Mackrell he would have to put off the crossing until the next day. So Mackrell and his mahouts stayed in a dak bungalow — or government guest house — on a cliff above the river. The packs were taken off the elephants and they were put to graze.

Dinner was cooked by Mackrell's personal servant of the past thirty years, an Assamese called Apana. He and Mackrell ate with the mahouts. Mackrell basically liked the mahouts, and when they were behaving well he called them his "boys", as in "made tea for all the boys", a frequent diary entry. He admired their skill, their closeness to the elephants. A mahout does not necessarily work with the same elephant but ideally he would do, and that's a lifetime relationship, since an elephant lives for between fifty and seventy years. The story is told of the Assamese mahout who was keen on drink — by no means a unique case. One afternoon, he came back from a lunchtime session and keeled over in a jungle clearing. Seeing that the sun was beating down on the small prostrate figure, the mahout's elephant stood over him for an hour while he slept, making shade. Elephants are as endearingly loyal to a single master in that way as dogs, which, by the way, elephants hate. There may have been extra fellow feeling between that elephant and his mahout because elephants, too, have a taste for alcohol. In his book *Elephants*, Richard Carrington writes, "Nearly every elephant worth his salt will knock back a gallon of beer with the enthusiasm of a cricket team after a thirsty match", and in *The Ivory King* Charles Holder mentions an elephant that could "draw a cork from a bottle of claret and drink the contents without spilling a drop". It was the habit of tea garden labourers of Assam — who lived in huts with mud walls — to keep rice wine in buckets or cooking pots. The elephants which also laboured in the tea gardens would sometimes use their trunks to punch a hole through the walls in order to suck up the wine. Having become drunk, they might then knock down the entire hut.

After dinner, Mackrell unpacked his portable HMV radio and sat on the veranda. All was dark below; a light rain was falling. He lit his pipe. If he had tuned into Radio Tokyo, he would have heard the announcer with the almost perfect English accent boasting that Japanese Imperial Forces had completed the liberation of the Burmese people. Or, if he wanted to take his mind off the war and the foaming river below, he might have tuned the dial until he picked up some light jazz, of the kind played in his favourite restaurant in Calcutta, Firpo's on Park Street. Either way he would have been sipping a whisky, while the mahouts smoked a little opium.

The next morning, Sunday 7 June, Mackrell and his men took their twenty elephants down to the sandy banks of the river. They were accompanied by some of the villagers, including the headman, Mat Ley. It had stopped raining, but the clouds were mustering for another downpour and the water still raced. While grateful for Mat Ley's offer of boats, Mackrell was determined to cross with the elephants. It would be no harder for them to cross with their loads than without, and the elephants were needed on the other side — for marching up to, and then crossing, the notorious Dapha. The mahouts roved up and down the white stones of the riverbank, looking for crossing places. Some of the elephants seemed keener on finding them than others. A few had wandered over to graze on bamboo leaves in a thicket some distance from the bank, as if to say, "River? What river?"

Mackrell had his eye on a particular mahout. He was called Gohain, and he was Mackrell's personal mahout, his chauffeur you might say, and he was aboard a male elephant called Phuldot. (All captive elephants are given names, but this is in order that they can be talked about rather than because they answer to their names. If you stand a few feet away from an elephant and call out its name, it will slowly fix you with a rather disparaging stare with its tiny white and bleary eyes, and that's about it.) Phuldot was a good elephant, and Gohain was a good mahout.

119

Phuldot was already knee-deep in the water, and Gohain was talking to him. He called Phuldot "samboyt", meaning "sir". The word "agad" would have featured, meaning "forward". Phuldot began walking through the seething water, Gohain bantering with him all the time — "We're in rather a hurry, sir, if you *don't* mind". He was lightly tapping Phuldot with the side of the sword-like stick called an ankus; he did not prod Phuldot with the sharp point — that was only used for a reproof. Midway over, Phuldot disdainfully lifted his trunk, a small accommodation to the seething river. He wavered slightly in the middle, but at no point did Phuldot lose his footing on the shifting rocks of the river bed. When Phuldot emerged on the north bank the tide mark only came two-thirds of the way up his body, and all the luggage he carried was dry.

By now, some of the others — elephants being herding animals — had begun to follow, but not all of them. One began to signal distress, waving its trunk and trumpeting when only a few yards in. Unprompted by its mahout, the elephant suddenly collapsed into the second amphibious mode: starting to swim with trunk upraised. But the tide was too strong, and it scrambled up onto the same bank further down. At this, three others began trumpeting, and turning away from the water. Their loads were removed, and the mahouts began trying to get them to swim across . . .

By the middle of the afternoon, Mackrell had got sixteen of his twenty elephants across the Noa Dehing. The other four remained on the north bank, in the care

120

of the villagers of Miao. Their loads had been distributed among the bolder sixteen, minus a certain number of rice sacks, which Mackrell left at Miao in the care of some men of the Second Battalion of the Assam Rifles, who would begin to create a support camp there — another staging post for refugees.

Over the next few hours, Goal Miri led the way through the thickening jungle, earning his 200 rupees, but Mackrell decided that the track he was using was not the most direct. For now, he pressed on and, with the light fading, the party came to that "small" tributary of the Dapha, namely the Debang river. After crossing the river, Mackrell noted, "We saw some Mishmis fishing." Now it will be becoming apparent that if you were going to meet anyone at all thereabouts, it was going to be Mishmi tribesmen fishing. These were not the same ones who had assisted Millar and Leyden, but they were equally accommodating. Mackrell explained in Assamese what he was doing, and the leader of the Mishmis ("a really splendid man") agreed, for a remarkably low fee of ten silver rupees, to guide his party towards the Dapha along wild elephant tracks — a shortcut, in effect, even if the mahouts did have to chop away at the trees as they progressed. On the evening of the 7th, Mackrell made camp in a clearing. During the night, it started to rain again, and we might picture the rain falling onto the mush of tea leaves left in the billy that stands near the smoking fire.

War And Tea (Part One)

In 1834, the free trade movement in Britain led to the East India Company losing its monopoly on the China tea trade. The Company's focus turned to India, where what seemed like a viable tea plant had been discovered in Assam. In the early 1830s, its viability was confirmed by research carried out at the Botanical Gardens just outside Calcutta, which was fitting since Calcutta would become a staging post for aspirant British tea planters in their journeys to the jungles of the north-east, and a visit to the Botanical Gardens would provide a foretaste of those jungles, a patch of which they would have to clear before settling down to their new lives.

In 1838, Assamese tea was marketed in London for the first time, and it went down well. It had a strong, malty flavour, making what we know today as "English Breakfast Tea", the name carrying the false implication that it is somehow of English origin. Through the production of this tea, the digging of coal mines, the establishment of brick works and railways, the laying out of cricket pitches and golf courses, the British would chip away at the exoticism of Assam.

India was not a colony in the literal sense. Its only settlers were the tea planters. In 1884, one George M. Barker published a book called *A Tea Planter's Life in Assam*, which was meant as a guide to becoming a planter but reads like one long attempt to put the aspirant off. The book begins: "A *mens sana in corpore sano* is absolutely necessary to resist this dreadful climate: the work is very hard, the sun is a terrible enemy." Having decided he can stand the strain, the would-be planter can look forward to the journey out: "The much dreaded and talked-of voyage is after all a miserably prosaic affair; uneventful, with scarcely an incident to break the monotony . . ." He arrives at the gateway to his adventure, Calcutta, capital of the Raj: "Calcutta — giant city though it is — boasts of only one fairly good hotel, the Great Eastern . . ."

After a few days in the capital, during which the traveller would be well advised to have some linen suits run up, and to recruit some servants ("The number of servants required in India is appalling") there comes the journey "up country". Then, as in 1942, it was not possible to make the whole journey by rail; the latter part would have to be by steamer along what Barker calls the Brahmapootra (Brahmaputra) up to the town he calls Dibrooghur (Dibrugarh). Barker suggests that shooting an alligator from the deck might alleviate the sheer boredom of the trip.

And so the planter arrives at his new home, Assam, summit of his life's ambition. Unfortunately, "The impossibility of rapid communications render[s] Assam anything but a charming place of residence . . ." A good

123

road is "traversable by buggy", but "for an average road the only means of locomotion are tats or a hatti, the latter for choice". A tat is a pony; a hatti is an elephant, and almost the only positive passages in *A Tea Planter's Life in Assam* concern elephants. The elephant is "the most useful brute in Assam". In discussing them, Barker's cynicism falls away: "A giant of strength, willing and docile, he goes about his work in a business-like way, dragging gigantic trunks of trees, or carrying heavy loads that would otherwise be a source of perplexity as to how they were to be moved." The elephant is the one animal he is against killing: "The indiscriminate slaughter of these splendid fellows, under the title of sport, has been rightly tabooed, and a heavy penalty attaches to anyone killing one without special permission."

Having cleared his bit of jungle with the aid of his elephants, and planted out his tea bushes, the planter could get into a routine of skirmishing with Nagas, arguments with the labour force ("Coolie management is the planter's worst trouble") and generally being ill. "But with quinine, chlorodye and a bottle of brandy, a man can do a great deal towards holding in check the various illnesses that are constantly besetting him." It is no wonder, says Barker, that "when struck down by fever, solitary and sick, they take to 'pegs'". The tea planters of Assam were reputed to take too many of them, especially as far as the cerebral types of the Indian Civil Service were concerned. In *The Ruling Caste*, David Gilmour writes that if one posting was more unpopular than malarial Burma, it was Assam, which was highly malarial *and* had tea planters: "Dismayed by the society of rough and heavy-drinking tea planters in Assam, the young Civilian might yearn for the panelled walls of his Oxford study."

A book of 1912, *In Abor Jungles* by Angus Hamilton, approvingly describes the tea planter as a law unto himself: "The tea brews in the planter much the same spirit of jovial independence and hospitality that the breeding of sheep and cattle does in the colonial run-holder." In the years immediately before the First World War, the planter was slightly less of a rough diamond than his Victorian predecessor, but he was still tough. The planter himself usually did not own the tea garden he cultivated. He took the heat — literally — for the owner, who stayed in London, thank you very much, and only went out to his garden in the cold season, if at all. The planter, whether employed directly by the owner of the garden or by a managing agency, was paid to be in the front line. He must withstand firstly the other planters, with their heartiness, sportiness, insistence on clubbability, which is why the planter's wife would also be interviewed when the appointment of her husband was under consideration.

For the planter's wife it wasn't a matter of finding a spider in the bath in the morning . . . One wife, who was in Assam during the 1950s, found a six-foot-long monitor lizard behind the sofa on her first day. A couple of years later (after her first bout of malaria, this was) the same woman suspected there might be rats in the attic of her bungalow, because she could hear scratching as she lay in bed. In fact, the rats had moved on. They had nested in the hessian that lay between the roof beams, and their urine had made the hessian soft, which in turn attracted snakes: a colony of very venomous banded kraits. One day, the ceiling dissolved, and a banded krait fell on her bed. She wasn't in it at the time, and she was by now acclimatized to Assam. (For example, she had christened the six-foot monitor, which turned out to reside in the drain of the swimming pool, Rodney.) "I just called in the bearer, and he bashed it [the banded krait] with a stick." She had "about a dozen household servants, but I'd rather not have had any — or maybe just one. They just sat around and stared at you. It was really irritating."

This was the rugged world that Gyles Mackrell entered when, on the eve of the First World War, he became an assistant manager with a company that ran a tea plantation at Lungla, Assam. This was 5500 acres in the Surma Valley, the second valley of Assam by its borders of the time after the Brahmaputra Valley. He was also a part-time soldier, having enlisted in the Surma Valley Light Horse directly upon his arrival in India. This small, decorative regiment of 300 or so men — one of about forty volunteer regiments in late Edwardian British India — had a training ground at Lungla. Mackrell must have been doing quite well, because the Surma Valley Light Horseman was not only not paid, but he had to buy his own uniform, which was pricey, what with the knee-high leather boots, the braided tunic and helmet with brass spike and chain; then there were the mess bills and he might opt to buy his own horse. For this, a "charger fund" had been set up by a group of tea agency houses in Calcutta — a clue to the day jobs of the regiment's members. In 1890, a Major Nicolay, who had examined the Sylhet Squadron, observed, "The majority of gentlemen forming this Corps are Tea Planters in the District, generally speaking, good riders and very fair shots, well acquainted with the roads and paths about the country, and . . . would render excellent service in time of need to Government."

The regiment's founding purpose had been to intimidate the surrounding hill tribes which were always liable to give trouble, and in this sense it was like an elaborate neighbourhood watch scheme for tea planters. But it was also recreational. There were polo tournaments, tennis days, mess dinners and lunches. The members of the regiment prided themselves on their resilience; on the other hand, they did not drill during the rains. A book called *Through Fifty Years: A History of the Surma Valley Light Horse*, by the Reverend W. H. S. Wood, contains photographs of beautifully dressed men posing in formation in arid fields. One shows a unit of men standing like a football team, while the commanding officer lounges in front like a glamour model. As with the Epsom College magazines, the book records no prizes for Gyles Mackrell, whether for musketry, horsemanship or sport, but there is an appendix headed "Decorations and Awards Gained by Members of the Corps", and here he *is* mentioned, although it would for something he would do shortly after leaving the regiment.

127

When war came, the Surma Valley Light Horse could not stand alone as a fighting force (too small), so it became a unit of the Indian Defence Force, which was a sort of part-time but conscripted home guard for India that lasted until 1919. Payment was introduced, together with route marches and drilling in the rains — all very regrettable to the old hands. But Gyles Mackrell had moved on.

In early 1916, after a period in North Africa with an Indian Army cavalry regiment, he joined the No. 11 Squadron of that predecessor of the RAF, the Royal Flying Corps. One thing we can say with certainty about any First World War pilot is that he was brave. The plane that recurs most often in the squadrons Mackrell flew with was the BE2, whose initials stand — rather discouragingly — for Blériot Experimental.

Mackrell trained in France before embarking on the most dangerous job possible: flying planes over enemy trenches in order to protect slower moving artillery observation aircraft. The pilots of No. 11 Squadron were the first "fighter pilots" in that they engaged enemy aircraft in aerial combat. But there were many other ways for them to be killed: by being shot by the enemy from the ground, or accidentally by their own side, or by the malfunctioning of their flimsy aircraft.

Gyles Mackrell was lucky still to be alive in April 1917, when he returned to England, now as a member of No. 33 Home Defence Squadron, patrolling the North Sea coast. His job was to look out for enemy aircraft or Zeppelins, but there weren't many of either,

128

and it is likely that, as a second lieutenant flight commander, he also trained pilots.

In February 1918, Mackrell was back where he belonged: in India, amid life-threatening weather. He was now flying with No. 31 Squadron, whose badge featured the star of India and the motto *In Caelum Indicum Primus*, meaning "First in the Indian Skies". They were the first RFC squadron to operate in the country. There was little private aviation at the time, so it follows that when, on 8 February 1916, two 31 Squadron officers looped the loop above the squadron's base at Risalpur (located within the North-West Frontier Province, sixty miles south of the Khyber Pass), this was the first time the feat had been performed in India. Exuberantly looping the loop over Risalpur became a routine activity for the squadron, and it suffered its first fatality in December 1917 when a pilot and mechanic were killed attempting a double loop.

As with the Surma Valley Light Horse, the original purpose of No. 31 Squadron was the intimidation of tribesmen, in this case those of the North-Western rather than the North-Eastern Frontier. The official history of the squadron recounts, somewhat implausibly: "At a Durbar held at Peshawar in February, 1916, two B.E.2's were demonstrated before all the chiefs of the trans-border tribes. The tribesmen said at the time that 'the machines were only large birds and no one could possibly be inside them.' However, when the machines landed and the Chief Commissioner was taken for a flight they remarked that 'the days of robbery and murder are at an end. Now the Raj can see all our doings.' "

In 1917, No. 31 Squadron was engaged in operations against Muslim Mashud tribesmen in the volatile territory of Waziristan, between Afghanistan and the North-West Frontier Province of India. British Political Officers attempted to control the territory by forming alliances with some of the tribesmen, and paid with their lives when the balancing act went wrong. The most rebellious tribe were the Mashuds. There had been skirmishes throughout the war, and, in early 1918, the Mashuds and their allies were emboldened in their campaign by the British entanglement in the Middle East, and the anti-British incitements of Turkish agents in Afghanistan. An official report called *Operations in Waziristan* contains sketchy maps that suddenly give way to a "vertical photograph" of the territory: this shows a rocky ravine resembling the surface of the moon. The photograph might have been taken from a plane flown by Mackrell himself. The pilots of No. 31 Squadron were involved in aerial reconnaissance, and bombing raids against the villages of the rebellious tribesmen. The tribesmen's houses were half underground and made of mud — very hard mud — and, because they were practically impervious to the 20lb Cooper bombs dropped on them, the pilots might aim instead for the adjacent flocks of sheep. (Cooper bombs looked like bombs in cartoons: teardrop-shaped with a fin at the rear end. Early in the war, they had simply been hurled down by the pilot, but by now they were

130

retained under the wings and released by the pull of a lever in the cockpit.)

It was said the tribesmen would attempt to counter the planes by casting spells on them, and that they would use the unexploded bombs (initially, Cooper bombs often failed to explode) to reinforce their houses. On the other hand, the tribesmen were excellent shots, and often had the opportunity to shoot *down* on British planes from the peaks of their mountains.

Most of the pilots operated from Lahore, capital of the Punjab. A note in the squadron records from summer of 1918 reads, "The climate conditions at Lahore, in the hot weather always the most unhealthy of Indian stations, have been unusually severe and work is almost at a standstill. Seventy per cent of the personnel at aircraft park are sick." *Operations in Waziristan* describes Waziristan itself as "the most unhealthy of the trans-frontier provinces . . . dysentery, diarrhoea, malaria and sandfly are rife". Summer temperatures hovered at around 125 degrees Fahrenheit in the shade. The planes could only operate in the early morning, otherwise the engines overheated and lost power. As it was, it might take a quarter of an hour to climb 1000 feet. The planes suffered a persistent — and one would have thought pretty fundamental — problem of supply, a shortage of tyres, so the pilots would sometimes take off and land on their wheel rims.

A history of No. 31 Squadron states, "Forced landings were fraught with great danger, capture resulting in mutilation and death by various very unpleasant methods." In his memoir, *First in the Indian Skies*, N. L. R. Franks gives more detail. "I should mention that on the Frontier we carried revolvers to destroy ourselves in the event of a forced landing in tribal territory, as it was said that the tribal women would remove one's genitals while still alive." To guard against this, Mackrell, like all pilots, would have flown with a chit written in Pashto in his tunic pocket. It promised a lot of money for his return safe and *intact* should he crash, and, because of the nature of the depredation to be guarded against, it was called a "goolie chit".

In early 1918, Gyles Mackrell was given command of "B" Flight of a sub-division of 31 Squadron, namely No. 114 Squadron, whose badge was a cobra's head and the motto "With Speed I Strike". From late 1917 to July 1918, this squadron was operating over Baluchistan, which lay south of the NorthWest Frontier Province, and was then defined, by the *Encyclopaedia Britannica* of 1910, as "a country within the borders of British India", although some of its ethnic groups would have had something to say about *that*. Britain attempted to govern Baluchistan from Quetta, where No. 114 Squadron was based. From here it conducted operations in the summer of 1918 against the Marri, a hill tribe located in eastern Baluchistan that had a track record of raiding into Sind and the Punjab. *Britannica* says of this region, "Its climate debars it from European occupation. It is a land of dust-storms and poisonous winds; a land where the thermometer never sinks below 100 degrees Fahrenheit in summer, and drops below freezing point in winter; where there is a deadly monotony of dust-coloured scenery for the greater part of the year, with the minimum of rain and the maximum of heat." As before, the tribesmen were elusive. A note of April 1918 reads, "fifteen flocks of sheep were observed. Five bombs were dropped on them with effect." The pilot is not named. Nor was any pilot named in the following: "Nothing further of note occurred until November 1918, when the Distinguished Flying Cross was awarded to two of the Squadron's officers." One of those two men was Gyles Mackrell. His DFC was given without citation; that is, no particular reason was given in public for the award of the medal, which may mean it was for general valour.

In 1917, our young flier had married a Mary Pullen at Newbury in Berkshire. If Mary Pullen seems a fairly common name, Gyles Mackrell does not. Various English telephone directories from the mid-1930s (when telephones became widespread) to the mid-1970s contain the name of a Mrs Gyles Mackrell, and this looks somehow like a defiant evocation of a marriage that had ended childless and in divorce, because Gyles Mackrell was in India throughout the inter-war period. Whatever emotional pain is subtly suggested by that directory entry, it must remain private, and if we are looking for a third party in any divorce, then India itself — a country that Mackrell clearly loved — might be put forward as a candidate.

By 1919, he had returned to civilian life as an area supervisor for Octavius Steel and Company, a managing agency for tea garden owners, and not to be confused with the abovementioned Steel Brothers. Company head office was in Calcutta, but most of the gardens it managed were in Assam, in whose capital, Shillong, Mackrell bought a house. By the time of the Second World War, Gyles Mackrell would be glancingly referred to in *The History of the Indian Tea Industry*, by Sir Percival Griffiths, as "a well known tea man".

War And Tea (Part Two)

Mackrell and all his colleagues were members of the Indian Tea Association, the trade association for the tea planters of India. It was created in 1888, the original purpose being to stop the planters poaching each other's coolies. Unlike Mackrell, *most* of these people had a quiet First World War. In *Green Gold: The Empire of Tea*, Alan and Iris Macfarlane write, "The Great War of 1914–18 produced the largest crop and the highest profits yet achieved. The troops in the trenches needed tea and they were not too bothered about quality . . . Few planters 'joined up' and the War did not touch India generally . . ."

In the inter-war years, profits rose, the result of mechanisation and growth of the tea habit in Britain, which by the time of the Second World War was the highest consumer of tea per capita. The planter was insulated by prosperity from many of the hardships inflicted by Mother Nature in Assam. His Indian labourers, the coolies, were not so protected, and the rise of Indian nationalism began to make them feel aggrieved at low pay and high mortality rates. In 1927 a delegation from the British Trades Union Council surveyed the conditions of Indian labour. It was highly critical of the conditions in which the tea industry coolies of Assam lived and worked, which it described as "the nearest approach to slavery". The ITA issued furious denials in the British press, and conditions did vary from garden to garden. The labourers, the planters argued, had good "perks". They were given homes (they lived in rows of huts called "labour lines"); the gardens had resident doctors, usually Indian, and schools on site.

The Second World War *did* touch the planters, and gave them a chance to restore their dented reputation. Tea was Britain's first ally in the war effort. About 10 per cent of photographs in any book devoted to the Home Front show people drinking tea, whether served to troops in a NAAFI canteen, or by the Salvation Army in bombed-out streets, or dispensed from watering cans to shelterers in Tube stations. Furthermore, a third of the planters joined up and left their gardens. (There was never any conscription in India.)

In March 1942 the government of India requested ITA assistance on the Burma-Assam border. The planters and their 450,000 labourers were asked, on a voluntary basis, to build motorable roads. These would be used to let the army out of, then back into, Burma; and to supply China. In addition, they were asked to provide humanitarian assistance to the refugees already flowing along the routes upon which the roads would have to be built.

There is no doubt the planters did as they were asked, but in *Green Gold* the Macfarlanes are cynical about their motives. They stress the road building for the military over the humanitarian relief effort, and the suffering of the coolies who built the roads, several thousand of whom would die on the job. The Macfarlanes assert of the ITA that ". . . right from the start it was less selfless patriotism than necessity that dictated their actions". The ITA's labourers were being poached by the military, and for this its members were compensated. The compensation must not be jeopardized by any foot dragging on the relief effort. Furthermore, the war boosted demand for tea. The Macfarlanes conclude that the ITA "must avoid the stigma of being seen to be unwilling, from selfish motives, to help the war effort".

But surely a desire to do the right thing often co-exists with a willingness to be *seen* to do the right thing. The story of the two main northerly evacuation routes from Burma is a story of humanitarian effort as much as military logistics. In the case of the first route — Tamu — Imphal — Dimapur — a rough track would be widened to make a motorable, if hair-raising, 200-mile road. This effort co-existed with provision of succour for the refugees. In the case of the second route, along the Hukawng Valley, the humanitarian work caused the building of what would become the Ledo Road to be suspended.

There was a certain constancy to the staging posts established by the ITA volunteers along the routes. They combined eastern and British hospitality: eastern in that the essential structures resembled the zayats (bamboo shelters with palm-leaf roofs) that occur in the remotest spots of Burma, built by locals for the convenience of travellers; British in the determination with which a certain warm brown beverage was dispensed. Here is a quote from an unnamed witness in Dorman-Smith's Evacuation Report: "The camps consisted of a series of bamboo barracks with well thatched roofs and floors built raised off the ground. At the entrance to each camp there was on one side a stall where tea was kept permanently brewing and on the other side was a dispensary with a doctor in attendance."

Note that the tea comes before the doctor. The British faced, in the Japanese, a tea-drinking enemy, but the British considered tea to be on their side. The symbolic role of tea to the British is that it asserts normality. That is why it is always served after an accident. Part of the appeal of tea is that its aims are modest. Its serving involves a reassuring but simple ritual, easily mastered. Tea provides caffeine, but not as much as coffee; it is a narcotic, but not to the extent of alcohol. It tastes better than water, which has to be boiled, and therefore purified, when tea is made. This is the greatest service of tea to humanity: it necessitates the boiling of water. The British exploited Indian labour in their tea gardens, but in inflicting the tea-drinking habit on the indigenous population — which they made the second largest consumer after the home country — the British did India a favour. Furthermore, the British style of tea drinking, with milk and sugar, increases the energy and protein value. The more scientists understand tea, the more virtuous it seems to become. It contains beneficial vitamins, minerals and anti-oxidants. It may offer protection against strokes and cancer. Tea leaves applied externally can be used as antiseptic, as any monkey in the jungle knows.

"On the road in-between the camps at about four mile intervals," the witness continued, "were ration dumps where coolies were sorted out and sent up the road with the supplies of rice, dhall, atta, bully beef, sausages and tea, which comprised our rations. At these ration camps tea was always ready for the wet and weary travellers."

There is something redolent of cosier outdoor scenarios from the mother country. The zayats did resemble shaggy bus shelters. And there is an echo of the dispensation of refreshments along the track of a cross-country run or a paper chase — kindness combined with a chivvying along. Refugees were "patched up", fed only a little at a time. The mantra was "Keep them hungry, keep them moving". In the early days, a little rum might be mixed in with the refugees' tea, but it was discovered that this could be fatal. Cigarettes were not withheld. The smoking of cigarettes to calm the nerves was considered just as sensible as drinking tea — which is to say very. The tea-planter heartiness, denigrated by the more refined members of the Indian Civil Service, was now an asset. Dorman-Smith quotes an observer of the ITA's effort:

The work of their officers and doctors (and labourers too) at the forward camps, living as they did for weeks at a time in appalling sanitary conditions, in great discomfort, with hardly more than coolie rations, handling mobs of terrified and therefore sometimes intractable refugees, with cheery sympathy but with firmness, is a fine record of which the Association may be proud. In many cases those staffing the forward camps suffered constant ill-health, but they carried on and hardly a man went sick.

But all this stiff-upper-lip stuff disregards the horror. A high percentage of the dead were found lying on their backs with their legs drawn up and their buttocks bare. It was said that 50 per cent of refugees had diarrhoea. In the later stages of the exodus, when the frailer refugees were coming through, almost all had dysentery. There was little solidarity on the routes. *Sauve qui peut* was about right. Older and slower refugees were abandoned by the faster and younger ones; children were left behind by parents, wives by husbands and vice versa.

Army officers recalling the evacuation tend to suggest that their men kept ranks. But in his report, Dorman-Smith wrote, "The worst feature of the Hukawng Valley evacuation was the misbehaviour of some of the troops, British, Indian, Chinese, they looted everywhere and everything . . . the Kachins were reduced to a state of starvation through the looting of their godowns and the mischievous destruction of their crops."

Those of the Chinese forces who took the evacuation routes to India were brave but wild men in uniforms of ill-fitting denim without badges of rank, and wearing sandals, which they preferred to boots. The Chinese private was paid about two shillings a month and had no supply lines to speak of. So he stole what he needed. Rice dumps were plundered; the radiators of army vehicles were drained — because the Chinese soldier liked to drink his water hot. Then again, British and Indian soldiers on the walkout also stole what they needed. In the British Army this is called "winning" an article . . . and how is stealing to be defined when there is no rule of law?

On the walkout, all soldiers were reduced to the status of infantrymen. When those soldiers who normally proceeded in tanks, trucks or cars turned to their infantrymen colleagues and asked, "How do we get to India?", the latter are said to have taken pleasure in replying: "You walk, mate."

To look briefly at the two main routes . . .

The core of the Tamu-Imphal-Dimapur route was a rough track stretching 130 miles from Imphal to Dimapur. Along this, the ITA had established its camps while coolie labour widened the track. Most of the refugees were ferried along this road in lorries supplied and driven by tea planters or their Indian labourers. The more southerly part of the route was fraught in a different way.

The first fifty or so miles, from the border town of Tamu, required more labour-intensive road building, there being less of a track to begin with. The refugees had to walk along this stretch, even as the road making proceeded. There was no jungle here, but arid, rocky

141

mountains, and the road being scraped into these was just a winding ledge of scree.

The oil-lit receiving camp at Dimapur was next to the railway station, but as engineers expanded the sidings, so, too, the cemetery beyond the camp grew every week. It was said that grown men would collapse with relief at the sound of the locomotives. But they were not about to board the *Brighton Belle*. The refugees would travel in rough and crowded goods wagons. There were no lavatories: the facilities consisted of ropes dangling from the side of the wagons, to which the refugees were expected to cling, and so the defecatory nightmare continued. But many refugees could not be put onto the trains without treatment in the hospital camp. And however busy its doctors, the Dimapur mosquitoes were busier still.

In May 1942, Dimapur was like a nightmarish parody of a Victorian town, with its vastly overworked postmaster, railway staff and gravediggers. It was a dispersal camp, not a rest camp, and the rule of thumb was that anyone who stayed there for three days would die. The superintendent, Alexander Beattie, manager of the Woka Tea Estate in Assam, has been described as "a practical-minded Scot", and he needed to be. He played host to 150,000 people, most of them ill in some way. He had brought with him the lorry from his own tea garden (about fifty miles from Dimapur), and seventy of his labourers. He ferried in vegetables, eggs and milk from his own, and neighbouring, tea gardens. His chief lieutenant was the wife of an officer in the

ITA's Scientific Institute, and she ran a team of planters' wives and their servants.

The Dimapur camp abutted a school building, and that was needed for storing the food, so the camp itself — and the hospital it incorporated — was of bamboo and palm thatch. There were no walls, but then the nocturnal temperature never dropped below seventy degrees Fahrenheit. The monsoon was coming, certainly, and the rain would then blow in, but it was assumed the flow of refugees would stop when that happened. But the monsoon came early and the people kept coming. Soon the floor was six inches of mud, the bamboo mats floating upon it and sanitation a lost cause. We might picture Beattie walking under the palm-leaf roof of the camp by night, the oil lamps swinging as they are buffeted by the monsoon, note-book in hand, perpetually organizing; the tea planters were great organizers, great logistics men.

On 10 May, the town of Imphal was bombed by the Japanese, and it is said that 60,000 died as a direct or indirect result. The raid sent a surge of refugees towards Beattie, who was beginning to run a temperature himself. He would die from typhoid on 12 July. The bombing of Imphal was the beginning of the end of Tamu — Imphal — Dimapur as a route for *civilians*, and the relief operation would be wound up by the end of June.

The Hukawng Valley route became the default option after the bombing of Imphal, even though it had been described, on that improvised road sign of April, as one of the "Valleys of Death", and here, too, a road was being built, or at least planned: the Ledo Road, the northerly replacement for the Burma Road. The Indian Tea Association volunteers and their paid tea garden labourers were supposed to have been assisted in its construction by a Chinese labour force sent by Chiang Kai-shek, but such was the chaos on the Burmese side that it was not possible to muster any such force, and work on the road was put off. (The Ledo Road would be built from December 1942 by American soldiers — mainly African Americans, 1000 of whom would die — and 35,000 local tribesmen and tea garden labourers, many more thousands of whom would also die.)

As mentioned, the starting point in Burma for the Hukawng refugees was the village of Shinbiwyang. There was a full ITA camp roughly every dozen miles thereafter, with sub-camps — manned zyats — in between. Each main camp had a small hospital, and those on the Burmese side carried out a programme of inoculation against cholera, which prevented an epidemic. The first goal for the refugees, and their reward for crossing the eight mountains and eight rivers in spate, was a village called Lekhpani, where the ITA had established its forward receiving camp. This was known as the "Tea Pot Pub" because of the meal refugees were served on arrival: tea, cheese and jam on biscuits. The sight of a tea pot must have symbolized the return to civilization.

There is an account of one group of refugees on the Hukawng route spending four hours trying to ignite damp bamboo in order to make tea. It was calculated that at Shamlung, a camp midway along the route, tea was consumed at a rate of five pounds per hundred people per day, in other words almost an ounce each, which is enough for ten cups; but then Shamlung was the camp that came before the highest part of the route, the 4000-foot Pangsau Pass, and the refugees needed fortifying for that. At the same camp, incidentally, the refugees consumed the same weight of Marmite as of tea.

After being given the once over at the Tea Pot Pub, the refugees left for the nearby railhead of Tipong. From there, they were taken by narrow-gauge train — built to serve the local collieries — to a reception camp at Margherita. This was in the heart of planter territory, as betokened by the rangy railway station, the telegraph poles, the bases of the roadside trees painted white with lime, giving the effect of the trees wearing bobby socks (it is done to deter ants), the dark green tea gardens rising gently on all sides, and the pretty nine-hole golf course on which the camp had been created. Here, finally, nature had been tamed. Bougainvillea flowered by the tees. The tents were on the fairways, and the camp HQ was the musty, wood-panelled interior of the clubhouse hall where tea and biscuits were always on the go, where many a dinner dance had been held, and where the names of past champions and club captains were proudly listed. From here, most began the 500-mile onward journey to Calcutta. The Margherita camp was overseen by a tea planter called Ronald MacGregor Thomson, a friend of Mackrell's who was equally keen on shikar, and known to all his many friends as Tom-Tom.

★ ★ ★

Some vignettes from the Hukawng route . . .

Late evening at a camp . . . two unshaven planters lighting cigarettes under broken brollies before setting off towards the Burmese side to look for stragglers. (These were called "back reconnaissances".)

The ITA camp at Nampong, on the Assamese side of the Pangsau Pass: half a dozen bamboo and palm-leaf huts — shaggy, lopsided bungalows with the rain falling on them and nobody about; the jungle rearing up vertically behind. (This was the destination for the elephants Gyles Mackrell had been dispatching from Namgoi Mukh.)

Another camp . . . a sea of black mud, with some rough lean-tos, a thoughtful looking soldier holding a rifle, rain falling and smoke rising from untended fires; a line of kerosene cans. It might be Passchendaele, except for the trees in the background.

Two teenage English boys in a zayat, one sitting on the bench watching the rain, the other reclining on the ground in front of him; but the one reclining is dead.

From late June, military purposes reasserted themselves on the Hukawng route. Back reconnaissances were sent out to pick up stragglers. In late July, the RAF flew the ITA Chief Liaison Officer, a man called Dudley Hodson, over the route. At Shamlung, he thought he saw a lone European man waving at him from among the abandoned huts. As far as the authorities were concerned, the principal evacuation routes were now closed.

But the drama was still unfolding on the other route to the north, another Valley of Death. In his book of 1946, *Forgotten Frontier*, Geoffrey Tyson speaks of "a more exclusive, clubbable route", as if a garden party were taking place in the jungles of the Chaukan Pass.

Captain Wilson Sets Out

On Saturday 6 June, when Mackrell encountered the Buddhist funeral at the village of Miao, our original pair, Millar and Leyden, finally arrived at the Indian Tea Association base camp on the golf course at Margherita. We might picture the flags that were left on the greens rippling in the hot monsoon wind as Millar and Leyden enter the clubhouse. They were received like heroes, or like ghosts. "Our arrival from the Chaukan," Millar wrote, "caused considerable surprise and stir." It would do. In late May an RAF plane had spotted a small party in the Chaukan; it had not been envisaged that it would ever come out. It is likely that Millar and Leyden were offered a very large number of cups of tea indeed.

Here they took tiffin with three officials: Tom-Tom Thomson, who ran the camp, Major General Ernest Wood, Administrator-General, Eastern Frontier Communications (a role that made him responsible for the overall Burma evacuation), and a senior police officer called Eric Lambert, who was designated Political Officer, Margherita. A Political Officer was an official administering an area of strategic or military importance, usually on the fringes of the Empire. Lambert was shortly to launch his own evacuation rescue — in his case he would locate the Chinese 5th Army, which had got lost in the Naga Hills during a monsoon. It is a testament to the Chinese reputation for unruliness that it was thought necessary to protect the head-hunting Nagas from *them*. Lambert had been a magistrate in the Naga Hills, and had led expeditions to try to stop head-hunting, so he knew the territory. He would find the Chinese (about 3000 men), then escort them into Assam, shielding the local Nagas from their depredations. As a reward, he would be presented by Chiang Kai-shek himself with the Chinese Army Medal (First Class) and, in spite of being Irish, he would be commissioned a general in that army. But that wouldn't happen until July.

Meanwhile, Lambert, like Thomson and Major General Wood, was in a slightly embarrassing position *vis-à-vis* Millar and Leyden: pleased to see them, but owing them an explanation as to why no ground party had been sent to look for them. Lambert explained that it was the combination of the Chaukan Pass and the monsoon that had been decisive. Nobody could survive *that*. Anyhow, the message from Millar and Leyden was that the party spied by the plane must have been the railway party of Sir John and the Rossiters, and that Gyles Mackrell had gone to look for them.

Guy Millar, ever eager to do anything but go to bed for about a week (to which he would have been thoroughly entitled), proposed a plan. He would be driven at speed to the airbase at Dinjan, where he would board a plane and be flown over the Chaukan. He would try to spot Sir John, or at least try to spot Mackrell, with whom he had arranged, during their nocturnal parley, a system of communication by signals. What Millar proposed to do next, having signalled to Mackrell, is not recorded, but it doesn't much matter, because Major General Wood scotched the plan immediately. He explained to Millar that three RAF planes had been "lost" flying over the Chaukan in search of evacuees. It seems it was as dangerous to fly over the Chaukan in the monsoon as it was to walk through it. There was the ever-present danger of crashing into a mountain, what with unpredictable thermals, lightning and the likelihood of the windscreen wipers being overloaded by rain.

On the other hand, the rescue could not be left in the hands of Mackrell who, even with his twenty elephants, was essentially undertaking a one-man mission. And so phone calls were made, telegrams were sent, runners were dispatched through the steaming rain and another, bigger, rescue party was assembled. It would comprise two units of Assam Rifles under the command of an amiable Yorkshireman called Captain John Reginald Wilson, who — very much *unlike* Sir Reginald Dorman-Smith — was known to all as "Reg".

Reg Wilson was born in York in 1902; his father kept a big stationery shop in the middle of the town. He attended a private school where he excelled at all sports. According to a surviving relative, "He loved sport, and he loved action." After leaving school, he began training to be a tenant farmer at a village just inland of Scarborough. He also joined the Green Howards regiment as a territorial — that is, part-time — soldier. Even so, rural Yorkshire did not offer a sufficiently dynamic life, and in 1927 he went out to India, probably having seen an advertisement in a paper seeking trainee tea planters. In Assam, he became the manager of a tea garden, working for the firm of Duncan Brothers, and Reg Wilson was the ideal tea planter. He was good-looking, with swept-back, pomaded hair, and as popular with his Indian staff as his fellow planters. He more than held his own at polo, tennis and golf. He was also — a further mark of amiability — a chain-smoker. All in all, according to the same surviving relative, Reg Wilson was "something of a playboy", but he was also a major jungle wallah, and in early 1942 he had volunteered to work as a civilian on the ITA relief effort in the Hukawng Valley. In mid-1942, he was made a captain in "V" Force, a unit created in anticipation of a Japanese invasion of Assam. It would engage in guerrilla attacks on the enemy, in cooperation with the Gurkha soldiery of the Assam Rifles.

Late on that Saturday, Reg Wilson was taken to the government bungalow at Margherita, where Lambert gave him a chit to the effect that he, and not the freelance Mackrell, was in charge of the Chaukan rescue. British Assam, like British Burma, was a small world (except physically) but Reg Wilson had somehow avoided meeting Gyles Mackrell, and he refers to him

151

in the early stages of the diary he kept as "Giles" Mackrell.

An indication of the urgency of his mission lies in the fact that Reg Wilson began packing to follow Mackrell at 3.45 a.m. on Sunday 7 June. He did so at the golf course in the pouring rain. He was not given any elephants. None could be mustered in time. Instead, he would have, besides his two detachments of Assam Rifles, forty porters, but these, unlike the Abors retained by Mackrell, were from the political porters, raised by the British from among the tribes of Assam — *professional* porters. They were known for their rigid working practices. They would walk a fixed number of miles for a fixed amount of money, and they tended to win any arguments about those terms of engagement by sitting down and refusing to move. Wilson also had his own Medical Officer, an Indian called Dr Bardoloi.

Besides such basics as rice and tea, here are some of the things Wilson asked the porters to carry:

Thirty-six umbrellas.

Eight bottles of rum.

One case of tinned sausages.

One case of Heinz Baked Beans.

One case of Bonax. (Wilson describes it as being "like Bovril".)

A hundred and sixty blankets.

He was told he would be able to collect mosquito nets from the village of Miao.

Elephant Trouble for Mackrell

As all these plans were being made to supplement Mackrell's mission, the man himself was being his customary, purposeful self.

In their jungle encampment, Mackrell and his mahouts woke early on the morning of Monday 8 June and struck out towards the Dapha river behind their newly recruited Mishmi guide. Mackrell led the men and their elephants over what he called "a wonderful road", which in that territory meant something about six feet wide with more rocks than red mud and with enough clearance above the elephants for the mahouts to sit up top without having to swing their axes at the oncoming branches. The party was ascending, and Lieutenant Colonel Charles Hugh Stockley wrote in his book *The Elephant in Kenya*, "The nautical roll of a big bull [elephant] going away slightly uphill is most pronounced, almost inducing one to break into a chanty."

It was raining heavily, of course, but Mackrell was noting with admiration "the really huge timber" — trees of 150 feet or more — and the great cliffs that bounded the Noa Dehing. But by 2p.m. the Mishmi guide was tired. He wanted to veer off the route and go to Tinguan, his home village along the Debang river, for a rest and a smoke of opium. And the mahouts made it clear that they quite fancied doing the same. Mackrell reminded everyone, in case they had forgotten, that "we were trying to save the lives of some starving people and that every hour might count". But he didn't just rely on windy exhortation. Mackrell doubled the Mishmi's fee to twenty rupees, and said he could ride on an elephant. As for the mahouts, he knew that they were keener on going to the village for a rest rather than a smoke. After all, they had their opium *on them*. He promised them a rest shortly, and he persuaded them — again, bribery may have been involved — to have a "whip round" of their opium. It came to about a quarter of a pound, and some was given to the Mishmi, so he had the prospect of a smoke when they came to their resting point. This satisfied the Mishmi who, as Mackrell acknowledged, "really was giving up a lot" in going so far out of his way to help them. He was giving up more than he knew.

Where did a man like Mackrell stand on the opium question? To have distributed the stuff, and encouraged men to smoke it, would have been not only frowned on in Britain, but was also illegal. It was illegal in Assam as well, but the illegality was only technical. The British did not want to alienate thousands of peasant farmers in Bengal by stopping the production of opium. And the British had been using opium to bribe Indians ever since the days of the East India Company. This was widely known back home, and objected to by some evangelical Christians, who in the early twentieth century would endeavour to wean Indians off opium by sending out a then-legal opium derivative sold in bottles that proudly proclaimed it to be "non-addictive" — namely heroin.

It was 2.30p.m. by the time all this had been sorted out and they got going again. The Mishmi guide warned Mackrell that there was no prospect of reaching the Dapha river that day, but they pressed on, into the sort of scenario that would have given most people a nervous breakdown, but that Mackrell tended to describe simply as "not very satisfactory".

"At 4pm," he wrote, "we ran into the middle of a very large herd of wild elephant, quite sixty of them." Soon, the wild elephants were on all sides amid the trees, and amid the rain, in the gathering darkness. Now, if you are surrounded by wild elephants, the one thing you must not do is come between a cow and her calf. That is one circumstance guaranteed to bring on a charge. The overriding purpose of a herd of elephants is to protect the calves. At any sign of danger the proper place for the calf is either immediately to the side of, or below, the mother. The main danger in the jungles of Assam in 1942 was tiger — a quarter of all elephant calves were killed by tigers at the time. Men are normally safe from wild elephants, but not if the calf seems threatened, and the calf has two particular bodyguards, neither of which is the father who, by the time the calf has been born, has become rather detached from the mother. But she has by then enlisted another female, a sort of "auntie" figure, to help with

155

the childcare, and this elephant becomes as protective of the calf as its mother, so doubling the danger to any humans who might be in the wrong place at the wrong time. And Mackrell and his men had "unfortunately" interposed themselves in just this way. So Mackrell walked warily, rifle in hand; he was afraid he might have to shoot, not that a loaded rifle is any guarantee against an angry elephant.

Then an aeroplane flew over; Mackrell didn't know what kind because it was hidden by the canopy of trees. Most likely it was one of the transport planes carrying supplies to Kunming — one of the "Chungking Taxis".

Whatever it was, it flew low and loud and elephants do not like noise. It is one of their endearingly middle-aged characteristics, along with their usually docile nature, and their appearance of wearing a pair of baggy corduroy trousers. Mackrell's own elephants didn't mind so much, but the wild herd began trumpeting, that is, screaming with rage. On top of this, the rain had increased, and Mackrell's own herd had come to a precipitous ascent with rivers of red mud flowing down between the trees, causing the animals to skid and slither, and in some cases topple over while others proceeded cautiously, on their knees, but even *their* loads would slide to the side, all of them being *overloaded*, the four elephants having been left behind at Miao. In addition, Mackrell and his men were beginning to be attacked by hundreds of leeches.

By 8p.m. it was pitch dark and they needed to camp; the mahouts were hungry, and the Mishmi wanted to smoke his opium. But there was no level place, no

156

water for the elephants, and when Mackrell lit his hurricane lamp and swung it before his face, he saw — through the hissing rain — that the ground was absolutely *swarming* with leeches.

A leech is a shiny, slug-like worm — a living ooze — with suckers at each end. Not all feed on blood; some feed on small invertebrates, eaten whole. Leeches progress like the proverbial inchworm, back end coming up to the forward end, making an arch, before the forward end moves on again. They breed in the monsoon, and wait on the ground, on tree trunks, on leaves, for their prey, which they detect by sound or vibration. As the walker approaches, the leeches begin moving hurriedly towards him, the ones on the leaves making the leaves shake. The walker feels he is the victim of an evil conspiracy. It is like being ambushed by a street gang: one attacker steps out from a doorway, another is already in your way, a third drops down from a window ledge (because a classic leech move is to drop into your hair, or down the back of your neck), and they close in from all directions. The anterior and posterior suckers engage, and the leech bites as the former is applied. An anaesthetic is secreted, so that the bite is painless, and an anti-coagulant. The leech drinks until it is full, and an engorged leech can be as big as a banana. It then drops off, perhaps bouncing as it lands. To remove a leech before that point, you can scrape away the suckers with a finger nail, but you have to be careful not to rip the teeth away: this will tear the wound and could cause it to go septic.

It was odd, Mackrell reflected. He had plenty of jungle experience, but not so much of jungle at night, and he had always been told that leeches were not active after dark. A man who knew leeches was Frank Kingdon-Ward, the great plant hunter. In a book about some of his wanderings of 1914, *In Farthest Burma*, he devoted a whole chapter to "Infinite Torment of Leeches":

There is nothing more horribly fascinating than to see the leaves of the jungle undergrowth, during the rains, literally shaking under the motions of these slender, bloodthirsty, finger-like creatures, as they sway and swing, then start looping inevitably towards you . . . Leeches entered literally every orifice except my mouth, and I became so accustomed to the little cutting bite, like the caress of a razor, that I scarcely noticed it at the time. On two occasions leeches obtained such strategic positions that I only noticed them just in time to prevent very serious, if not fatal, consequences.

Kingdon-Ward knew a good method of dealing with them. "The easiest way to get rid of a leech is to drop salt on it; the pressure set up through its porous skin soon sucks it inside out practically." The trouble was that ". . . one does not as a rule carry a salt cellar in one's pocket". Another method — and one favoured by your typical heavy-smoking British soldier — was to touch the leech with the burning end of a cigarette. This causes the leech to release its bite, and it is satisfying to imagine the foul thing screaming in agony, but the defence mechanism that causes it to widen its jaws might also prompt the leech to vomit its stomach contents into the wound, increasing the risk of infection.

When the leech has fallen off, the wound bleeds, perhaps for more than a day, because of the anti-coagulant. If the wound is quickly cleaned with soap and water — or if the jungle walker is lucky — the bite will leave nothing more than a sore that lasts a couple of weeks. Mackrell's remedy for those that landed on him or on his butler, Apana, was to snip them in half with his nail scissors. The two stopped to perform this ritual every fifteen minutes, in which time each man had acquired forty or fifty.

Mackrell, like all the British jungle wallahs, did not dress properly for the war on leeches. There was some merit in wearing few clothes, like his mahouts. You could then see exactly where the leeches had attached themselves, and they could be scraped off with a razor-sharp kukri, or you could spit the juice from the betel nut you might be chewing onto it — that would make it release its hold. Or you could wear puttees, with trousers tucked in, as the Japanese did. But Mackrell wore a long-sleeved bush shirt, shorts, socks and boots. The Burmese called the British "the trousered ones" because they did not wear the skirt-like Burmese longyi, but the British were only half trousered, either as civilians or soldiers, and many veterans of the Burma fighting would never wear shorts

again after the war, their legs being covered in sores
that never healed.

At 8p.m. Mackrell and his men were still progressing
in the dark, on foot or elephant, every man holding
either a torch or a hurricane lamp. All around, the
jungle seethed with the rain, the warm wind and
the leeches.

At 11p.m. Mackrell sensed that the mahouts were on
the verge of mutiny "and small blame to them". He
called a halt in a clearing near a small stream that was
clattering its way towards the Noa Dehing. They did
not bother with the tents, but rigged up some
tarpaulins; a fire was lit. They were near a great, dark
rock — a salt lick, but no animals came to lick the salt.
The mahouts cooked a meal for themselves; being
Hindus they had strict dietary rules, and would always
eat separately from non-Hindus. Mackrell must have
eaten something, too. Tinned sausages and rice,
perhaps. But all he mentions in his diary is tea — "hot
tea with rum in it".

The Mishmi smoked his blob of opium, which would
have been greyish, about the size of a cherry, and soft
but slightly gritty, like marzipan. He smoked it through
a bamboo pipe, with a clay bowl inset for the burning
of the opium. Before lighting up, he would have cleaned
out this bowl with a knife, building up the anticipation,
and so the pleasure.

It is likely that Mackrell was smoking his own pipe of
tobacco, as he observed the Mishmi. And what would
the Mishmi have observed as he took the first of the
dozen or so inhalations? The rain would still have been

160

crashing down; the jungle would still have been fizzing with leeches, many of which would still have been crawling inexorably towards him, but all this would have seemed . . . rather mildly amusing, or simply irrelevant compared to the overall benignity of the world.

The next morning, Mackrell and his men woke early. Their campsite was so exceedingly uncomfortable that it was easy to persuade everyone to an early start. The first job — after the brewing of tea — was to round up the elephants, and it turned out one was missing — an elderly female who'd been made particularly restive by the nearness of the wild herd. So they were now down to fifteen elephants, and the loads had to be redistributed again. It was — as usual — raining heavily; they wanted to get on, and the job was perhaps done hurriedly.

They set off along a track that came to border the cliff of the Noa Dehing. There was steep jungle to the left of this narrow path and a drop of "several hundred feet" to the river below on the right. At this point, one of the haulage pads strapped to one of the elephants slipped, so that it was beneath the elephant rather than on top of it. All the elephants were stopped on the cliff edge, and Mackrell and the men tried to refix the load. It was imperative that all the elephants remained absolutely still; the least slip would have sent them down the gorge, and the path was becoming more viscous with every minute, such was the force of the pelting rain. To refix the pad was a tricky job. The straps had to be cut away, and new ones tied on. But the job got done, and they continued on their way.

After a whole further day's hike, they began to hear another roar rising above the roar of the rain, and the roar of the Noa Dehing. It was the big one: the roar of the Dapha river.

Mackrell Reaches the Dapha River and His Work Begins

Elephants generally like water. They have been recorded as swimming along rivers for six hours or more at a time. In *Elephants*, Richard Carrington writes,

Elephants will sometimes go swimming, or wallow in muddy pools for the sheer joy of being in the water. An elephant bathing party is a most entertaining sight. The animals splash and trumpet, squirt water over themselves, or lie at full length with the contented expressions of elderly gentlemen surf bathing at the edge of the sea. The calves dash about on the shore in playful pursuit of one another, squeaking with excitement and pushing each other into the water. The cheekier among them butt their recumbent mothers playfully in the ribs or squirt water from their trunks in the general direction of some dignified old bull.

But this was different.

A full hour after first hearing the roar of the Dapha through the trees, the Mackrell party was still cutting through steeply descending jungle. At the foot of the incline, they arrived at the top of a cliff. In the gorge below was the Dapha. The cliffs bordering the river varied from sheer drops of 250 feet to 50-foot slopes. They found one of the latter, and took the elephants down. The margins of the river within the gorge were ambiguous: there were low plateaux or marshy tracts on which grew lemon trees and ten-foot-high grasses, and there were strips of rocky beach. This ambiguity made the river additionally dangerous. You'd think you were beyond the edge of it, then with a sudden surge it would reach out and pull you in.

Here the wild elephant track they had been following veered away from the water — which was very sensible of the wild elephants. Mackrell, his men and their own elephants stood next to the sagging shelter in which Millar and Leyden had spent the night after their own crossing and they contemplated the river. They did so in silence, because its noise made speech inaudible. They stood in a vast, right-angled valley. The Dapha thundered madly south, where it crashed into the Noa Dehing, immediately and crazily — like one drunk meeting another on a wild Saturday night — falling in with *its* plan of thundering *west*. The two rivers met in a great steaming cauldron hundreds of yards wide. As with Millar and Leyden, Mackrell sensed that he was intruding upon the private trauma of Mother Nature, and he would write in awed terms, "Few if any had ever seen the Dapha in the Monsoon before."

164

Mighty tree trunks were bobbing around in the water, looking about as significant as human hairs being whirled down a plughole. These logs were "a terror to the elephants", and some would not approach the river even after Mackrell and the mahouts had cut a pathway through the scrub to the water's edge. Mackrell climbed up behind his personal mahout, Gohain, on the big tusker called Phuldot — the one that had taken the lead crossing the Noa Dehing at Miao — and they walked the elephant to the river's edge. From here, ten feet up, Mackrell had a better view, and he saw amid the rainy mist a small grass-covered island in the middle of the river.

There were men on it.

None of them was Sir John Rowland, who at that moment was marching through the rain about 120 miles to the west. These were small men, in ragged remnants of army uniforms, some wearing wide-brimmed felt hats: Gurkhas — sixty-eight of them. Mackrell did not know this, but they were the bulk of the party that had stayed a single night at Sir John's camp, having arrived in the wake of those escapees from Japanese capture, Fraser and Pratt.

It was unusual for Gurkhas to need rescuing. As a rule, they were the ones *doing* the rescuing. They had, of course, put up some heroic military performances on the retreat from Burma, sometimes near water — and they had a great reputation as bridge builders. Dorman-Smith described one episode from the walkout in his Evacuation Report, with no location or date given:

. . . the Gurkha units maintained at all times their customary standards: at a difficult river crossing there was no bridge and the river was swift and deep . . . Hundreds waited on the bank. They had to cross or starve. A party of Gurkhas volunteered to take a rope across. They were not all skilful swimmers. A round dozen went. Only seven reached the other side alive, but the rope spanned the breach and many lives were saved. The names of those who died are not known, but — Thappa or Guring or Rai — the Indian Army and Nepal may be proud of them.

If there was a chink in the resilience of the Gurkhas it was indeed that they generally could *not* swim, which is perfectly understandable. Their homeland, Nepal, is landlocked and its rivers are torrential and freezing cold. A notorious incident of the fall of Rangoon had occurred when the British prematurely blew up the bridge over the Sittang river. Allied soldiers were trapped on the wrong side of it, and attempted to escape the Japanese by swimming. Hundreds of Gurkhas drowned, and thereafter swimming lessons were included in their training.

. . . Not that anyone could have swum the Dapha in the monsoon, and the island on which the sixty-eight Gurkhas were stranded was being rapidly eroded. They were also starving: their emaciated state made that clear enough, and they underlined the point to Mackrell by repeatedly gesturing to their mouths.

The mid-river island was only about sixty yards from the bank on which Mackrell and his men stood. Gohain rode Phuldot into the river, while behind him Mackrell, or somebody, filmed the attempt. In the film the water seems not so much to flow as fly, and the island is not visible in the rain haze. You can see the concentration that Phuldot puts into resisting the river. He progresses slowly, every so often stopping, as if calmly deciding: "Actually, this is impossible." Gohain keeps looking round, as if to say, equally mildly, to Mackrell: "This is not going to work", and the elephant is eventually recalled. The trouble was that the rain, combined with the force of the water, had washed away the shingle on the river bed, leaving no binding between the boulders. Therefore Phuldot couldn't walk across the river, and if he had tried to swim he would have been swept away.

The Gurkhas had attempted to bridge the river. One of the passing tree trunks had been ensnared, and they'd pushed it lengthways from the island, with their end of it weighed down by stones, so that it stuck up over the racing water, but it didn't reach more than a quarter of the way across.

There was the possibility of a Plan B, however. Mackrell and the mahouts went a little way into the river with some of the more willing elephants. When the next suitable log came bounding past, they managed to stop it, and the elephants carried it to the bank. (Elephants move logs as dextrously as men move planks about.) This second log was extended out from the bank so as to meet the one coming out from the island. A mahout went out on an elephant with a roll of rope over his shoulder. He would try to join the projecting end of the logs together. The Gurkhas tried to push their own tree a little further towards Mackrell's, but as soon as its anchor of rocks was disturbed, the trunk was swept away, taking the other log with it. Mackrell would write, "Until dark, we tried over and over again, up and down the river but failed to get an elephant anywhere near them, and the Khampti Mahouts took terrible risks of being washed away and broken to pieces in trying to get over."

At dark, they gave up: "and I shall never forget the line of dejected figures crawling and stumbling back to their meagre grass shelters. They had been so full of relief and hope when they saw us first . . ."

The elephants were put to graze; the tarpaulins were strung up, and an evening meal was cooked on Mackrell's side of the river. Mackrell and his men would have suppressed any appearance of enjoying the meal, what with the starving Gurkhas only sixty yards away. Afterwards, Mackrell lit his pipe and watched the river in the fading light. Then he had another idea. Picking up one of the hurricane lamps, he walked over to one of the pads that had been removed from an elephant. He took it out and began to assemble his fifteen-foot fishing rod. Working under a tarpaulin, with his pipe in his mouth, and the hurricane lamp by his side, he rigged up a line, "fishing line first to be cast [towards the Gurkhas on the island] . . . attached to a light rope which in turn was attached to some of the elephant tethering rope to which we intended to tie bundles of food in tarpaulin". That's how he described the plan in his diary, but there's a whimsical note to the passage which sounds like something from a fairy story . . . Rapunzel letting down her hair. It never came to anything, and Mackrell carried on watching the river until midnight, when he put out his pipe, wrapped himself in a tarpaulin and went to sleep.

But it was another very light sleep, and "at 2am a different tune in the roar of the water brought me wide awake". Mackrell unwrapped himself from his tarpaulin and walked to the river's edge. The level was falling; the flow was slower, the river more translucent and altogether better behaved, although still playfully flinging the occasional log about. By four in the morning the river was three feet lower than it had been the night before. The Gurkhas were stirring from their grass shelters on the island, as were Mackrell's mahouts, who needed "no urging" — and no breakfast — before beginning the rescue attempt.

The first elephant they rounded up and prepared was not Phuldot but Mackrell's other favourite: another male called Rungdot. Three weeks before, when he'd been setting up his refugee food distribution camp at Namgoi Mukh, Mackrell had needed to cross the Namgoi river, but the monsoon had started and the cane rope suspension bridge at that point had been washed away after a landslide, which is what tended to happen to those bridges. Rungdot was the elephant that got him over.

At 5a.m., in the clearing haze of dawn, the Dapha was a reformed character and, according to Mackrell, "singing merrily". It had taken on a relaxed, green tinge as opposed to its rabid, foaming white of the evening before. Even so, Mackrell, Rungdot and a mahout unnamed by Mackrell walked a good way west along the riverbank before they found what looked like a safe place to enter the water: a point where the channel split into six or seven streams, with relative shallows in between. Mackrell was not aboard the elephant when it went in — only the mahout. Space on the elephant was at a premium. If the crossing was successful, it would be necessary to accommodate as many Gurkhas as possible on Rungdot's back.

Mackrell watched Rungdot enter the river, feeling his way with the genteel caution of any elephant on the move. The elephant lurched, steadied himself, lurched again. Suddenly, the merriment seemed to have gone out of the river, as if it resented having its good manners put to the test. The mahout was talking to Rungdot continuously as they were buffeted, paused, resumed their slow progress. Mackrell held his pipe, but did not put it into his mouth.

By 5.30, Rungdot was climbing out of the river on the far bank, with the tide mark four-fifths of the way up his side — that mark that always looks so unfortunate, like a new suit that's been ruined. By 7a.m. Rungdot was back at the camp with his mahout and the first three Gurkhas on his back. Mackrell wrote out a chit, and gave it to Rungdot's mahout. It was a promise of a hundred rupees, to be paid to him when back at the base at Margherita. (The reward was duly paid, and it is to be stressed that the mahout had not undertaken the rescue in anticipation of it.)

170

By midday, all sixty-eight of the Gurkhas were back on the south side of the Dapha. As the rescue was proceeding, the biggest tarpaulin was strung between two trees to make a rain shelter for the Gurkhas. Normally, the fire would have been lit beneath this tarpaulin, but there wasn't enough room for a fire *and* the men. So Mackrell's butler, Apana, got a fire going underneath an umbrella that he had to hold to keep upright. He kept tea continually brewing in an old kerosene tin, with the aim of immediately serving tea to the rescued men — together with a very small amount of sugar, since Mackrell was low on sugar. Because the umbrella was over the fire, and not over Apana, and since he was in a clearing with no trees above, Apana was very badly soaked, with serious consequences.

As the elephants came in, Mackrell, being the biggest man present, lifted the Gurkhas down. He was particularly worried about one man, who couldn't have weighed more than five stone. The Gurkhas didn't have any luggage as such, but one carried a rifle. Refugees were not allowed to carry weapons, but the man with the rifle said he wanted to hand it over personally to the commandant at the Margherita camp. He had carried it all the way from Burma, whereas most men had thrown their guns away, so Mackrell thought this was an achievement and he let the man keep the gun. Mackrell wrote, "All were so genuinely grateful and said 'By the mercy of God and the help of your honour, we are alive!'" Most of the rescued men were from the Lashio Battalion of the Burma Rifles, or the Burma Frontier Force. They had been on the Dapha island for seven days, and they

171

would all certainly have died had Mackrell not turned up. They told Mackrell that some of their comrades were following on behind, and that there was a European party — Sir John and the Rossiters — several days back, but the Gurkhas didn't know whether they were pushing on or staying put in the hope of rescue.

The Gurkhas had made it through to the Dapha partly because the rivers they had encountered had not been in full spate.

Even so, they were not yet safe.

As Mackrell wrote, "our troubles began with the actual arrival of the rescued party". He did not have enough food or cooking utensils for sixty-eight starving men. On coming down from the elephants, some of the Gurkhas spurned the shelter of the big tarpaulin and immediately ran over to where Apana had been cooking the night before. There they found, and devoured, some dried potato parings. Those under the tarpaulin were served in the first instance one cream cracker and a cigarette tin full of milk made from an American brand of powdered milk called Klim ("Spell it backwards!" joshed the label) that had long been a staple for jungle explorers, and would soon become one for jungle fighters. It lasted forever in its tin and for about a week after the seal was broken. Those of the mahouts who had no caste objections to cooking (that is, the less orthodox Hindus among them) began boiling rice on a fire they had managed to get going, but it wasn't much of a fire, what with the rain and the wind. The Gurkhas said they wanted to get their own fire going, so as to cook their own food, and Mackrell made the mistake —

172

"since this was my first experience of dealing with starving people" — of believing them. In fact, on being handed the rice to cook, they immediately ate it raw. So Mackrell had "several cases of colic to attend to".

When the meal got formally underway, the rice was flavoured with Marmite, and a lucky few of the Gurkhas got tinned sausages with it. Mackrell then began dressing the sores and wounds. Having left in a hurry, he had only the small wooden medical box that had been his constant companion on his hunting trips. It was capable of dealing with "a normal camp", but not sixty-eight Gurkhas, especially since many of its contents had been used on his own men. (Mostly septic leech bites.) But he did what he could with diluted Dettol and a pot of Iodex (an ointment containing iodine, available in India since 1919, under the slogan "Pain Should Not Come in the Way of Your Life"). For bandages, one of Mackrell's spare bush shirts was torn up and used.

Once the Gurkhas were fixed up and fed, Mackrell broke the bad news to them: he had not enough food to keep them in the Dapha camp; they had another ninety miles to go to the golf club base at Margherita, and only about twenty of them would be able to get a lift on an elephant. He would be sending ten elephants back with them, together with mahouts, and as much food as he could spare. Not having settled down, so to speak, in the camp, the Gurkhas took the news well, and so, in the late afternoon, the ones who could walk trailed slowly away into the jungle behind the elephants carrying the Gurkhas who could *not* walk.

The mahouts on the elephants had instructions to pick up rice from the dump Mackrell had initiated at the crossing point at Miao, then return to the Dapha.

Sir John Encounters His Principal Enemy: The Tilung Hka River

The Gurkhas rescued by Mackrell had not known whether Sir John Rowland and his party were staying put or pushing on. In fact, they were pushing on. We last saw Sir John and the Rossiters — with their own sixty Gurkhas in attendance as porters — on 6 June, when he had been traversing yet another "vile pathway". On that day, they had travelled about four miles. The seventh of June was "another terribly wet day" (you really do want to shake Sir John by the shoulders, and say, "It's a monsoon, man!"), much of it spent trying to climb "a 1000 foot high hill which was very difficult to negotiate due to its steepness and the slippery surface caused by continuous rains". On 8 June the going was good *and* bad, and they travelled five miles, striking camp on the cliffs of the Noa Dehing, which was in full flood below. On 9 June, Sir John Rowland was trudging on, and he still couldn't get over the rain: "Another perfectly damnable day. It rained heaven's hardest most of the morning, all the afternoon and evening." Sir John spent much of that day wading waist-deep through the outer edge of the Noa Dehing, no other pathways being available. On 10 June, the day on which Mackrell performed his first rescue at the Dapha river, Sir John wrote, "Another truly vile day's march in pouring rain." He had invested all his hopes in the two parties he had sent on ahead: firstly Millar and Leyden, secondly the young Commandos.

On 11 June, Sir John's railway party, the Rossiters and the Gurkha porters cut their way through to a clearing at the intersection of the Noa Dehing and one of its many tributaries, the Tilung Hka.

The Tilung Hka was relatively small by the Lost World standards of the Chaukan route but it was now in flood. In the course of looking for a crossing place, one of Sir John's party, the Indian railway store clerk who was not so young any more, C. V. Venkataraman, missed his footing on the muddy bank and slid into the river. He was immediately swept out of sight. Some of the Gurkhas ran along the bank, following his shouts. Venkataraman travelled 200 yards in about two minutes, before arriving with a bang at a large rock, which was close enough to the bank for him to be pulled out. The river could not be crossed.

The light was now fading; it was time to strike camp, which they did about a half-mile away — on the banks of the larger river, the Noa Dehing. The fires were lit, a bed sheet was hoisted on a bamboo pole to attract passing planes, rice soup was cooked up. At this point Sir John's number two, Manley, who himself had been ill, was lagging several miles behind in order to keep pace with his elderly servant, Appalswamy, who was not well.

That evening, the Gurkha Jemadar (a rank designating a junior Indian officer), whose name was Rattan Singh, took Sir John aside. The progress was too slow for his men's liking. Unless allowed to progress at their own speed they were sure they would starve. Therefore they could not agree to carry on as porters. Sir John called a meeting ... and another desperate lunge was decided on. After Millar and Leyden and the four Commandos, a third breakaway would be fired off — "double marches" and all — towards civilization, with a brief to explain to anyone they met on the way that Sir John's railway party and the Rossiters were camped together and "desperately" short of food. But first this latest breakaway party would have to cross the Tilung Hka. It consisted of the Oriental Mission unit: Major Lindsay, Captain Cumming, Corporal Sawyer, plus Kendall, the railway surveyor on the Burma-China construction, and Eadon, the Anglo-Indian anti-malarial inspector on that railway, plus the sixty Gurkhas under Jemadar Rattan Singh — and every man in it would be his own porter. We will call this party "Lindsay's Men".

The remainder of Sir John's party and the Rossiters would remain behind, on the wrong side of the Tilung Hka. They had little choice without their porters. They had only progressed about fifty miles beyond the Chaukan Pass, but the bulk of their party, being debilitated by age or, in the case of Mrs Rossiter, pregnancy, were exhausted, and they did not have enough food for the sixty miles that lay between them and the Dapha.

Sir John's number two, Edward Manley, walked into the camp towards midnight. His servant, Appalswamy, had died of exposure and heart attack about half a mile back.

On the morning of the next day, 12 June, the latest hares having gone on ahead, Sir John, who liked proper "form", called another meeting, which convened in a bamboo lean-to, under the rain, on the wrong side of the Tilung Hka. Sir John created a food committee, and, magnanimously forgoing the chairmanship, he appointed Manley to that position. The committee "checked up all available food" and found it to be "exceedingly little", the Gurkhas having been inadvertently given the rice rations meant for the Rossiter faction of the party. There could be reckoned to be six *full* days of food left as things stood. Therefore everyone was put on quarter rations — that is, a quarter cigarette tin of rice per day, to be taken with boiled water as a thin soup with some fern fronds and "wild plantation tree hearts" floating about in it. It was pointed out by Dr Burgess-Barnett — referred to by Sir John as Principal Medical Officer — that there was no nutrition in either of the latter, but it did form bulk and might help spin the rations out to twenty-four days, "after which," as Sir John wrote, "if no relief party or aeroplane arrive with rations it is recognized we must die of starvation".

He added that, "Some of the party did not take kindly to this idea", whether of being on quarter rations or dying of starvation or both he does not say.

★ ★ ★

If Edward Wrixon Rossiter was keeping a diary, we do not have it. He is therefore upstaged in the jungle by Sir John. It is a shame we don't know more about Rossiter's personality, because it seems there was a lot of it. He has so far appeared to us as a man free-willed or capricious enough to have considered escaping Burma via China, and resentful at having finally been pressured into going through the Chaukan Pass. We have noted his impatience to get on (he had not thought it necessary that everyone should wait for the sick man Milne), and there is a note in the young Commando Bill Howe's diary to the effect that Rossiter feared being "left in the lurch" with his pregnant wife and child. The Commandos and Lindsay's Men having gone on ahead, he was the youngest man left in what might have been thought a party of crocks, given the ages of Sir John, his deputy, Manley, the Indian railwaymen and Dr Burgess-Barnett. And the Royal Engineer, Captain Whitehouse, was beginning to be in a very poor state of health.

Then again we have also seen Rossiter cooking curry and cake in the jungle, and demonstrating knowledge of arboriculture. Perhaps our native Dubliner had what is thought of as a Celtic temperament, veering between morbidity and high spirits.

Rossiter is presented as a dashing, rather dangerous figure in a book called *Lords of the Sunset*. It is a travelogue of Upper and eastern Burma, written by a romantically minded Irishman called Maurice Collis, and published in 1938. The "Lords of the Sunset" were

179

how the Shan peoples were referred to by the Kings of Burma, which would have been a compliment except that the Kings of Burma referred to themselves as the Lords of the Sunrise. The book details a tour through the Shan states on the Burma — China border, where the Shans — who administered themselves with the "assistance" of the British Burma Frontier Service — formed a series of dynasties with no kings but many lords or princes . . . and many princesses.

Collis presents the Shan states as a flower-strewn arcadia, with bright green hummocky hills, peaceful lakes and waterfalls, a landscape from a children's story, and his travels are punctuated by a series of meetings with the Shan princesses, usually when their princes are away. It's all kept on a very courtly level, but the Shans are a subtle, sophisticated and attractive people, and Collis is clearly entranced by the princesses. One has "a caressing idiom" to her speech, and a "lithe vitality in her movements"; another, all lyricism abandoned, is simply "very pretty". Collis says of one of the princesses, "she knew Rossiter of course". The book was written in the mid-1930s, when Edward Wrixon Rossiter was Assistant Superintendent of the Burma Frontier Service for the Shan district of Loilem (this was before he moved north to Putao). Rossiter escorts Collis on some of his travels. Rossiter elegantly defined his duties to Collis: "to advance the Sawbwas' [the princes'] authority and their people's interest". He briefs Collis on the niceties of Shan etiquette and acts as an interpreter for him, translating the names of some of the princesses: Soft Tiger, for example, or Lady Magic Mirror in the Palace of the Million Umbrellas.

Rossiter and Collis eat fifteen-course dinners with the princesses, in the dimly lit halls of their rural palaces (this being Burma, all the courses are put on the table at the same time), and smoke cigarettes with them afterwards. They swim naked in a lake in front of one of the princesses, who holds their towels and looks on amused. Afterwards, Rossiter challenges this princess to a barefoot running race; they josh about something in Shan, and she playfully throws his towel back at him. At another dinner, the mother of a princess teases Collis about when he is going to take a Shan wife. She does this via Rossiter, in his role as translator. She then asks Collis what he would require in a wife. Rossiter leans forward confidingly and answers without consulting Collis ... at which he (Rossiter) is roundly, but playfully, slapped by the woman, and all the attendant servants fall about laughing.

"Eddie" Rossiter is presented as a bachelor. Certainly no wife is mentioned, and this indeed was some time before Rossiter met Nang Hmat, who would accompany him into the jungle in 1942. But things were not quite so simple, as we shall see, and it might be that carefree "Eddie" alternated starkly with the more severe Edward.

The Man in Sunglasses: Captain Fraser Falls into the Tilung Hka, and Brings News of the Commandos

At the camp made by the Rossiters and Sir John Rowland, on the east side of the Tilung Hka river, it is still 12 June, and it is now evening.

As the light faded, a bedraggled figure in sunglasses came staggering through the darkness into the camp: it was Captain John Fraser, the man who had escaped from the Japanese together with Sergeant Pratt, and who — with Pratt — had gone ahead with that earlier advance guard, the Commando party. He came into the camp from the wrong direction: that is, from the direction of the Tilung Hka. Sir John would have been surprised to see him, and possibly apoplectic. The Commandos were meant to be miles ahead.

Captain Fraser was half soaked, but then so was everyone. In Fraser's case it turned out to be river water, because he, too, had fallen into the Tilung Hka. He was given a change of clothes, and installed in the camp's main lean-to, which now had a good fire burning at one end. Ironically in view of the food committee's grim conclusion of a moment ago, he had come back to Sir John in order to get a meal, since his pack had been washed away in the river, and the other Commandos had almost run out of food. He was given a full cigarette tin of the rice broth with the ferns in it, which Sir John's party would henceforth refer to — without affection — as skilly soup. Fraser consumed it rapidly, having taken off his sunglasses, because the soup made them steam up.

When he'd finished eating, John Fraser put his sunglasses back on and told the story of his encounter with the Tilung Hka, the necessary preliminary to which was the story of what the Commandos had been doing since they'd left Sir John's railway party on 1 June in order to make their "double marches".

The first thing to say is that the Commandos did not encounter the Indian rescue party promised by the radio message. That was because there wasn't one. They had — like Sir John following behind — shadowed the right bank of the Noa Dehing, sometimes wading through its edges, sometimes climbing near-vertical wooded hills as steep as the walls of houses, with sheets of red mud flowing down on either side. It was all "up and down" country, although broadly they were descending from the high point of the Chaukan Pass. The "forestry men" in the party had known what to expect; the others had just been appalled. Whereas the railway party and the Rossiters had made diffuse camps, combining tents, grass huts and suspended tarpaulins, the Commandos had built a single bamboo hut every night, with a roof made of bamboo leaves.

They all then lay down next to each other, and if one turned over, they all had to. The rain would always come in somewhere, and it was a lottery as to who it fell on. The thing was to stop counting the drops and go to sleep.

The Commandos carried both army packs (rucksacks) and haversacks (shoulder bags). Young Second Lieutenant Bill Howe carried one change of clothes, a groundsheet to roll his blanket in, a kukri, "the old-fashioned long-barrel services revolver", a long-sleeved pullover, a petrol lighter and an aspirin bottle full of petrol, and "a few personal things". He also carried a rain cape, which he would later throw away, since it was too heavy to carry.

Ritchie Gardiner carried two pairs of shorts (he would later decide that his chief lack was "a pair of long trousers"), two bush shirts, one short-sleeved pullover, one towel, two blankets, a .38 Colt automatic pistol and a .44 Winchester carbine rifle, both of which seemed to become heavier with every passing day, and he had jettisoned most of the cartridges for the rifle early in the walk. His pack weighed so heavily upon his emaciated frame that he threw away the orchids he had collected in the Chaukan Pass, all but the copper-coloured one, "which I am going to call the Chaukan orchid as it was my first find".

And he determinedly retained a sterling silver "Eversharp" propelling pencil (advertised throughout India as being "For the Man of Action"), which he would hold onto even when he became so weak that it began to constitute a burden. The other Commandos said this was because he was Scottish. In fact, Gardiner — a man of action who usually "avoided the pen" — had become addicted to keeping a diary: "I really suspect that it began to be a substitute for alcohol (of which of course we had none) for every evening about sundown I would feel the urge to write come over me." He used any old scrap of paper, "including some which normally is used for another purpose altogether". Gardiner had been worried about his knees, but these were "behaving like bricks", and he gradually transferred his anxieties to his feet. He wore a pair of rubberised snipe boots "borrowed" from Rowes Gentleman's Outfitters of Dalhousie Street, Rangoon, "during the demolition period". Snipe boots are essentially low wellingtons, meant for splashing, gun in hand, through the marshes in which the snipe lives. Gardiner regretted that they were not better fitting *leather* boots, since his ankles were beginning to swell, which might be the cumulative effect of hundreds of leech and sandfly bites, or the first stages of beriberi. Gardiner did not know.

Sergeant Pratt had done most of the cooking: such delicacies as rice and tinned cheese, or rice on its own, or — a speciality of Pratt's — Marmite soup. A couple of times he'd got up early and cooked porridge, and they'd all appreciated that. The Commandos generally had a lot of trouble getting fires started, and had all been very badly bitten by sandflies.

On 2 June, they'd seen a tree cut and a knife-cut inscription to the effect that a party from the 10th Gurkha Rifles had been that way on 29 January 1942

— early evacuees, in other words. This inscription was taken to be proof that the Commandos, Sir John and the Rossiters had been in the Chaukan Pass after all. So Moses, the Dutch Jew, now accompanying the Commandos, had been right.

Later on 2 June, Ritchie Gardiner had shot a muntjac deer that was being swept along by the Noa Dehing; they managed to get it out, and had a really good roast dinner around a big fire. That (sandflies apart) had been a red-letter day. There'd been another treat six days later on 8 June, when white-bearded soap manufacturer, Jardine, the "old man" of the party, had become even older. He turned forty-five on that day, and he produced a large slab of chocolate, so that they all had one square with their usual midday lunch: a single cream cracker. They were all extremely hungry all the time, and everything they ate that was not rice tasted "absolutely first class". In spite of his great age, Jardine was doing "damn well", and the only reservation about him was that he turned out to be an ardent Catholic, and would alarm them all by periodically dropping to his knees to pray for deliverance for them all.

But what happened on the banks of the Tilung Hka suggested that no one was listening.

That river had checked the progress of the Commandos, and in the late afternoon of 12 June they were joined on the river-bank — as they prowled the long, man-high marshy grass looking for a place to cross — by the previous day's breakaways from Sir John, namely Lindsay, Cumming, Kendall, Eadon and their accompanying Gurkhas. It was hot, and it was raining. The water level was rising fast, so a quick decision was required. The first idea was to ask the Gurkhas if they wouldn't mind chopping down a couple of big trees to make a bridge. But halfway through the chopping, the plan was abandoned.

The men spread out again, looking for a crossing place. Young Bill Howe found what might be a good bet: two fallen trees, one on either bank. They remained attached by their roots to the banks, and the ends where the branches were had become partly wedged in river rocks; parts of both logs were under the water and other parts above it. The trouble was the gap of churning water in the middle. Howe walked along the river, calling out to summon the others, who were widely dispersed. The first to arrive at the crossing point were Lindsay's Men plus the enigmatic Dutch surveyor, Moses, but minus the radio operator, Corporal Sawyer. It seems that while Howe was trying to round up the others, Lindsay's Men and Moses crossed the river, because they were nowhere to be seen when Howe returned to the fallen trees with the Commandos. So the second breakaway party from Sir John had overtaken the first, acquiring Moses in the process, but leaving behind Corporal Sawyer. Lindsay's Men were always going to be the quicker party, with their Gurkha porters, and it seemed they were on their way.

The level of the river was rising fast, which is why Lindsay's Men hadn't waited for the others. Captain Boyt went first over the logs, and he had no trouble.

187

That was to be expected: he was the true commando of all the Commandos. Howe, Gardiner and McCrindle also crossed. Sergeant Pratt was next. At the end of the first log, there was a gap of about ten feet to the second, but this second one was slightly downstream of the first, so it was a matter of going with the flow of the water, and trying to veer right towards the second log. Halfway across the gap, Pratt went under. But he came up holding onto the second log. "Old Man" Jardine was next and despite a too sedate looking breaststroke, he managed to get from the first to the second log.

Then it was Captain John Fraser's turn. He'd been the slowest of the walkers, possibly because of the ankle swellings caused by the Japanese ropes, and as he inched along the first trunk he kept stopping to push his prescription sunglasses up towards the bridge of his nose. This was not promising. At the end of the first trunk, he took his sunglasses off, and put them into the top pocket of his bush shirt. He came to the point where the first log was almost completely submerged, and the force of the water on his legs sent him cartwheeling over, and into the water, where he immediately grabbed hold of a smaller passing log, which carried him crashing into a boulder. Fraser remained pinned against this boulder by the force of the water, with only his head above the water. Ritchie Gardiner, who had already crossed over, now sacrificed his position of safety; he dropped into the freezing water, and allowed himself to be swirled towards where Fraser was trapped. Fraser's pack had become entangled with the log that trapped him, and Gardiner freed Fraser by cutting it away with his kukri. The pack rolled away in the water. It had contained six packets of biscuits, a tin of cheese, a tin of butter, a jar of Marmite. Now Corporal Sawyer, radio operator of the Oriental Mission, was astride the first tree trunk. He had hesitated before beginning to cross, thinking he had better go to the aid of Fraser and Gardiner, but from the water Gardiner signalled him to start.

Sawyer wore his pack on his back, and over the top of it his rain cape, since he'd decided this was *not* a superfluous luxury in a monsoon. He inched along the first trunk, went into the river, fought the freezing water for a minute then grabbed hold of the second trunk and hauled himself onto it. Young Bill Howe was sitting astride the second trunk, waiting to grab onto Sawyer, and he had actually got hold of Sawyer's arm when Sawyer spilled off the tree trunk. He was instantly out of reach, owing to the force of the water on his rain cape, and within a few seconds he'd disappeared around a bend in the river. Meanwhile, Gardiner, half wading and half swimming, dragged Fraser back to the first bank. So for Gardiner it was back to square one: he had returned to the wrong side of the river. Both he and Fraser were exhausted, and they walked — "like drunken men", Gardiner wrote — through the tall grass of the riverbank back to a fire the Commandos had made the night before. "We were lucky to find the fire still in and wood to build it up, so stripped nude and got half dry and warm which served to bring us round." Corporal Sawyer was never seen again (early the next morning, Ritchie Gardiner would find one of his socks further along the river), and nor was his pack, which had contained a tin of cheese, some butter, Marmite and all of the Commandos' salt.

That night, as we have seen, Captain Fraser, half dried out, walked back alone to Sir John's camp, where he spent the night. It did not rain during the night. At dawn the next morning, Fraser returned to the river where his comrades the Commandos were waiting for him. They got him over, and they pressed on through the jungle again, aiming for the Dapha river, with Lindsay's Men and their Gurkhas a few miles ahead. The Commandos had roughly seven days' food left, allowing half a cigarette tin of mouldy rice with a little Marmite, one biscuit and about half an ounce of cheese per man per day. They also had very little tea left. At their present rate of progress — they were averaging about six miles a day — that food would carry them twenty miles. But it was sixty miles to the Dapha river and Gyles Mackrell.

Mackrell Consolidates at the Dapha River

Mackrell had now decided to stay put on his riverbank just as Sir John had on his. It seemed that others would soon need his assistance in crossing the river.

Mackrell's servant, Apana, had become ill, which was put down — perhaps not very logically — to his having brewed the tea in the rain. Apana had also been sleeping in wet clothes, as had Mackrell and the other men. He had a high temperature and a pain in his chest. He sat under the big tarpaulin and Mackrell gave him Sloan's Liniment to inhale. This made Apana cough, and at one point Mackrell thought he'd choked him.

That day, Mackrell did the cooking. He also supervised the creation of a proper camp in the lee between two river cliffs. Bashas were built, tents erected. The wide tarpaulin became the focal point, and the sacks of rice were stored here. A bamboo fire was kept constantly burning. Mackrell unrolled the two white oilcloths he'd brought, and made a big letter "T" on a flat patch of ground, the crossbar of the "T" being placed in the direction of the prevailing wind. This was a guide for aeroplanes, and a target for any food drops.

The rain drummed down on the white "T" and on the wide tarpaulin. Mackrell sat under the tarpaulin, and watched the river.

Mackrell's diary is silent about Friday the 12th, the day on which the Commandos were doing battle with the Tilung Hka, but the entry for Saturday the 13th begins with a sigh of relief expressed in the single word: "Sun." Bed rolls were opened out and dried; clothes were washed, and Apana came out from under the tarpaulin. The Sloan's Liniment had "put him right" after all. Towards evening, Mackrell noted, "Saw three large buffaloes." Here was the young naturalist of Epsom College speaking, the boy who had taken *Acidalia trigeminata*. He seems pleased to have seen the buffaloes — which were in the tall grass near the river — but most people would not have been. Wild buffaloes were considered by the tea planters of Assam (who called them "buffs") to be the second biggest menace after tigers. Like tigers, they might attack without provocation. They would come up and stare at you, and it was fatal to turn away and run. You had to outstare them; then they would usually shamble away. By the same token, a buffalo was the second most prized "bag" for an Indian white hunter after a tiger, as Mackrell well knew.

We saw earlier that he feared he might have to shoot a wild elephant. The problem was not that he couldn't shoot a wild elephant; it was that he didn't want to. In one of his most famous essays, "Shooting an Elephant", George Orwell describes his own shooting of a rogue elephant while a policeman in Lower Burma. After his first bullet, the elephant went down, but it got up again after the second. Orwell expended five bullets from one rifle and "bullet after bullet" from a second one but "The tortured gasps continued as steadily as the ticking of a clock." It took half an hour for the elephant to die. Even a Burmese policeman doesn't come across rogue elephants very often, and Orwell had never shot one before, and would never do so again, whereas if the shooting of rogue elephants ever did come up in conversation, Gyles Mackrell could mention that he had shot twenty of them.

Most of the tea planters hunted, usually informally. After a hard day's work they would plod down to the nearest watering hole and blast some duck. But for a longer break, they might go on a proper hunting expedition, a shikar, thus themselves becoming shikari.

Mackrell ran a shikari business as a sideline, which is why he took up cinematography: to provide mementos for his customers. Certainly, the film archive he left behind shows many white men and women in sola topees standing behind dead tigers or dead elephants, or sometimes live elephants with dead tigers strapped to their backs, and always with a penumbra of Indian servants. The Europeans don't quite know how to act. Every so often, one will go forward and change the position of the tiger.

Mackrell only shot elephants if they were rogue, and by the 1930s the British in India were becoming slightly embarrassed by the proliferation of tiger skins in their bungalows, and it was becoming necessary to have a reasonable pretext for shooting tigers as well. So Mackrell would keep an ear out for Assamese villages where tigers were attacking livestock or people. He would then arrange an expedition to that place, and we have an account of one of these written in 1934 by a woman called Elswithe Williams, the wife of a man who was being shown the ropes by Mackrell. The letter is headed, "In camp, near Kokrajar" (a town in northern Assam), and addressed "Dearest Family". It begins, "We really are having the most marvellous time, this place is literally alive with tiger . . ."

Not for long, it wouldn't be.

Besides her husband, Fred, Elswithe was also accompanying a man who was probably her brother. He was called Oliver, and he had been set up for a shoot by Mackrell. A tame buffalo had been tied to a tree. A machin, or small house, had then been built in the branches of a nearby tree, and Oliver had been installed in this for the night with his rifle poised, and an electric torch on the end of the barrel, which Elswithe describes as "a very creepy business but awfully interesting".

Oliver killed the tiger when it came for the buffalo and, hearing the shot, the villagers came out and escorted him in a celebratory procession back to the village with flaming torches held aloft to deter other tigers, all of which Elswithe also thought "a very creepy business, I should think", although it saved Oliver having to wait for the elephant that Mackrell planned to have sent out to collect him at dawn.

194

Oliver had only killed the tiger after it had killed the buff, and this did bother Elswithe — a bit. "It sounds rather cruel to tie up a live beast, but actually it doesn't seem to worry them, you see they are tied up somewhere anyhow, and the tiger kills them immediately, they hardly make a sound, spring on them and break their neck."

Another nearby village was being terrorized by another tiger, and one of Mackrell's guests, referred to by Elswithe as "The General", had been assigned to this tiger; he had "various shots at him and made a complete mess of things, just letting buffalo after buffalo get killed". The villagers had got "pretty fed up" with The General, and so had Mackrell. He decided to do the job himself. So one of the half-eaten buffs was laid under a tree, and Mackrell went up another one. He didn't bother with a machin or anything like that, but just strung a cane chair up in the branches, and parked himself on it, with his pipe on the go. "Sure enough he [the tiger] came back at about 8.30pm, and Gyles got him," Elswithe wrote. "There is no nonsense about this camp," she continued, "Gyles is excellent, and we jolly well have to do as we are told. He won't let us women sit with them [on the tiger vigils] since it is far more difficult for two people to keep absolutely quiet than for one . . . but he has promised that, if the chance arises we shall sit up with him, so I do hope it does." She concludes that Fred, her husband, had shot a deer, "so he is by no means disgraced."

Mackrell had dispatched the Mishmi guide he had recruited for ten rupees back to his village, Tinguan. In

195

return for more silver rupees, he had asked the guide to come back with some more Mishmis, and on the morning of Sunday the 14th the man returned to the Dapha camp with a further "fifteen splendid fellows". Here were the makings of Mackrell's own advance party, since they were willing to cross the Dapha and go forward with rations to look for anyone else who might be coming from the Chaukan. But before a party drawn from these men could set off, extra supplies would have to be brought up to the Dapha. Mackrell was banking on these coming from two sources: first, on the backs of the ten elephants he had dispatched with the rescued Gurkhas, and, secondly, on the backs of the elephants that Mackrell's associate at Namgoi Mukh, the Kampti Raja called Chaochali, would bring. Chaochali, a very reliable man, was about due, according to Mackrell's calculations. As for the ten elephants, Mackrell calculated that, since they had left on the 10th, they should be at Miao, and its store of rice, on the night of the 12th. Provided they set off back from there on the 13th, they ought to reach the Dapha camp on the 16th at the latest, then "all would be well". Meanwhile, Mackrell was "dangerously short of food".

The good news was that the Dapha was down. The hot rain continued to pour, but the level of the river was determined by the weather miles away. So on the afternoon of Sunday the 14th, Mackrell and Millar's "boy", Goal Miri, crossed the Dapha by elephant carrying sacks of such food as could be spared. The aim was to create food dumps for anyone else who might turn up with the river uncrossable once again. They went into the jungle beyond the river, but could not locate the path Millar and Leyden had taken, which roughly followed what Mackrell called "the Chinese cut" — that is the succession of tree cuts made by the Chinese cold weather survey of late 1941. That track had skirted the right bank of the Noa Dehing, and was now submerged beneath the seething and *still rising* waters of that river.

The problem was this: if the level of the Noa Dehing dropped, and the Millar-Leyden track reappeared, anyone coming from the Chaukan would likely be on it. Therefore they would miss any food left at a higher point. Mackrell and Goal Miri found compromise trees midway between the two routes, and Goal Miri climbed them and tied the sacks out of reach of wild elephants. Mackrell then made a cut in the bark to alert any passer-by to what was above.

While recrossing the river that morning — after leaving two sacks of food suspended from two trees — Mackrell and Goal Miri saw elephants arriving at the camp from the direction of Miao. Sitting on the first of them was the dignified figure of Chaochali, the Kampti Raja — dignified but ill. He had brought more supplies, but was feverish and "quite done up". Mackrell gave him aspirin, then quinine, and put him to bed in a tent. In the afternoon, Mackrell wandered along the river towards the crossing point again, rifle in hand. Looking east through the mist, he saw a grassy plateau above the riverbank on his own side. There were deer on it, but they were no more than vague brown shapes amid the rain and the tall grass. He couldn't "get at them" with his rifle. He then looked *across* the river, seeing more mist, more tall grass.

And then a turbaned head: a Sikh soldier. There were Gurkhas with him as well — about thirty men in all. No shout could carry over the river, but Mackrell signalled to the men that they should stay put. He then ran back to the camp, and returned with some elephants on which the men were brought over. They were all starving — apparently proof of the failure of Mackrell's food drop of that very morning. In fact, the Sikhs had seen the tracks made by the elephants that Mackrell and Goal Miri had been riding on — the freshly broken branches, and the fresh elephant dung (elephants excrete turnip-sized lumps fairly frequently) — and they'd thought these must be the tracks of *wild* elephants in close proximity. Therefore they had avoided the tracks — and avoided the sacks of rice in the process. These men were the balance of the hundred soldiers who had come into Sir John's camp behind Fraser and Pratt, plus — it appears — some men who'd avoided the orbit of Sir John altogether. Either way, fifteen of these men's comrades had died of starvation before reaching the Dapha. They explained this as they sat under the tarpaulin drinking tea just brewed in the kerosene tin, and eating biscuits. Rice was on the boil some distance away — Apana had lit his cooking fire under trees this time, even if they *were* crawling with leeches.

When the rescued men had finished their meal, Mackrell had no dall or salt left, and the Sikhs had had to take their tea without sugar, since there was none of that either. Mackrell had also given the last of his quinine and aspirin to Chaochali.

Chaochali (who had now developed dysentery) had not brought enough extra food, but early that evening Mackrell sent the fifteen newly arrived Mishmis off over the river with all he could spare. They would try to establish a line of food dumps to sustain anyone approaching from the east. Mackrell made sure the Mishmis had plenty of tea with which to greet anyone they might encounter, and tins of sausages (already established as Mackrell's trademark "rescue" meal), rice and Marmite. He also armed the Mishmis with an open chit — written in Assamese and English — urging anyone who met them to treat them well, and take only such food as they needed in the immediate term, since the Mishmis were on a mission of mercy. Mackrell himself would wait at the camp, in the hope that the ten elephants he'd dispatched would come back soon with a lot of food on their backs.

Under the tarpaulin, Mackrell took out his stationery wallet and wrote a chit. He put it in an empty can of Klim, to protect it from the rain, and gave it to one of the Mishmis together with some silver rupees. The chit was addressed to the officials at the Margherita base camp. It began, "It would have been easy just to say we heard people were likely to be here and we came and got them, but it would have been unfair to the mahouts and elephants to minimise the difficulties. The report can wait. The important points are these." He then asked to be told what arrangements were being made to receive the men he was sending back to Miao.

199

He added, "I must have medical help." It was futile really because the chit would take a week to reach Margherita, and Mackrell needed food before then.

He lit his pipe; it suppressed appetite.

Captain Wilson Arrives at the Dapha, and a Gurkha Sergeant is Dispatched to Look for Sir John

Tuesday 16 June was the day on which the ten elephants were due to return from Miao to the west. They did not do so. Instead, there was an arrival from the east: another thirty-eight Gurkhas and Sikhs, all waving from the far side of the Dapha, all starving. They were brought over and taken under the wide tarpaulin, where they were given biscuits and tea — not only now without sugar, but also without Klim, since that, too, had run out. They were then given a small amount of rice each. First thing the following morning, Mackrell spotted "another batch" on the far bank, "mostly Gurkhas and Nepalis and Garwalis". He brought them over as well.

Mackrell was now running a veritable refugee camp-cum-ferry terminal, yet he had run out of food. Where were his ten elephants?

In the early afternoon, there *was* an arrival from the west, but it was not the ten elephants. Instead, Captain Reg Wilson walked into the camp accompanied by his sixty "political porters" (actually, more like fifty now, some having defected in disgust on the way from Margherita), the two detachments of Assam Rifles, Dr Bardoloi, and *four* elephants that looked vaguely familiar to Mackrell. Mackrell took his pipe out of his mouth and watched the approach of Wilson. He had been expecting no such personage, and he was on his guard. As the two men shook hands, Chaochali, the Kampti Raja, stood beside the tent in which he'd been lying ill and watched the Assam Rifles. All these uniforms, all of a sudden. None of the tribes of Assam (Chaochali was a Naga) were very keen on the Assam Rifles, whose job it was to keep them in line.

Mackrell asked Wilson to join him under the wide tarpaulin, where Wilson showed him the chit by which he, Wilson, had been placed in charge. Mackrell read it, nodding, and handed it back. Tea was served — tea with sugar and milk (or, at any rate, Klim) in it, thanks to the extra supplies that Wilson had brought. Under the tarpaulin Wilson smoked, but Mackrell did not relight his pipe. This was going to be a rather tense conversation. Mackrell was looking at the four elephants. He asked whether by any chance Captain Wilson had seen the other six? Wilson nodded. He would come to that in a minute.

He explained that it had not been an easy journey from Margherita via Miao. Yes, they had begun by punting canoes along the Burhi Dehing river from Ledo to the place the British called Simon. But beyond Simon they had been "foot-slogging" through the low jungle, following the trail made by Mackrell's elephants, which was clear enough . . . the elephants' feet having made nine-inch watery holes in the mud, into which Wilson and his men kept stumbling. On 9 June, as they approached Miao on a hot, dark, dank day, the leeches attacked. In his diary, Wilson had marvelled, "Some places if you stop they catch you faster than you get others off." On 10 June, they arrived at Miao, where they had to cross the river. By now, Wilson was liberally decorated with Elastoplasts covering his leech bites. His boots, he noticed, were full of blood. He wrote, "ABCD vitamins should soon counteract this!" which seems, incredibly in the circumstances, to have been some sort of jungle wallah's in-joke.

Wilson met the village headman, Mat Ley, who told him that Mackrell had left with sixteen elephants, but he couldn't say exactly what supplies he'd been carrying on them. Mat Ley offered to cross Wilson by boat, just as he had offered Mackrell. Wilson, not having any elephants, accepted, and Mat Ley supplied some long canoes and oarsmen, for which Wilson paid him a hundred rupees. But the river was raging, and they could not cross. Wilson killed some of the intervening time by dismantling — with Mat Ley's authorization — a couple of semi-derelict bamboo houses in Miao. He then loaded the pieces onto one of the boats. The houses could be reassembled later at any jungle camp.

On 13 June, a fine day, they crossed the Noa Dehing. They then had what Wilson called "a dirty march" towards the Debang river, which, in the absence of elephants, they crossed by making a bridge of tree trunks. This was "rather difficult". One of the Gurkhas of the Assam Rifles "fell off the tree and was dragged under by the stream; one man just got him, but it took five to ten minutes to get him out and keep his head above water". On 15 June, Captain Wilson saw, coming the other way through the jungle, the sixty-odd Gurkhas whom Mackrell had rescued and the ten elephants he had sent with them. The Gurkhas told Wilson that Mackrell was encamped at the Dapha, that he had saved their lives; they also told him they were extremely hungry, so Wilson "gave out a feed to all". This took some time, which delayed the ten elephants whose progress Mackrell had been wondering about. Wilson then decided to keep four of the elephants for his own party, so many of his political porters having defected, which delayed the other six Miao-bound ones still further as the loads were rearranged. Having quizzed the Gurkhas about the state of the Dapha camp, Wilson then set out a list of additional kit — above and beyond just sacks of rice — that ought to be collected at Miao and brought back to the Dapha. The rounding up of these additional stores would mean the elephants would have to spend longer at Miao, increasing Mackrell's perplexity.

Having absorbed all this, Mackrell asked about the condition of the Gurkhas, and Wilson mentioned that one of the men had been carrying a rifle, and that he had taken the rifle off the man since it was against regulations for refugees to be armed. Mackrell explained that he had made a point of letting the man keep the rifle.

Exhaling smoke from his cigarette, Wilson said, "I did what I thought was right", and he could easily have pulled rank in a much more forthright manner. The awkward fact was that Reg Wilson represented officialdom, albeit in an easy-going Yorkshire guise. Furthermore, Wilson was an army captain, and, while Mackrell had been a squadron leader, he was counted merely a civilian in 1942. Yes, he was designated an ITA Liaison Officer, but so too was almost any man who acted in any capacity for the ITA. As well as being the senior man, Wilson was also thirteen years younger than Mackrell, which can't have helped.

Mackrell was never pompous or officious. For a start, he did not move in a world that allowed him to be. He was no box wallah, insisting on bureaucratic precedence, and there was no room for pomposity in the jungle, or in dealing with elephants and mahouts. You would soon be found out. But he did like to be in charge. He liked to be his own man; that's why he spent half his life in the jungle. He had been a tea planter, and the planter might be socially constricted even if he did live miles from his neighbours; but, then, Mackrell had taken care to become an area supervisor in the tea industry, a man with a roving brief. On the hunting expeditions he organized, he was in charge, and therefore free, and he had spent much of the First World War in the skies over Baluchistan, which is about as far from being a box wallah as you can imagine. It may be that school and marriage had restricted his freedom, and now Captain Wilson seemed likely to do the same.

Wilson began a tour of the camp. Meanwhile, Chaochali, still standing by his tent and eyeing the Assam Rifles whom Wilson had brought with him, called Mackrell over and asked how long they would be staying. After walking around the Dapha camp with a somewhat proprietorial air, Captain Wilson ordered an armed guard on the rations. Mackrell wrote, "I am not sure I like that in a volunteer camp like mine where all has gone so smoothly under most difficult conditions."

As Wilson carried out his inspection, his political porters were having a good sit-down. Mackrell wrote, "I have asked Captain Wilson to put some of his porters to build shelters [many of his rescued Indians were sleeping under crudely rigged tarpaulins, and were too ill to build their own] and as soon as they are rested, this will be done. I wish I could rest my people!" Mackrell would conclude that these political porters "apparently have to rest as soon as they arrive anywhere", which is just about his only criticism of any Indian in his entire diary, because Gyles Mackrell was a Home Counties public school man who had to some extent gone native.

Take the mahouts. They shared their leader, Chaochali's, dislike of the Rifles, and by extension the commander of those men, Captain Wilson, who'd already had a few run-ins with the mahouts of the four elephants he'd commandeered. In his diary Wilson described the mahouts as "a putrid crowd", and he marvelled at Mackrell's ability to handle them, and at

Mackrell's knowledge of their charges. "Mackrell," wrote Wilson, "knows what an E [an elephant] can do." In spite of the initial prickliness, Wilson's diary is consistently admiring of Mackrell, and the two men would soon settle down as a team, jointly signing chits and looking out for each other's health. Mackrell in turn was grateful for the food Wilson had brought, even if it wasn't enough (Wilson not having known about all the unexpected Gurkhas) and he was "very glad Capt. Wilson had brought Dr Bardoloi", who seemed "a very conscientious type". But the doctor was also thin and frail, and Mackrell wondered whether he would stand up to conditions at the Dapha.

In mid-afternoon, a further few Sikhs and Gurkhas were crossed over the Dapha and fed. Then a plane flew over. It was RAF. The plane circled once, then dropped something on the riverbank. One of the Rifles retrieved it and handed it to Wilson: it was a tin of Klim, or a tin that had once contained Klim. Wilson prised off the lid, and there was a piece of paper inside: a chit. Wilson read it, then handed it to Mackrell. The message was from a Political Officer, not Lambert at Margherita but another man based at a bungalow in Sadiya, the most north-easterly administrator of the Indian Empire in fact, and the closest one to the Chaukan Pass.

The chit said there was a food dump at Miao. Mackrell already knew that, since he'd put it there. With surreal irrelevance, it continued to the effect that "your party" should cross the Noa Dehing if possible, so proceeding towards Miao on its left bank. Realization dawned. The message had been dropped on

Mackrell's camp in the belief that it was the camp of Sir John Rowland, and it was just as well the mistake had been made, because if Sir John, or anyone else coming from the Chaukan, had acted upon the message they would have drowned in the Noa Dehing. And if they *hadn't* drowned, they would have starved, since they would have missed the Dapha, and Mackrell's Dapha camp and its supply of food. So Mackrell didn't think much of *that*.

The plane flew on, a further sixty miles east above some of the densest jungle in the world, and then it flew over a clearing in the crook of two rivers, where a fire burnt, a bed sheet on a bamboo pole sagged in the rain, and Sir John Rowland, Edward Rossiter and their two parties waved frantically at it, but, as Sir John noted, it "ignored our signals".

Havildar Iman Sing

On 18 June, two days after the arrival of Captain Wilson at the Dapha ferry terminal, Mackrell crossed "a few more Gurkhas and Sikhs". Later that day, the other six elephants he'd dispatched finally turned up again, together with additional food, and "some tarpaulins" that Wilson had irritated Mackrell by sending for. The elephants were accompanied by more of the political porters recruited by Wilson, who immediately set about having a rest. Some of the earlier arrived political porters had already absconded. There were now about seventy refugees in the camp, which was beginning to look like a village, with a dozen or so bamboo and palm huts, and the big tarpaulin as the centre of operations, and the place where Dr Bardoloi had his surgery.

On 19 June, Wilson and some of the porters rebuilt one of the houses he had dismantled at Miao. They put it on "the point", a promontory of the riverbank overlooking the crossing place. They put food and medical supplies in it, and this new house was for the benefit of any refugees who might be too ill to progress the further 500 yards through tall grass to the actual camp.

In the afternoon, Wilson and Mackrell asked one of the Gurkhas of the Assam Rifles who'd accompanied Mackrell, a man called Havildar (sergeant) Iman Sing, if he would be willing to be taken across the river together with two Gurkha sepoys and as many rations as they could carry. Iman Sing agreed.

He and his three comrades had a slightly different brief from that of the fifteen Mishmis whom Mackrell had sent over the Dapha five days before. Sing would strike out immediately towards the Chaukan Pass in an attempt to meet Sir John. He carried a chit signed by Mackrell and Wilson, "setting out the position". (Whatever the "position" was; it seems to have said little more than "We know you are there, and we are trying to get you out.") Sing would spend the next ten days marching fast through the jungle looking for the Rossiter and Rowland parties.

Soon after the departure of Sing, Chaochali recovered from his fever and dysentery and, taking Mackrell aside, he said he wanted to return to Namgoi Mukh, a jungle encampment he vastly preferred to the one he was now in. Mackrell wrote that his friend "obviously hates Dapha and wants to get away from the Rifles etc". Chaochali did leave, together with the ten elephants and "a big batch" of the rescued soldiers.

The Commandos Despair of Reaching the Dapha, but then a Star Appears

The Commandos had finally crossed over to the west side of the Tilung Hka on 13 June, having lost Corporal Sawyer and having nearly lost the bespectacled Captain Fraser the day before. The 13th was a fine day, and they made good progress until, at 1 p.m., they came upon a small hut built by Lindsay's Men, who had gone on ahead after their faster crossing of the Tilung Hka. The Commandos decided to stop there for the remainder of the day, washing and drying clothes, getting "lots of odd jobs done" and resting after their river trauma.

The next day they spent in that staple activity of Chaukan refugees: clambering over the rocks on the edge of the Noa Dehing. It took them three hours to do the first two miles. At 2 p.m. they came to another tributary of the Noa Dehing. It was wider than any British river, but they had no name for it, even so. It turned out to be fast but shallow and they crossed it by means of a complex of stepping stones and driftwood, as laid out, they presumed, by Lindsay's Men. In the afternoon, the Commandos made speedy progress, having found a track at a higher level, and in the evening — which was fine — they built a shelter at a place they called "Python Camp". Why? Because young Bill Howe saw a python hanging from a tree. He took out his revolver and finally shot it after a fusillade of misfires (damp cartridges) that caused the barrel to burst. The Commandos chopped up the snake with their kukris and ate it over a big fire: a feast of python soup, python cutlets, rice-in-Marmite and tea. They decided it tasted like tough chicken and was "quite good", but then they *were* half starved. Of his busted revolver, the irrepressible Howe noted, "One less thing to carry!" That night, Ritchie Gardiner baited two fishing lines with python liver. Nothing bit.

The next day was much worse. Most of it was spent on or in the margins of the Noa Dehing river, and even Howe was starting to get "browned off" with it. The water was making everybody's boots disintegrate. Actually, Captain Boyt's had split apart some time since, and he was now lagging behind with swollen and septic feet. There was little conversation between the Commandos. According to Howe's widow, "They just thought about food all the time."

On 16 June, the day of Captain Wilson's arrival at the Dapha, the Commandos came to another hut built by Lindsay's Men. They looked inside and saw a figure lying on a bed of ferns: it was the Anglo-India railwayman, Eadon, who had gone forward with Lindsay's Men. The anti-malarial inspector had succumbed to malaria and couldn't continue. Lindsay's Men — all on the point of starvation — had promised

212

to send help back to him, as now did the Commandos, but they knew this might be a hollow promise. They were making for the Dapha, but they didn't know that anybody would be there. All they knew for certain was that they would have to cross the river. They had no firm idea how far away the Dapha might be, because they couldn't fix their position on any of their maps. Eadon had some food with him, but was not up to eating. The Commandos couldn't carry Eadon; they could hardly walk themselves. They made him a drink of tea; they did not think he could last very long.

They pressed on, and passed by the corpses of three Indians.

Towards the end of the next day, 17 June, the Commandos came to another hut with another man dying inside: this was Moses, the controversial surveyor and International Boy Scout. In his diary, Ritchie Gardiner wrote that he was "alone in a hut by the river. Apparently he fell in trying to cross a trib [a tributary]. He had been swept along, minus his pack, to this hut. He had lain for five or six days without food." Moses was "Quite compos mentis but very weak". His many open wounds were crawling with maggots. The Commandos could do nothing but promise to come back for him. Ritchie Gardiner gave Moses his spare sleeveless jumper, because Moses said the nights were cold.

On 18 June, the Commandos went up and down a series of gorges — valleys that ought to have held Dapha tributaries but didn't. Then they came to one that did. They managed to cross it, but they were

213

exhausted that night, and both Boyt's and Gardiner's boots were completely shot. They camped on the bank of the Noa Dehing, on a beach two feet above the water. They counted the rations: eleven cigarette tins of mouldy rice, nine packets of mouldy cream crackers; one tin of cheese, one jar of Marmite. Young Howe, a good-looking chap, carried a mirror. He risked a glance into it and was appalled at his sunken cheeks. In the night the roar of the river became louder as the water rose towards the hut. They all lay awake, looking at the roof. Rainwater was coming in from there, but the bigger problem was whether the river would come in from *below*. By dawn, the river had subsided, but none of them had slept.

The next day they brewed their tea in the dawn light, in the rising mist. Boyt tried to put on his boots, but gave up. There were no boots to put on, just fragments of leather and string. He and Gardiner would find it very hard to complete another day's march. Jardine, the Catholic, was kneeling down and facing away from the others. In the words of Howe, he was looking at "a bright star shining through the mist that gave the impression of a large cross in the sky". They all saw it. Ritchie Gardiner wrote of "a clear sky in the east, and a single large star shining".

They set off, climbing up — in Howe's words — one "awful" hill, then coming down an "appalling" one. They saw a large monkey in a tree, and Ritchie Gardiner shot at it, but his gun misfired. Damp cartridges again. Later, the same thing happened with a partridge.

At midday, as they looked down at the river from a cliff, they saw some rough rafts on the rocky beach below. Why not ride them down the river towards the Dapha tributary? You'd be going with the current, and you'd be going fast, as Gardiner and McCrindle enthusiastically pointed out. But everyone else pointed out that you'd be going far *too* fast. The idea was a symptom of their desperation. At one o'clock, they set off again, and they'd gone only a hundred yards or so when they saw seven Mishmi tribesmen standing in their way. They were the Mishmis who'd been crossed over the Dapha and sent forward by Mackrell on 14 June, and they carried a chit from Mackrell saying that food, shelter and medical assistance awaited. Gardiner wrote: "Never was there a more welcome sight."

The Commandos all shook the Mishmis' hands, which bemused the Mishmis. Communication was difficult, but the Commandos tried to explain about Eadon and Moses, stranded in their bamboo shelters. To show that elephants would be required for their rescue, they attempted to imitate elephants by lurching about waving their arms in front of their noses. The Mishmis had no "stores" as such with them but what Howe describes as a "little" rice, which was a lot by the standards he'd become used to. At camp that night the Mishmi headman caught two masheer (large game fish) and Ritchie Gardiner wrote, "Every mouthful was appreciated in a way that would make a Firpo dinner look second rate." (Firpo's was the Italian restaurant in Calcutta regarded as a culinary peak of India by more than one person in this story.) The Mishmis then

215

handed round some of the black tobacco they carried, and every man rolled himself a cigarette.

There was still twenty-five miles to go before the Dapha was reached, and, while the Mishmis would carry the Commandos' packs, they did not have elephants, so everyone would have to walk. Boyt, whose feet were the worst, would be supported between two Mishmis. On the face of it, Gardiner, McCrindle, Howe, Boyt, Fraser and Pratt were now saved, but what about Lindsay's Men, who, supposedly, had gone on ahead together with their Gurkhas? We know that Eadon and Moses had fallen away from that party, but what of its other members?

The Mishmis would not have known what had been happening back at the Dapha camp since their departure. But, as already noted, Mackrell landed parties of Indian soldiers, mainly Gurkhas, on the 16th, 17th and 18th, and these were the ones who had been portering for Lindsay's Men. It appears they had gone on ahead in the closing stages.

On 20 June, as the Mishmis were escorting the Commandos towards the Dapha river, Major Lindsay, Captain Cumming and Kendall, the surveyor, were spotted across the Dapha by Mackrell, and brought over by elephant. (In other words, they had reached the Dapha without encountering the Mishmis.) Mackrell himself went over to arrange the transfer, carrying a flask of hot Bovril and a packet of cream crackers for his first European guests. Major Lindsay, he noted, had a huge abscess on his leg, Cumming was not too good, while Kendall looked "desperately ill". Once they'd crossed over, Dr Bardoloi opened the abscess on Lindsay's leg. Cumming was given morphine, Kendall quinine.

Major Lindsay briefed Mackrell about the Commandos following on, and Eadon and Moses languishing in their huts. Mackrell sent an elephant back over the river with a chit for the Mishmis, explaining what Lindsay had said, but by now the Mishmis already knew about Eadon and Moses, having been told by the Commandos.

Major Lindsay wanted to leave Dapha immediately in order to speak to RAF top brass in Delhi, with a view to getting a food drop started for Rowland and Rossiter. Mackrell agreed, and that night he gave his own tent to Lindsay, so that he would be rested for his onward journey. He also prepared a special elephant pad, in order that Lindsay could ride with his bad leg stretched out. Early on the morning of the 21st, Major Lindsay and Captain Cumming left by elephant for Miao, but Dr Bardoloi had told Mackrell that Kendall the surveyor was far too ill to be moved. The doctor was very worried about Kendall.

Later on that Sunday, a few miles west of the Dapha camp, Sergeant Pratt and Captain Boyt of the Commandos were walking with their Mishmi rescuers with the other Commandos in the rear when they saw two elephants standing in their path. Pratt and Boyt tried to scare them away until dissuaded by the Mishmis. They were tame elephants, sent forward by Mackrell, and their mahouts were smoking nearby. It was a case of: "Your carriage awaits." In mid-afternoon, the Commandos were put on the elephants to cross the Dapha. Ritchie Gardiner observed "a strong and deep current which we could never have made without their assistance". Even so, his elephant "nearly fell over, fifty yards from goal".

On the other side Mackrell and Wilson — "Both charming and so kind and helpful", wrote Howe — greeted them with Bovril, chapattis, and very hot, very sweet, tea. The canvas bath was unfolded and water boiled. Gardiner "Had a HOT bath and borrowed a CLEAN vest from Mackrell". Dr Bardoloi attended to Gardiner's feet while he "lay back with a pipe of real tobacco — it would have to be Barney's of course . . ."

Wilson kept making tea all day. Gardiner "had six mugs, with plenty of milk and sugar and sweet biscuits". Later, the Commandos were served the full welcome dinner — tinned sausages, tinned cheese, the works — and more "lovely hot, sweet tea". Howe noted with delight that, after his "wonderful dinner", he "felt quite ill from too much food". They were told that a runner would be leaving for Miao the next day, so they drafted messages for telegrams.

Grand Tiffins and the Squits: The Commandos Recuperate at the Dapha, but Mackrell Falls Sick

In the last week of June, the Commandos stayed at the Dapha camp. They had to wait for elephants to come back from delivering earlier refugees to Miao. This shuttle service worked far too slowly for everyone's liking, and it still wasn't bringing in enough food. Gardiner, rapidly turning into a belletrist, used the time to elaborate his diary, adding not only a prologue but also an epilogue on fancy writing paper that had been brought to the Dapha by Captain Wilson (who was, after all, the son of a stationer).

Young Bill Howe was up and down over those few days. On 22 June, the day after his rescue, he wrote, "Porridge for breakfast with lots of milk and sugar followed by fried fish. I have still got a hankering for sweet stuff, but have already lost the awful ache just for food."

On 23 June, the Commandos bathed on the safe margins of the river, shaved and "spruced up" for a photograph, taken in the rain. The picture survives and they look terrible. "Old Man" Jardine looks like a white-bearded skeleton. Fraser gazes myopically from behind his prescription sunglasses (which look alarming like the heavily shaded spectacles worn by the blind). Howe and Boyt, with pipes in mouths, manage to look wryly amused (as well as ill); Pratt, with folded arms, still looks determined. Gardiner, Kendall and McCrindle look too thin, and waterlogged, Kendall especially: he hangs back, and seems to glow with pallor. Somewhere along the line, he had been bitten by the mosquito called *Plasmodium fulciparum*, the one that carries the most dangerous form of malaria: cerebral malaria. Three Indian servants, unfortunately unnamed, crouch in the foreground. It seems they came through with Lindsay's Men. Behind the party, a mahout sits on an elephant under an umbrella; he is not posing, he just happens to be there, much as a double-decker bus might find its way into a group scene in London.

Gardiner spent much of his time watching the Dapha river and thinking of ways to describe it in his diary. Gardiner, who had collected the Chaukan orchid, was of all the Commandos the one who took the most interest in his surroundings. Mackrell explained to him that the Dapha flowed at never less than eight miles an hour, or fifteen miles an hour when the level was up. The ceaseless roar came from the shifting of the boulders on the river bed. Mackrell also pointed out the snow-capped peak of the 15,000-foot Dapha Bum mountain to the north-east. (The mountains of that part of the world are called "bums" — not quite as hilarious as it looks, since the word is pronounced "boom".)

The next day, the effervescent Howe caught a chill, and that combined — as he admitted — with overeating gave him the "squitters". The Commandos all agreed they were going to ask for a month's leave when they returned to their units. "What I want now," wrote young Bill Howe, "is more comfort and fancy things and civilisation." In a footnote to the diary, he writes, "This seems to suggest we were starting to think of wine, women and song." Later, there is an advance on that: "My legs rather bad and feeling very lazy with no particular desire to do anything, but I shall be glad now to get moving and have these boils properly attended to and get to those desires we are still looking forward to as keenly as ever!" which is followed by the note: "Looks as if sex is rearing its ugly head!"

There was one item of reading matter in the Dapha camp: a back number of *Men Only*. Who brought it to the camp? We can probably rule out the elephant men: Mackrell, the Kampti Raja, the tracker Goal Miri. The Mishmis couldn't have brought it. *Men Only* is not available in the Assamese jungle, and they wouldn't have understood it anyway, although they'd have got the gist. The reader was vouchsafed one photograph of a naked woman per issue, coyly posed so as to reveal only the breasts, or perhaps the buttocks and the side of one breast (it being morally as well as anatomically impossible to display both breasts and both buttocks at the same time), and coyly captioned something like "Firelight study", or, if outdoors, "Wood nymph".

Otherwise it was wordy, sub-Wodehouseian humour: "RC. Robertson-Glasgow on why he prefers his male friends to be fat . . . Perhaps this almost morbid love of adiposity comes to most of us as we reach that age and port when comparative strangers tap us on the fourth waistcoat button and say, 'O-ho.'", or quite funny cartoons (posh fat man to waiter in restaurant: "May I enquire WHY there is no more Château Lafite?") The adverts must have had an odd resonance in the jungle: "You wanted Schweppes, of course, sir?" "How to eke out your Brylcreem. With so much less Brylcreem in the shops we all need to make the most economical use of what we've got." (The secret? Add water.) "Dri-Ped shoe leather, always completely waterproof." "Wetherdair waterproofs are in short supply . . . You may have to go out of your district to get one." "Headache and neuralgia quickly banished by Cephos." "Specify Redi-Bilts, the interlinings that keep your suit in shape."

It is not impossible that clubbable and handsome Captain Wilson had packed this publication at Margherita, along with the thirty-six umbrellas.

On the other side of the river, the Mishmis, political porters and Assam Rifles were making probes forward, looking for Eadon and Moses. And Havildar Iman Sing was marching in the presumed direction of Sir John. Sometimes Mackrell went over, sometimes Wilson, but communication between the two sides was impeded by the fact that the river would become uncrossable for twenty-four hours at a time. Wilson spent a lot of time in or outside the house he had built at the point, looking through field glasses to see any sign of new arrivals on the other bank, but he couldn't look for long because the steam from the rain would make everything go blurred.

The shortage of elephants persisted; many of the porters had absconded; many of the Indians in the camp were ill. The Mishmi headman — the guide Mackrell had recruited at the Debang river — had dysentery. Late on 23 June, it was necessary to move the camp away from the rising waters of the Dapha. Mackrell and Wilson went upriver on elephants in pouring rain ... and they had to *keep* going, along jungly ledges, looking for a plateau that would be safe. They eventually found a site more than an hour's elephant ride from the original camp. The new one was established in relays, but journeying along the route between the camps became difficult, and on the night of 25 June the logistics broke down and Mackrell was left alone at the new site with food but no bedding and no tent. It rained all night, and Mackrell, sleeping under trees in his rain cape, woke with a high temperature and a "racking head". He could not concentrate properly, and had to stop writing his diary. He took to his tent, which disturbed everyone, like an enormous tree being felled. (In spite of the rain, the tent would become suffocating during the middle of the day, so that Wilson would urge Mackrell to come out and sit under the main tarpaulin for some of the time.)

On 26 June, Ritchie Gardiner borrowed McCrindle's razor and slashed the abscess on his foot. "Then the

223

doc gave it the coup de grace with his unprofessional looking thorn."

He discussed the Chaukan Pass with Captain Wilson, who said the Mishmis would go fishing high up the Noa Dehing but not as far as the Chaukan Pass. *Nobody* went up there. Gardiner found that "easily understandable".

On the 29th, the Commandos were transferred to the new camp, when what they really wanted was to be transferred to Miao, that staging post on the way back to the golf course at Margherita and the civilization it represented.

The new camp gave a better view of the Dapha Bum, and on the evening of the 29th there was no rain and no mist, giving Ritchie Gardiner an opportunity to use his silver pencil: "a piece of pure Alpine scenery: slate blue and brown rocks, jagged peaks and large scattered snowfields." He was fascinated that snow could be visible from the muggy banks of the Dapha. Gardiner read extracts from his diary to the Commandos, and was secretly delighted when they nodded approvingly. He noted: "It ought to serve."

The previous day, despite being ill, Mackrell had tried to cross the Dapha on two elephants with supplies for the Mishmis on the other side. He tried for hours with two mahouts. Wilson had wanted to come along, but Mackrell said he would not be required. To Wilson, the mahouts were "not trustworthy" and he thought a below par Mackrell would need help to keep them in line. The whole relationship between Mackrell, the mahouts and the elephants continued to baffle Wilson.

He blamed the mahouts for the shortage of supplies coming through from Miao. "The elephants seem to go all over the place once they leave Mackrell's immediate control ... It's a puzzle to me that Mackrell has managed them [the mahouts] but so far he has."

Mackrell failed to cross the river on that occasion, and by the 29th they were "down to brass tacks" on rations both at the new Dapha camp and at the staging posts being created on the other side of the river. No concerted forward push could be mounted without a reserve of food and more elephants.

And what of Sir John Rowland?

Both his party and that of the Rossiters were still stuck on the wrong side of the Tilung Hka, still living, or slowly dying, on their skilly soup. Sir John's diary for the last week of June records business as usual: terrific thunderstorms, incessant rain, passing aeroplanes paying no attention to them, and the deterioration of everyone in the camp. People were light-headed, dizzy; they walked between the communal fires and their individual huts without saying a word. On 29 June there was another check on rations, and, as regards mouldy rice, the parties were found to be "slightly in hand". Even so, Dr Burgess-Barnett advised Sir John that, if no help came within five days, they were finished.

225

The Drop: Linkage is Established, By Land and Air, Between Mackrell at the Dapha and Sir John at the Tilung Hka

On the morning of 30 June at the Dapha camp, Captain Wilson was standing next to his "house" on the point with binoculars in hand, when he saw the Mishmis on the other side of the river. They had with them the anti-malarial man, Eadon, and the International Boy Scout, Moses.

To enable them to cross the Dapha, Eadon and Moses had been put on the same elephant. Its mahout was having difficulty persuading it to step into the river, which was running fast. It did enter the water, but kept stopping, seeming to reflect, seemingly sighing at the absurdity of the feat it was being asked to perform. Mackrell, still sick, was at the house on the point with Wilson. The Commandos came to the riverbank, too. The elephant teetered; Mackrell folded his arms and muttered something that Wilson couldn't hear over the roar of the water. The elephant stabilized itself, sighed again, closed its eyes and with an air of distaste lowered itself into the water and began to swim . . . and so Eadon and Moses were brought over.

226

Howe wrote that the pair were "literally back from the grave", which was very *nearly* true. "It made my relief and happiness considerably more to know they too were safe." Gardiner wrote, "They looked if possible dirtier and more disreputable than we did on arrival." They had been saved in the first place by the Gurkha Havildar, Iman Sing, who had been dispatched from the Dapha on 19 June, and had found Eadon and Moses dying in their huts as he attempted to reach the Rowland and Rossiter parties. He had then fed them and handed them over to the Mishmis.

Eadon and Moses had entered a camp where tea was once again drunk without milk or sugar; there was little else but rice left, and much of that was mouldy. Almost all Wilson's political porters had absconded. On the 29th, most of the remaining porters were sent back to Miao for more rations. None of those sent would return.

As mentioned, Major Lindsay of the Oriental Mission had departed the Dapha camp on 21 June, with his leg up on a special elephant pad. He intended to pull some strings in order to get a food drop started from the air, and he was armed with an accurate map position for the Dapha camp, and a more or less accurate one for Sir John and the Rossiters (provided they stayed put). As further moral blackmail he planned to invoke Rossiter's pregnant wife, Nang Hmat, and her baby boy, John.

Mackrell and Wilson obviously had faith in Lindsay's persuasive powers because, within two days of his departure, they had laid out on their unfurled white

"T" the message "DROP MESSAGE HERE". They made the letters using small stones; each one was about six feet high, but they did not need to write out those three words in full. Instead, they used a three-letter code taken from the code book used in that particular theatre of war, and designed to speed up the sending of Morse messages. Pre-arranged three-letter codes existed for such elemental messages as "DROP MESSAGE HERE", and, as a pilot trained in the days before radio, Mackrell would certainly have known them. As well as bags of food, they wanted information about what, if anything, the authorities intended to do about Sir John and the Rossiters.

The thirtieth of June was fine, in fact very hot. Even so, Mackrell kept to his tent. In mid-morning a plane came over the camp. It ignored them; it was the Chungking Taxi. In the afternoon, another plane came over. It was a DC3 like the Chungking Taxi, but this had no Chinese writing on it. Instead it carried the RAF roundel, and the RAF called their DC3s Dakotas. The Dakota circled the camp twice, then sacks began spilling from it. The men at the camp had to dodge the sacks, but nobody tried to catch one (as one all too grateful refugee in the Hukawng Valley had done: he died six weeks later in hospital). One sack landed with a tremendous whump two yards from the tent in which Mackrell lay. A few seconds later, another landed directly on top of the first. Mackrell put his head out of the tent, and in spite of everything he looked pleased. It was like Christmas. Wilson counted sixty-nine sacks on the ground, and each one contained another sack, folded over, with food in it: tea, sugar, rice, tins of sausages, baked beans, Marmite, Klim, cigarettes. Wilson wrote, "About 30% of tins broken, but it's a good lot just the same." Actually, having the previous day been on the point of starvation, he now became something of a gourmand: "Only 1 tin of marmalade, which is a pity . . ." Some of the sacks landed on the "DROP MESSAGE HERE" ground, but there was no *message* in any of them.

We will follow that Dakota as it continues east.

The pilot was Wing Commander George Chater, and he had taken off half an hour or so before from Dinjan airbase near Dibrugarh, Assam. After the Dapha drop, he followed the course of the Noa Dehing for sixty miles or so, looking out — in conference with his navigator — for its junction with the Tilung Hka. Here they turned left, descending over jungle towards what looked like a tribal village: a collection of bamboo and palm-leaf huts, two smouldering piles of bamboo, a white sheet on a bamboo flagpole. Chater descended to about a hundred feet; he circled deafeningly four times, so that people began to come out of the huts — thin, dazed people, British, Indian, Anglo-Indian, and in the case of one woman holding a baby, Burmese. The wing commander couldn't help noticing that falling sacks had almost killed some men at the Dapha camp, and so he was now alerting these new recipients of his largesse. As a further precaution, he planned to drop the sacks on the margins of the camp, half in the jungle. He had also noticed that many of the earlier sacks had burst, so he descended lower, to about a hundred feet, apparently skimming the tops of the tall trees (the pilots regarded a jungle drop as a sporting challenge, and it was not unusual for Dakotas that had done them to return to base with foliage in their undercarriages). The men in the cabin behind Chater opened the side door, and begin hauling and kicking out the sacks.

The next day, 1 July, was still hot, but raining again. At 6 a.m., the Commandos left the Dapha camp for Miao, riding on three elephants spared by Mackrell from ferry duty on the Dapha. Kendall, the surveyor, had left earlier in the morning, carried on a litter by four of the remaining Dapha porters. On 3 July, Wing Commander Chater once again approached the Dapha camp in his Dakota. He dropped more sacks, and Captain Wilson noted, "It looks as though Major Lindsay has been busy." It seems the man who had left Dapha for Miao and civilization on 21 June had indeed pulled strings, and he had pulled them *hard*. This time, Wilson was pleased to see tinned and dried fruit in some of the sacks, this being "just what Mackrell wants". Mackrell had been lamenting the absence of fruit in the camp, but the man himself was still keeping largely to his tent with a high temperature and a severe headache. Dr Bardoloi had told Wilson that Mackrell "did not react to quinine in the normal way". If he *had* done, he would have been better within a week, but he had now been ill for ten days. And just because the quinine was not helping him does not mean that it wasn't producing its familiar, charming side effects: persistent nausea, headaches, ringing in the ears.

Wilson himself was also feeling ill, and his arms and legs had gone septic with leech bites.

As before, there was no message from Wing Commander Chater, so Mackrell and Wilson still did not know whether Sir John and the Rossiters had been fed as well. (What Mackrell and Wilson *had* received in the 1 July drop was a teddy bear, presumably meant for Nang Hmat's baby.) Also as before, Wing Commander Chater flew on east, following the big river. Sir John's camp was found again, and more sacks or, as Sir John wrote, "Manna from the skies", were sent down. He does not say "from heaven". Sir John had disapproved when his colleague Eric Ivan Milne had proposed saying prayers for their deliverance. According to Milne, Sir John "couldn't pray if he tried", but after Chater's first drop he had made what Milne described as "a sort of speech thanking the Almighty", and he hadn't objected when Milne had then led communal singing of "O God, Our Help in Ages Past". But many sacks were lost deep in the jungle, or in the Tilung Hka river, and it was a slow process to round up the remainder, owing, as Sir John wrote, "to the extreme weakness of most of the party".

There was "still another happy surprise" late in the evening of 3 July. The intrepid Gurkha Havildar Iman Sing — who had been dispatched by Mackrell from Dapha on 19 June, and had rescued Eadon and Moses on his way to Sir John — walked into the camp, explaining that he was the vanguard of a relief party that would soon be mounted, and telling Sir John all about Mackrell and Wilson. Iman Sing also brought

231

cigarettes, which were particularly gratefully received by Milne, who'd been reduced to smoking bamboo leaves. So ended what Sir John called "a day of miracles".

Sir John now had a month's rations for all (even if baby John did not have his teddy bear). Early in the morning on 4 July, Sir John and Edward Rossiter jointly composed a chit to Mackrell and Wilson. It was headed "Camp", with the salutation "My dear Mackrell or Wilson". It listed all the people in the camp — "25 persons, which includes . . . Rossiter's wife and an eight months old baby". It said that, although they were now receiving food, they were still too ill to move, and their joint parties would need porterage of between sixty and seventy men to take them through the jungle to the Dapha. It concluded, "So will you please rush through transport here immediately in charge of someone responsible to get us to safety (your camp) as quickly as possible". Then came the hopeful salutation: "Au revoir and good luck", and there was a PS. "Should there be any long delay in getting transport for our move forward, would it be asking too much to contact the nearest aerodrome for a further supply of rations to be dropped here." And a PPS: "Also please a few tins of Glaxo for the baby — by plane." Being pregnant, Mrs Rossiter would not have been breast-feeding her baby, and it seemed she considered Glaxo tinned milk superior to Klim.

This chit was handed to two of what Sir John rudely called the two "Gurkha coolies" who had come in with Havildar Iman Sing, and they set off back to the Dapha camp, with Sing himself remaining at Tilung Hka. The two Gurkhas would deliver this chit to Mackrell on 12 July. By then, however, Mackrell and Wilson *knew* that Sir John's party were being supplied from the air because on 5 July, not long after the two Gurkhas left Sir John, Wing Commander Chater came along the Noa Dehing once more in his Dakota . . .

Chater was evidently a man who did things in his own good time, and now he *did* drop a message on the "DROP MESSAGE HERE" site laid out by Mackrell and Wilson at the Dapha camp. It was a chit in a tin, taped up in a cloth bag. It stated firstly that "the Chaukan Party" had received food drops since 30 June. It then asked a series of numbered questions that could be answered "yes" or "no". While Chater circled above the camp, Mackrell — still ill — went to his tent and retrieved his aeroplane Morse signalling lamp, which at the press of a trigger emitted a light bright enough to be seen in daytime. Mackrell first signalled the number of the question, then gave his answer. To "Do you have enough people to rescue Sir John?" Mackrell answered "No". "Would thirty more porters be useful?" "Yes." "Is it possible to get them [Sir John's party] out during the rains?" "Yes." "Or should we wait until after the rains?" "No."

Chater then flew on to Sir John's camp, where he dropped more food — "fairly bombarded" them, Sir John noted with approval — and also a message addressed to Sir John himself, summarised by the latter as being on the following lines: "Not to worry . . . we're on the job, soon get you out, etc etc" and signed

"George Chater, RAF". Sir John was doubly reassured to see that name, because he realized that he knew George Chater socially. He was "Terence's friend" (whoever Terence was), and Sir John and his wife had had him to dinner a couple of times in Rangoon. Now George Chater was giving *them* dinner, so to speak. But that message of his might have signified bravado as well as bravery. It was becoming more dangerous every day to fly that Dakota. As the humidity rose to its peak in early September, unpredictable thermal currents were fermented. And Japanese Zeros occasionally flew over Assam in the summer of 1942; they were fighter planes and the Dakota was not. No more food was dropped on the Dapha camp after 5 July; and there would only be one more drop on the Tilung Hka camp. Many of the dropped sacks had been lost, and despite the newly arrived food, a serious vitamin-deficiency problem was developing on the banks of the Tilung Hka. Nonetheless, Wing Commander George Chater had forestalled starvation, and there was more good news at Sir John's end of the jungle: the weather was getting better.

Momentous Decisions: Mackrell Leaves the Dapha Camp Just as Sir John Decides to Strike Out for It

. . . That is to say, the rain had eased . . . but the heat and humidity were rising, and more or less everyone at the Dapha camp was ill. The larger amount of food had brought a larger number of insects and dysentery was rife. There was a shortage of porters, and a shortage of elephants. More of either went to the base at Miao than ever came back from it. The porters would abscond even if they were owed money.

The Mishmis were also fleeing. Mackrell and Wilson might have been able to keep more of them if they'd had more opium, but in early July they only had the small amount that Commando Boyt had brought with him, which prompts the question of whether Boyt himself ever put two and two together and smoked the opium he carried in the pipe that he also carried. Another difficulty with the Mishmis was that their headman, the one who had originally guided Mackrell to the Dapha for ten rupees, was now severely ill with dysentery. He was attended by Dr Bardoloi, but did not improve because, Mackrell wrote, "he refuses to diet". He was too ill to command his men, and they would not take orders directly from Wilson or even Mackrell.

The ninth of July was a particularly grim day at Dapha. The air was unbreathable; the camp was swarming with insects, attracted by the spilled food sacks. And one of the few remaining porters, a Naga, who was working on the east side of the river, stocking the camps along the track towards the Tilung Hka, died that day. His brother, also employed at Dapha, confronted Mackrell and said that his brother had died because he had been pressed into portering some of the way for Iman Sing, bearer of the chit for Sir John. This surviving brother said he would wait until Iman Sing returned, and then he would "cut him up". Mackrell eventually talked the Naga man down, and he (the Naga) left for Miao that evening, as did the very ill Mishmi headman.

The next day, two elephants arrived at Dapha from Miao. Sitting up behind the mahouts were a Lieutenant Colonel Pizey and a tea planter called Black, a senior man in the Indian Tea Association. They were emissaries from the government bungalow at Margherita. Word had reached Margherita that Mackrell and Wilson were ill, and Pizey and Black had come to talk them into leaving Dapha and reconsidering the rescue effort.

Tea was served beneath the big tarpaulin, and a conference was held. Mackrell was happy to agree to the proposal as long as "reconsidering" meant establishing the effort on a stronger footing. That night

Black and Lieutenant Colonel Pizey stayed at Dapha. Both were kept awake all night by sandfly bites. The next day, Pizey left, taking Captain Wilson with him.

Mackrell insisted on lingering at Dapha because he was sure that Iman Sing would be back imminently with a reply from Sir John (an expectation he had concealed from the porter who wanted to murder Iman Sing). The senior ITA man, Black, insisted on staying at Dapha in case Mackrell's fever, which was generally abating, should incapacitate him once again. And so Black was kept awake for another night with sandfly bites.

On 12 July, as already noted, Iman Sing's two men did return to Dapha, carrying the chit from Sir John and Rossiter. In his diary, Mackrell speaks highly of the two Gurkhas. They had done the trek from the Tilung Hka in just eight days, and on very little food. They were brothers, and he records their names: Tami and Gunga Bahadur. Mackrell made a meal for the brothers and pondered the chit in which Sir John said he was being fed from the air (which Mackrell knew by now) and that he was staying put, being in want of sixty or seventy porters. So Sir John was not expected imminently. It seemed a few days could be spared in which to return to base, and solicit help for a bigger and better rescue attempt.

On the evening of 12 July, the senior ITA man, Black, left the Dapha camp for Miao. The plan was that everyone remaining in the camp would then leave with Mackrell.

On the 14th, Mackrell and Dr Bardoloi were attending to the stores in the camps on the east side of the river — it was the familiar chore of rigging up the sacks in the trees so they would be out of the reach of wild elephants. This was a precautionary measure. Nobody was expected at the river in the immediate future, but that had never stopped people turning up. Suddenly a plane came low over the trees, and it was not the sociable George Chater in his Dakota; this plane did not display the RAF roundel. It displayed the red Japanese rising sun. Mackrell and Dr Bardoloi walked briskly — they did not run — into the jungle "in case of machine gunning". The plane circled twice, went away, then came back.

It circled two more times before heading east.

On the 15th, half a dozen elephants came through from Miao, and these would enable Mackrell to quit the Dapha. Before doing so, he rearranged the white stones that had spelt out the code for "DROP MESSAGE HERE" so as to spell out the code for "PROPER TO ABANDON POST AND MARCH WEST". This was to forestall food being dropped on an empty camp. On the 16th, he saw another plane approaching, and he was pretty certain this *was* RAF. To underline his rearranged message, he threw kerosene on some of the bamboo huts and set fire to them. They burnt fiercely as the plane circled above.

Mackrell left the Dapha camp on 17 July. It was a very hot day, and, as his elephant awaited, he lit his pipe and gazed at the burning bamboo huts, the collapsed tents, the hundreds of sacks, many containing rotting food from split tins, each sack surrounded by a cloud of flies. As he puffed on his pipe, he reflected knowledgeably on the insects and their associates. This, after all, was the boy who had taken *Acidalia trigeminata*: "Early dim-dams, then huge horse flies, all day leeches, at dusk midges and at dark and onwards sandflies in myriads and some mosquitoes. No wonder this area is uninhabited."

But of course it *was* inhabited, and he had just listed its inhabitants. As Mackrell and the mahouts, the remaining Rifles and porters and Dr Bardoloi trailed away through the hot mist, its rightful owners regained possession of the Dapha camp.

As Mackrell departed from the Dapha river heading west on 17 July, Sir John Rowland was beginning to consider approaching it from the east. He was tired of being "in the blue", which is how he referred to deep jungle. True, on 3 July he had received the chit from Iman Sing saying help was at hand, but that help seemed to be a long time coming, and Sir John had rather lost faith in rescue parties. By the 17th, two weeks had passed since he and Rossiter had dispatched their reply to Mackrell and Wilson, and for all they knew that reply had never got through.

The two parties had enough food for a few more weeks, but much of it was mouldy and illness was rife. Most of those encamped on the Tilung Hka had the first signs of the condition called wet beriberi, the vitamin deficiency disease that would have been avoided if they'd been eating brown rather than white

239

rice. The symptoms were swollen ankles or fingers and a loss of mobility, and the condition could cause heart failure if left to develop. But it would be rectified by the early restoration of a proper, balanced diet and Sir John — who had swelling of the fingertips — wanted to move while he still could. He was also suffering intermittent bouts of malaria.

In spite of the hopeful chit he had received, he suspected the decision would be made to postpone any rescue until after the rains, in which case Mrs Rossiter would have to give birth in the jungle and some older members of the party would die. Sir John would take as many as possible away with him, and he would demand that a rescue party came back for the rest. Certainly, the weather was propitious. For the two weeks after 6 July, Sir John records, "Another fine and sunny day . . . Another fine day . . . the fourth fine day in succession . . . Still another fine day . . . Another fine sun-shining day . . ." With each successive fine day the level of the Tilung Hka had been falling, as Sir John verified by a series of increasingly satisfactory evening strolls to the river and back.

The trouble was the old one: a lack of porters. But on the morning of 18 July forty more soldiers, mainly Gurkhas, arrived at Sir John's camp from Burma. On the morning of the 19th a further twenty arrived. The need to accommodate these new men — who were mainly from the Burma Frontier Force — made the newly replenished larder seem a rather less formidable bulwark against future disaster. On the other hand, Sir John had been wishing for sixty men — he had said as

240

much in the chit he had written to Mackrell — and here *were* sixty men. It was uncanny, when you thought about it.

Of course, Sir John had wished for sixty *fit* men . . .

Sir John ordered the PMO, Dr Burgess-Barnett, to hold a sick parade and found three of the new arrivals seriously ill with malaria; others were suffering from septic sores and swollen feet and ankles from leech bites. Sir John ordered Burgess-Barnett to "doctor them up", and he himself fed them up.

Sir John's mind was made up. Despite being sixty years old, and ill, he would lead a party through to the Dapha. He knew that not everyone in the camp would be fit enough to accompany him. For a start, the pregnant Mrs Rossiter and baby John could be counted out, and of course her husband would have to stay with her. Sir John did not regret the fact that Edward Rossiter would not be accompanying him, and we will soon see more evidence to that effect.

On 22 July, Sir John held a roll call of the men in the camp and offered the fittest ones the chance to accompany him. He put together a party of about seventy-five, the majority of whom were the newly arrived Gurkhas. Mackrell's messenger, Iman Sing — blissfully ignorant that a tough Naga porter had wanted to chop him into pieces — would also undertake the journey back with Sir John. Of his own original railway party, Sir John took the forty-three-year-old District Traffic Superintendent, Eric Ivan Milne, and the Indians, namely Naidu, the divisional accountant, Venkatachalam, the office superintendent, and

241

Venkataraman, the store clerk, even though each man was well into middle age. The other railwayman, fifty-six-year-old Edward Lovell Manley, his senior colleague on the Burma-China construction, would finally have to separate from Sir John. He was not fit enough to walk sixty miles through thick jungle.

Although perhaps fit enough himself to make the trek (but he wasn't completely well) Dr Burgess-Barnett would stay with the twenty-five or so remaining, who also included the less fit Gurkhas, some Indian servants and the bespectacled Captain Whitehouse of the Royal Engineers, who was beginning to have difficulty in walking.

On the afternoon of 23 July the rain had stopped and the sun was out; Sir John was ready to lead his seventy-five away towards the Dapha. But Gyles Mackrell had left the Dapha six days earlier, so who would be there to cross him over the river?

Mackrell Returns Temporarily to Civilization, While Sir John Attempts to do the Same on a Permanent Basis

On 17 July, Mackrell and his men and his elephants trailed back the way they had come, through the lower jungles towards the camp at Miao. At the Debang river, he diverted to the village of Tinguan to see the Mishmi headman who had shown him the shortcuts to the Dapha. The man's condition had not improved. He lay in his hut under a suspended hurricane lamp, looking "desperately ill". Mackrell paid what he owed him, plus a bonus of a hundred rupees. He also gave him rum, Klim and the small quantity of opium that he had about him. He gave chits to the other Mishmis who had helped him at Dapha — invoices for the wages owed.

That night, Mackrell slept in a spare hut in the village. He set up his camp bed and mosquito net well away from two holes in the roof, and, as the rain thundered down, the water ran in a sluice under his bed, so it was quite a satisfactory arrangement in that he himself was not wet. He was about to go to sleep when he heard a scrabbling on the side of his bed. Then he felt something climb effortfully onto his chest. He sat up, and a giant wet rat, squeaking with fright, leapt onto the mosquito netting, from where it fell onto Mackrell's head. He seems to have seen the funny side: "I had much difficulty getting out without getting bitten!"

On Saturday 18 July, Mackrell and his party crossed the Noa Dehing at Miao "with all elephants", although both rivers were rising. On the afternoon of the next day, in the bungalow on a cliff above the river, Mackrell had a meeting with Black, the senior ITA man, who introduced him to two new men who had been co-opted to the rescue effort: Captain Street of the 2nd Rajputan Rifles, and a man called Webster, a police officer. The two had arrived at Miao with a detachment of Assam Rifles and some political porters. After introductions had been made and tea had been poured, Webster explained to Mackrell that he, Street and Black would be going to Dapha to organize a fresh rescue expedition. We might imagine Mackrell moving his pipe about in his hands, but not lighting it. This would have been another tense encounter. Mackrell had been removed from the scene of the action, and these three men — all a good deal younger than him — would be taking his place. It seemed he was being pensioned off; and yet he had made a promise to Millar and Leyden that he would rescue the Rowland and Rossiter parties. It would be churlish to quibble about who rescued them; the main thing was that they should be rescued. It was therefore difficult to know what to say.

244

It became less difficult when police officer Webster continued to the effect that the aim of the new expedition would be to meet the Rowland and Rossiter parties, which had set off from their camp on the wrong side of the Tilung Hka and were moving west. Now Webster was imparting this information to Mackrell on the afternoon of Sunday 19 July. On 12 July, the Gurkha brothers working under the Havildar Iman Sing had handed Mackrell the chit from Sir John to say that he and the Rossiters were staying put because of a lack of porters. Soon after writing that, Sir John had, as we have seen, been miraculously supplied with porters and decided to leave for Dapha. But he would not set off until 23 July, and all the evidence as of that Sunday 19 July suggested he was indeed staying put. Mackrell put this to Black, Street and Webster . . . who begged to differ.

They explained to Mackrell that a plane flying over the Rowland/Rossiter camp a couple of days previously had seen a message: "PROPER TO ABANDON POST AND MARCH WEST". Moreover, they said, Sir John had burnt his camp to underline the message. Mackrell immediately saw that the game of Chinese whispers had just taken another lurch into farce.

"I don't think that is correct," he said.

Mackrell told Black, Street and Webster that he himself had set out that very message before firing the Dapha camp. What, he enquired, were the chances of Sir John having done exactly the same?

Silence in the room. Rain falling outside.

Certainly, it was agreed by Black, Street and Webster, that would be a remarkable coincidence. But then again, the 31 Squadron boys had been very sure of what they'd seen . . .

And there the meeting broke up, in stalemate, or limbo, it being unclear exactly who was in charge of whom.

The next day, that matter at least was resolved. As Mackrell trailed back west through the flat, steaming jungle towards the intermediate camp of Simon he saw an elephant coming towards him. On top of it sat a Gurkha of the Assam Rifles, a new Havildar, and we have his name: Dharamsing Curung. Mackrell introduced himself, and said, "Were you looking for me?" Dharamsing Curung rocked his head gently from side to side. In Assam, that means "yes". He had a chit for Mackrell, written by a government official called Pearce at the Margherita bungalow. Pearce was the Refugee Administrator for North Assam. Anyhow, he was in a position to determine superiority among the Dapha men, and his chit stated that, although Mackrell was being recalled for consultations, he — Mackrell — was the senior man. This is exactly what Mackrell had hoped for; he was pleased, and slightly surprised, since he was, after all, a civilian.

Mackrell pocketed the chit, and as the party, now supplemented by Dharamsing Curung, pressed on for Simon, the rain began to come down in a deluge. It would turn out that the endorsement Mackrell had received was equivocal, but for now he had the

246

important chit in his pocket, and he was developing a plan.

Mackrell arrived at the Margherita golf club base at 8p.m. on Tuesday 21 July. Half an hour later, he was lighting his pipe on the clubhouse veranda, and looking out over the course, where the refugee tents were pitched, and where about twenty people were dying every day in spite of the tea planter's ministrations. He had on his lap his stationery case wrapped in its oilcloth and a glass of whisky and water. He finished his drink, and began to write a chit. It was to Captain Street of the 2nd Rajputan Rifles, who was on his way to Dapha. Mackrell informed him of the chit placing himself (Mackrell) in charge. Mackrell also told Street that he (Street) was in charge of the police officer, Webster. He gave the chit to a runner, and it would proceed by a relay of runners to Dapha via Simon and Miao. There were then meetings at Margherita, and further chits and telegrams were sent, and telephone calls made.

On Thursday 23 July, the day Sir John set off from his camp on the Tilung Hka, Mackrell took an early tiffin at the golf club with ITA people. He was then driven to the airbase at Dinjan, home of 31 Squadron. Mackrell had been in the squadron himself, so it might have seemed to the younger fliers like a family visit, the social call of some terrifically energetic uncle. At Dinjan, he boarded a Dakota loaded with sacks of rice, atta and tea. He was carrying his 16mm film camera, and a half-full tin of Klim. First of all, the plane flew over the Hukawng Valley refugee route from Shinbiwyang to Margherita, which was close to being wound up.

However, sacks were dropped onto the camps at Shinbiwyang and Nampong, and Mackrell filmed the dropping. It was a crude process, with all the finesse of feeding time at the zoo: the soldiers stand by the wide-open cabin door — through which comes a blaze of white light, the 23rd being a fine day — and kick out the sacks. Mackrell's film doesn't show the camps, but mainly the gaping door, the soldiers' boots and the black and white jungle rearing about below.

He then asked the pilot to fly towards the intersection of the Tilung Hka and the Noa Dehing rivers. On the way, Mackrell studied the Noa Dehing. All along the banks were landslips, where the risen waters of the monsoon had dragged mudbanks and trees — and such riverbank tracks as existed — into the river.

They came to the site of Sir John Rowland's camp. No drop was made, but Mackrell had wanted to test his theory that the camp was still there.

It was. If Mackrell had ill advisedly leant far out of the cabin door — which he probably *would* have done — he would have seen the circle of huts, the tents, the white bed-sheet flag. It being fine, the camp was astir, and Mackrell saw a vigorous looking, but not young, man in consultation with "some rifles". This, as he later deduced, was Sir John Rowland. The point was that the camp was not burnt, and there was no signal about moving west. That Sir John was at that very moment making the arrangements to *start* moving west — that this was the whole reason the camp was astir — Mackrell could not have known from 200 feet up.

The plane then flew towards the Dapha camp. Here, too, the plane circled, and Mackrell saw a scene that would remain branded on his mind. Black, the senior tea man, Webster, the policeman, and Captain Street of the 2nd Rajputs had just arrived, together with their detachment of Assam Rifles, and forty political porters. Mackrell could tell they'd just arrived because the elephants, grazing by the river, were not yet unloaded.

Captain Street was bathing on the edge of the river and Black was standing on the bank.

Mackrell asked the pilot to keep circling while he wrote out a chit, explaining what he had apparently just verified: that Sir John was not decamping. He placed the chit into the half-full tin of Klim and dropped it towards Black, who ran to pick it up, and waved towards the plane to indicate he had received it, and understood that Sir John was in his camp, and not going anywhere.

But Sir John *was* coming.

As mentioned, Sir John and his party set off on the afternoon of 23 July, a "fine-sunshiny day".

The party crossed the Tilung Hka by wading through chest-high water. They then progressed in the traditional manner: along the rocky shores and precipitous banks of the Noa Dehing. Sometimes they encountered the landslips Mackrell had seen from the air, and these required detours inland. Sir John and his party travelled six and half miles on that first day.

In light rain they built a camp near the river. By the early hours of the morning, the rain had increased in

volume so that it drowned out the river. Not many in
the camp slept, and those that did were woken by a
fusillade of thunder at four in the morning. As dawn
broke, there were repeated flashes of lightning, showing
the river, the river cliffs, the landslips and the trees —
like forewarnings of a difficult time to come. In
mid-morning they came to a tributary of the Dapha in
heavy flood. It took two hours for the Gurkhas to make
a tree-trunk bridge. At three o'clock they abandoned
the day's march, and built a camp in torrential rain.
They had progressed four miles.

Sir John was removing between five and six hundred
leeches from his person himself every day. He ordered
regular returns to the river, so that the party could
bathe on its margins, using the force of the water to
assist in the removal of leeches. But on 26 July, Sir John
— the consummate colonialist — was noticing with
interest "several traces of good coal occurring in soft
sandstone".

On 27 July, incidentally, there was another — and
the final — food drop on the Tilung Hka camp that Sir
John had left behind. A message was dropped with the
food, futilely addressed to Sir John from the Margherita
bungalow, and telling him to stay put. It was probably
opened and read by Edward Wrixon Rossiter.

Midday on the 27th found Sir John clinging to a
bamboo clump on a near vertical bank of the river.
While reaching for a second bamboo bush, he lost his
handhold, then lost his *foothold*, and he slid down the
red mud of the riverbank, scrambling all the way but

250

unable to stop the slide; then he was scrambling in the water, and moving fast away from the men of his party.

He managed to get out, but he would take another "header" into the river a few hours later. The twenty-seventh of July was also particularly bad for leeches: "The forest paths were literally teeming with millions of them, bushes, trees, everywhere was alive with them." But on 30 July, Sir John was noting again "several more traces of good coal". The thirtieth of July was showery, and presented what Sir John called "6th big avalanche".

He and Milne supported Naidu, the railway accountant, "whose feet and ankles are so bad that he can hardly walk". Sir John himself was not coming through unscathed, and swollen ankles were slowing *him* down as well. On 31 July, Sir John and his party were approaching the west bank of the Dapha river, which was being its usual riotous self. They were looking for a camp staffed by men called Mackrell and Wilson, as per the chit delivered by Havildar Iman Sing, who was now returning with Sir John. But the party could see no sign of Mackrell or his camp, and they needed to contact someone — someone with elephants — otherwise they would be trapped on the wrong side of the river. So Sir John and his men built a big bonfire, making as much smoke as possibly by piling on green bamboo. After two hours, this fire elicited the sublime vision that had greeted the initial Gurkhas, Lindsay's Men, the Commandos, Eadon and Moses: elephants — two of them — with mahouts on their backs. Some Assam Rifles next appeared, then a

251

beaming Captain Street of the 2nd Rajput Rifles. We have a description of Street from Sir John: "a grand lad, full of life and quite a good looker, tall and well set up." The two shook hands warmly. Sir John and his party were crossed over the river by elephants, and came into the rebuilt Dapha camp, where they met Street's colleague, "a young police officer". Sir John provides no description of Webster, but then he would have more cause to recall Captain Street, as we shall see.

Over tea at the Dapha camp, Sir John asked about Mackrell, and was told he was preparing for another rescue push. Sir John was now convinced that his personal troubles were over, but he was determined that those he'd left behind at the Tilung Hka must be brought out, and he hoped Mackrell would do the job.

What of these left-behinds?

Captain Whitehouse of the Royal Engineers was suffering badly from Vitamin B deficiency, specifically Vitamin B12, which is contained in all the foods he was *not* getting: fish, liver, milk, eggs. He had acute pains in his legs. He walked about the camp less and less every day; he was losing feeling in his hands and feet and was often sick. He kept removing his tortoiseshell spectacles and rubbing his eyes. His eyeballs would move about independently of his will. His condition was known at the time as Peripheral Neuritis, and it can be fatal.

As for Mrs Rossiter, the odds were against her keeping her baby boy alive insofar as the odds would have been against *any* baby in those conditions. Dysentery, cholera, malaria — all were more likely to be contracted, and prove fatal, in the case of a baby. As a pregnant woman, the odds were against her own survival as well. Both Sir John's deputy, Manley, and Dr Burgess-Barnett were increasingly debilitated. And a dozen of the remaining twenty Gurkhas were sick.

They had to be got out. Elephants would be required, and they would have to be taken deeper into the blue in the monsoon than any tame elephant had so far been.

Mackrell in Shillong and Calcutta (Where He Can't Find Marmite but Settles for Horlicks)

On the hot evening of 25 July, when Sir John was two days into his march, Gyles Mackrell drove from Margherita west to Shillong, capital of Assam, and Mackrell's home town. Shillong was beautiful, famous for its high pine trees, spacious colonial bungalows, and one of the highest incidences of rainfall a year, upwards of 500 inches — not as much as the Chaukan Pass, where, as Sir Reginald Dorman-Smith wrote in his Evacuation Report, the rainfall "might as well have been measured in yards as inches".

Knowing he would be living in the jungle for some time, Mackrell had let out his house, but as he approached the front door there were no lights on and no signs of life. He entered the dark house and lit an oil lamp, since the electricity wasn't working. We can be confident of strewing a couple of tiger skins about in those wide, white rooms, and we might place some buffalo horns over the fireplace, and a locked gun cabinet in the corner of the study. On the bookshelves

... not much actual literature perhaps: rather, some maps, accounts of big game hunts, a history of the Royal Flying Corps. Mackrell wrote, "My tenant had run away, leaving no address, so servants had also bolted."

Mackrell had only been paying a call, but he now took his kitbag out of his car and moved in for two nights only.

At lunchtime the next day, Sunday, he drove through the hot rain until another white bungalow loomed beyond the swishing of the wipers: here lived the family of Dr Burgess-Barnett, who was still stranded at Tilung Hka. On that Sunday, Mackrell didn't know that, two days before, Sir John had left that camp with his party of seventy-five. The doctor's wife and two daughters, with whom Mackrell now took tea, didn't know that either. But they were quite right in assuming that their primary concern, the elderly doctor, was still out "in the blue" many miles from civilization (if the Dapha camp could be called that). Mackrell assured the ladies that the party was receiving food drops, and he promised that he would bring the doctor home to them, just as he had promised to rescue Sir John. It might be objected that, while undoubtedly saving numerous lives, Mackrell had not quite been able to keep his promise in the case of Sir John — that Sir John had rescued himself. But this would be to forget the air drops that had saved the Tilung Hka party from starvation. A necessary precondition of these had been the emergence from the jungle of Major Lindsay, with his map showing the location of the Tilung Hka camp,

255

and that wouldn't have been possible had Mackrell not established the *Dapha* camp.

On Tuesday 28 July, with his kitbag on the back seat, Mackrell now drove further west, to the ramshackle riverside town whose name he spelt Naraingunj, the Brahmaputra river port of Dacca. Here, he boarded a steamer and travelled through the evening, past the dark green outline of the intersecting valleys, through the rain. He disembarked at Goalundo, where the Brahmaputra and the Ganges meet. Here he boarded the night train to Calcutta, the *Dacca Mail*. He arrived at Howrah station in Calcutta at five in the morning.

Even then the Howrah Station tannoy was blaring, in English and Bengali. Having had to contend with the strong currents of rivers, Mackrell now had to contend with the strong currents of people. At one side of the main concourse were trestle tables loaded with documents, where sat officials already at work behind a cordon of military police. These were the reception committees and sub-committees for the refugees from Burma.

Most of the refugees ended their journeys at Howrah station, where they would also have to begin the rest of their lives. It has been recorded that on one day alone — 11 April 1942 — 15,000 people approached those tables for help. The first priority of the officials was to arrange food and clothing. There was also a customs check, which seems rather provocative in the circumstances. Then came the fraught questions of money and employment. There were separate committees for each community — Hindu, Muslim,

256

Indian-Christian, Anglo-Indian, European, Burmese Chinese (although most Chinese had gone eastward, towards Yunnan and, in most cases, malarial death) — and the tables at Howrah represented the front offices of the camps and hostels established in the already teeming city of Calcutta.

Let's take one community. "The Muslim sub-committee cared for some 113,000 evacuees and served about 460,000 meals, in addition to obtaining valuable assistance from the Islamic Hospital, until a special evacuees' hospital was established. Over 14,000 patients were treated by the Muslim medical officers." That was written by Sir Reginald Dorman-Smith, who added the characteristic remark: "The situation was not an easy one to handle."

But Mackrell did not trouble those harassed and sweating bureaucrats. Instead, he was met outside the station by one C. M. Macpherson, a fellow director of the firm of Octavius Steel and a former chairman of the Indian Tea Association. Macpherson drove Mackrell over the khaki-coloured Hooghly river into downtown Calcutta. He did so by the old Howrah Bridge. Alongside it, a new cantilevered bridge was being completed: two giant cranes inching towards each other, a slow courtship in the swirling rain. This new bridge would be strong enough to withstand the marching of thousands of men who would make for the Howrah trains, and head north-east to retake Burma. Mackrell stayed at Macpherson's house for two days, making plans and arrangements.

Calcutta, July 1942 . . .

The hot rain falling on the peeling stucco palaces. The Hooghly flowing fast through the middle of the town, as though it has more important business elsewhere and doesn't mind who knows it. The brown water is high at the Babu Ghat, where the ragged Hindus stand, thoughtful, half immersed. The water threatens the wharves and the dock railway that runs along the bank just there, between the river, and the Gothic High Court, which resembles the Palace of Westminster. The Houses of Parliament in the rain, then . . . except that the temperature is 105. The streets reek of diesel fumes; the rain drums on the roofs of the taxis, on the skeletal rickshaw wallahs, and on the bicyclists, some of whom veer about under umbrellas . . .

The traffic was even worse than usual that summer because the widest and straightest road, the Red Road — which skirted the maidan, or park — had been cordoned off and turned into an airstrip. Spitfires and Hurricanes stood upon it; ambulances were parked on the edges of the maidan; army tents billowed in the rainy gusts. Most of the Allied troops converging on Calcutta were quartered in Fort William, which stood on the maidan, but the fighter pilots were billeted at the white-stucco Grand Hotel on Chowringhee, which despite — or because of — the stucco that was perpetually peeling, looked as though it belonged in Brighton. The Grand was convenient for many bars and restaurants, the labyrinthine bazaars of the Hogg Market, and not too far (for those tongue-tied in the presence of Wrens, Waafs and nurses) from the brothels of Sudder Street. Of his own wartime furlough in the city, George MacDonald Fraser wrote, in *Quartered Safe Out Here*, of the pleasures of being "shaved by a squatting nappy-wallah, who used no lather but your own sweat and left your skin like glass ... After which there was nothing for it but to rest in Ferrazini's and linger over the Desert Sunrise, which was about a gallon of ice creams and syrups of every flavour and colour." He mentions that a Laurel and Hardy film was showing at the Lighthouse Cinema, a Betty Grable at the Tiger Cinema. In Calcutta — the Americans called it "Cal" — a young serviceman could enjoy himself while he waited to move north-east for the fight to reclaim Burma.

Calcutta had been displaced by Delhi as capital of India in 1911, but it still housed the head office of the Indian Tea Association, and Mackrell held some meetings in its offices, located behind the white pillars of the grandly classical Royal Exchange building on Clive Street. Its chairman in 1942 was another Octavius Steel man, one C. K. Nicholl. It's likely that Mackrell also visited the offices of Octavius Steel, on Old Court House Street. In Assam the tea was still growing, still being harvested, so there would have been some "civilian" business for him to attend to, and some letters of congratulation to read.

Mackrell steps out of the Royal Exchange Building ... Difficult to imagine this connoisseur of unspeakable weather going to the trouble of carrying an umbrella. A white linen suit, then, a sola topee and a Mackintosh cape. He looks at the parked aeroplanes with a feeling of . . . well, jealousy might have come in to it. Here were young men, performing life-threatening and life-saving missions over dangerous territory in appalling weather — just the kind of set-up he liked.

For the moment, anyway, he has time to kill. So he heads a little way north, let us say, towards Dalhousie Square, where he lights a cigarette in the doorway of one of the Calcutta gun shops. He enters the shop — a shadowy, dusty place smelling of incense, with buffalo horns around the walls. The Indian proprietor knows Mackrell, and they have a talk about the war. Difficult to avoid that subject in Calcutta, what with all the beery soldiers, and that airstrip running through the middle of town.

Japanese warships are menacing the Bay of Bengal. For some Indian nationalists, a Japanese incursion might be welcomed as presenting an opportunity, the enemy's enemy being one's friend. Britain had added insult to years of injury by declaring that India was at war without consulting the chief independence movement, the Congress Party, which was in danger of being outflanked by more radical nationalist forces.

In January of the previous year, Subhas Chandra Bose, a sometime mayor of Calcutta, a former President of Congress, and rival to Gandhi (in that Bose advocated the use of force to evict the British) had escaped from house arrest in Calcutta. Although an unlikely looking adventurer — bald, bespectacled and chubby — Bose had then apparently entered a John Buchan novel. Disguised as a bearded deaf mute, he fled India via Afghanistan and Russia (which was still allied to Germany at that point). From Moscow he was whisked to Berlin, from where the Nazis transferred him, by submarine, to Japanese-occupied Singapore. In 1943, he would be running the state of Azad Hind, or "Free India", which, fortunately for the British, was confined to the Andaman Islands in the Bay of Bengal.

As for the Congress Party, it had terminated its role in provincial governments in protest against the ruling power's unilateral declaration of war, so direct British rule had been imposed. But with India menaced by the Japanese advance through Burma, Britain needed the support of Congress in order to ensure the continued recruitment of Indians into the British Indian Army. Britain did not impose conscription on India, and, indeed, there had been a healthy flow of volunteers so far, because most Indians — the imperial grievance aside — were sympathetic to the Allies. In order to try and capitalize on this, Sir Stafford Cripps, who in spite of being a Marxist was a member of the War Cabinet, was deputed to negotiate with the Congress leader, Jawaharlal Nehru, and the Muslim leader, Ali Jinnah. He offered what was tantamount to full independence after the war in return for cooperation in the meantime. But it seems that Cripps was undermined by his own Prime Minister, that imperial diehard Churchill, and by the Indian Viceroy, Lord Linlithgow, and his offer was rejected by Congress as lacking in credibility, as not going far enough and carrying the taint of federalism. (The proposal envisaged secession for both the princely states, and the Muslims — two lobbies that Britain also had to appease.) Speaking for Congress, Gandhi described

261

the Cripps offer as "a post-dated cheque drawn on a crashing bank". He wanted immediate full self-government in return for war cooperation, and on 8 August, he would initiate the "Quit India" movement, the most fervent of his civil disobedience campaigns.

Soon, Quit India would cripple the transport connections between Assam and Calcutta, so threatening the defence of the north-eastern border. But Gyles Mackrell would be back in the jungle by then. Even though well disposed towards Indians, it is unlikely that Mackrell was an Indian nationalist. But most people saw the writing on the wall, in that summer of 1942, and it would have been clear that the sheer ranginess of the life he had lived could not continue. On the other hand, all the important elements of that life — the physical risk, the engagement with nature and landscape, the logistical talent — might be compressed into one last jungle mission. One thing is certain: if Gyles Mackrell were to be evicted from India with immediate effect, the gunsellers of Dalhousie Square would lose a good customer.

. . . Cordiality in the gun shop, then.

On the afternoon of Friday 31 July, Mackrell walked through the rain to the Bengal Club on Chowringhee. Independence was coming, but for now a Union flag drooped in the rain from each of the corner turrets of the club, with a particularly big one on the central cupola. Mackrell walked through the door beneath that dome, where he gave his cape to a doubtfully grateful white-turbaned servant, and was greeted, as arranged, by a wiry, brown-skinned man — brown-skinned but not Indian. The Bengal Club did not accept Indians as members until 1959. This was the intrepid plant hunter, and loner, Frank Kingdon-Ward.

Towards the end of his Evacuation Report, Sir Reginald Dorman-Smith had written, by way of an aside: "Mr Kingdon-Ward, the explorer and naturalist, had been in Putao, which he left on the 15th May; avoiding the Chaukan Pass, he struck north and crossed the Diphu Pass, at 15,000 feet, and so, passing through Rima on the Tibet border, eventually reaching Sadiya in North Assam, after covering nearly four hundred miles in a period of just two months." It sounds simple when you put it like that. But the number of white people on earth who knew of the Diphu Pass was probably in single figures.

So here we have the two tough middle-aged bachelors and leech magnets, comparing notes over their whiskies and water (no ice in either case). They would have spoken about Millar, that original emissary of Sir John, whom they both knew; they would have talked about jungle routes on the Burma-Assam border; they would have talked elephants. Probably, Kingdon-Ward would have got on to plants and even though his mind was on other things — namely boats, as we will see — Mackrell, as a veteran of the Epsom College Natural History Society, would have listened with more than merely polite interest. They both liked a drink and a smoke, so their session might have carried on for some time.

Afterwards Mackrell walked around central Calcutta trying to buy some jars of Marmite, since he suspected he was going to have to deal with cases of beriberi. But everywhere he went it had sold out. He bought some jars of Ovaltine instead — not much use against beriberi, but he thought it would soothe people who'd been through jungle trauma.

Later that day, Mackrell fulfilled another social engagement. He went to Firpo's on Park Street, to be congratulated and bought dinner by that faithful Catholic, soap and perfume magnate, Mr Jardine, late of the Tilung Hka and Dapha camps (at forty-five, he had been the white-bearded "Old Man" of the Commandos) and Mrs Jardine. Their dinner might have been ravioli and ice cream, because Firpo's was an Italian restaurant. It would have been a good dinner anyway, because Jardine was well off. Under the wobbling fans, and with light jazz playing, Jardine — who was quite deservedly putting on weight — filled Mackrell in on what had happened to the Commandos after they'd left the Dapha camp on 1 July.

Ritchie Gardiner, holding an umbrella as he rode on his elephant, had been continually bitten by leeches. The mahout then gave him a "salt stick": a two-foot-long stick with a linen bag of rock salt on the end. If you only touched the leech with this, the astringent effect of the salt caused it to fall off, much to Gardiner's delight. Young Bill Howe, with a rain cape wrapped around his shoulders, had also been very uncomfortable on his elephant, but he couldn't walk any distance because of boils on his legs. At one

264

point, Howe fell off his elephant, bursting a boil on the back of his leg, and he noted in his diary that "the thick green stinking pus simply poured out", though whether Jardine recounted this detail over dinner is not known.

At Miao, the Commandos crossed by boat. They had then continued by elephant to Simon, then by boat to the golf course camp at Margherita, where they arrived on 6 July. From there Kendall was taken immediately by ambulance to hospital. All agreed that "he looked bloody".

Jardine then presented to Mackrell a silver cigarette case, inscribed with the names of all the Commandos he had plucked from the jaws of death at the Dapha river. Jardine had undertaken the job of having it made up and engraved.

The Commandos had hatched the idea for the cigarette case on their long march. They were going to have one each for themselves, because at that point they didn't know about Mackrell. They planned it as they slept in their bamboo huts, all in a row, staring up at the leaking roofs. One of them had suggested a gold sovereign be set into the case, but when they came out of the jungle, and stopped being quite so light-headed, that part of the scheme was dropped. The original plan had been for an inscription somehow commemorating their joint adventure, but the one decided upon after the advent of Mackrell read, "In gratitude for having saved our lives", and Captain Wilson would also receive one. Aside from the inscribed signatures of the young

Commandos, the name of Corporal Sawyer, drowned in the Tilung Hka, was engraved in capitals.

Directly after dinner, Mackrell took a taxi to Howrah station, where he boarded the 10p.m. *Dacca Mail*.

The Society of Tough Guys: On His Way Back to Dapha, Mackrell Finally Meets Sir John, and Tragedy Strikes Twice

On 6 August, Mackrell was back at the Margherita golf club base, where he had a conference with the Political Officer, Pearce (Refugee Administrator, North Assam, and the man who'd put him in charge at the Dapha), the camp supervisor, Ronald "Tom-Tom" Thomson — and a man called G. D. Walker, who had taken over from Lambert as Political Officer, the latter having gone off to look for the Chinese 5th Army. Mackrell explained the plan he had formulated, and it was met with some scepticism, even amusement. But it was approved, and Tom-Tom had already made arrangements with boats in connection with the plan (Tom-Tom knew about boats and boatmen; he often used them on his hunting trips). He also gave Mackrell some plum cake wrapped in cellophane as a treat for the rescued party, should Mackrell succeed. (Both men were interested in cellophane, a relatively new way of keeping expedition food fresh.)

267

Sitting in on the conference was Sir John Rowland, the man whose plight had triggered the whole adventure. He shook Mackrell's hand, and later wrote that he formed the idea that Mackrell would "make the grade", being "part of the society of tough guys". Sir John briefed Mackrell on the likely condition of those left in the jungle. He thought Captain Whitehouse and Dr Burgess-Barnett were "not at all well". What he said of Mr and Mrs Rossiter and baby John we do not know.

If Mackrell was delighted to be on his way back to the Dapha, Sir John was equally pleased to be coming away from it. He had had a quick transit from Dapha. He stayed only one night at the river, which was a fine one, enabling him not only to wash but also dry his clothes. ITA man Black, Captain Street and policeman Webster had had two elephants to spare. Sir John had left the camp riding behind the mahout on one of them; behind Sir John sat Milne, and behind Milne sat the railway accountant, Naidu, who by now couldn't walk even if he'd wanted to. Five Gurkhas who'd become sick on the trek were accommodated on a second elephant. The rest of the men who'd come out with Sir John walked.

We will stay with Sir John for a few days.

On 8 August, he had the enjoyable chore of shopping for new clothes in the small town of Margherita. The next day he was driven to the airbase at Dinjan, where he thanked his former dinner guest, Wing Commander Chater, for having dropped food on the Tilung Hka camp. The wing commander then flew Sir John — in the very Dakota from which the food had been dropped

— 600 miles through heavy rain to Dum Dum aerodrome, Calcutta, the rail and ferry connections between Calcutta and Assam now being out of action by Congress-inspired Civil Disobedience, which had flared into riots, as those campaigns tended to do.

On arrival in Calcutta, Sir John found his favourite hotel, the Great Eastern, to be full so took a taxi to the only other option for a man such as he, the Grand. The Grand had rooms even though it was bulging with servicemen. On the 11th, Sir John had a decent hot-weather suit made up more or less instantly by a tailor on Chowringhee. He found difficulty in getting the trousers over his left ankle because of the swelling caused by Beri-Beri, which he had identified as his major remaining enemy. (He always spelt it with two capital Bs.) However, on returning to his hotel room, he took immediately to his bed for another reason: "a sharp attack of malaria".

While Sir John had been flying to Calcutta, Mackrell had been collecting "vital supplies" in Margherita. These included plenty of fruit (which he had felt the lack of on his first expedition) and a crate of whisky. On the evening of 15 August he, and all his supplies, arrived at the intermediate camp of Simon in a flotilla of canoes punted along the Buri Dehing by Mishmi tribesmen. The low jungle on the riverbanks contained "Imperial pigeon by the hundred", and numerous wild elephants, balefully trumpeting in the descending gloom for no reason that Mackrell could see. Along the way, the Mishmi boatmen had proposed calling a halt

269

and striking camp, "because it was raining!" (the exclamation mark is Mackrell's). At Simon, Mackrell took delivery of a number of Kampti elephants, as pre-arranged. In the negotiations at Margherita, he had been offered Burmese elephants, but had rejected these because his mahouts were not used to them. It has been mentioned that a hired elephant usually came with its mahout, like a taxi with its driver, but in this case most prudent mahouts might not want to go where the elephants were going. So Mackrell assembled separate teams of mahouts and elephants, then put them together. These were new mahouts, not the ones who'd been with Mackrell at the Dapha the first time around — all except for Mackrell's personal "chauffeur", Gohain, who was accompanying him once more.

The plan was that the party would continue on foot to Miao, but insubordination was in the air in India that August and the mahouts went on strike over pay. They were "put up to it", Mackrell wrote, by a particularly bolshie "opium mahout" (that is, a man badly addicted), name of Ragoo. For once Mackrell's powers of persuasion failed and he had Ragoo arrested by a military policeman at Simon, not for refusing to work but for inciting the others. The others then agreed to continue at existing rates of pay if Ragoo were released, and this was done.

On 16 August, Mackrell was still accumulating elephants at Simon when a runner came in from Miao. He carried a chit that had been brought to Miao from Dapha by an earlier runner. It was written by Black, and it said that Captain Street at the Dapha camp had a bad fever. The next day, another runner arrived with another bulletin from Black about Captain Street. That "grand lad, full of life", as Sir John Rowland put it, had committed suicide at the Dapha camp. He had shot himself in the head with his revolver. This was the first news Mackrell had received from the Dapha camp since the new men had taken over. Given that he himself had dispatched several chits about how he was preparing to return, he found this odd. But he thought he knew the reason . . .

At 5p.m. on 19 August, Mackrell arrived at the cliff-top government bungalow at Miao, the one overlooking the Noa Dehing where he had listened to his HMV radio on 6 June. He waited here a day to rest the elephants.

Mackrell departed for the Dapha on the 21st, just himself and a dozen elephants and mahouts. Soon after setting off, he saw a man coming the other way on an elephant. It was Webster, the military policeman who had been at the Dapha with Black and the late Captain Street. Webster dismounted. He explained that an attempt had been made to get through the jungle to "Rossiter", as the stranded party was now known, Edward Wrixon Rossiter having taken over the titular role from Sir John Rowland.

Webster, Black and Street had set off with forty porters. It had been raining heavily, and all the rivers were up. After two days, Street became feverish and returned to camp, where Dr Bardoloi, installed once again as MO at the Dapha, had been unable to bring down his temperature. Street became delirious, talking nonsense, walking about without a hat on a day of hot sun. Behind Dr Bardoloi's back he took a large dose of an antibiotic called M&B. He then bathed in the freezing Dapha to try and cool down. He shot himself after coming out of the river.

Malaria, the most likely cause of Street's delirium, can bring with it demonic visions, and these did not need much encouragement at the Dapha camp. Some of the treatments can also cause depression. On 4 July 1941, for example, General Orde Wingate, who, as leader of the Chindits would go on to lead a guerrilla campaign in the retaking of Burma, attempted to kill himself while suffering from a bad bout of malaria. In his room in the Continental Hotel in Cairo, he stood before the bathroom mirror and stabbed himself in the neck with a knife. He was saved because an officer in an adjacent room heard a suspicious combination of sounds: Wingate locking his hotel room door from the inside; then the crash from his bathroom as he fell. He was at the time suffering from a sense of professional failure, and Captain Street may have felt the same after turning back from the jungle.

As for Webster, Black and their forty porters . . . after six days, when they were still only halfway to Rossiter, their rations ran out, and they, too, had been forced to turn back.

This full-blown rescue attempt came as news to Mackrell. He had been sending chits forward to the Dapha suggesting only that food dumps be created along the first twenty miles or so of the route to Rossiter — this in preparation for his own attempt.

Webster went on his way, Mackrell on his.

After crossing the Debang river, that hors d'oeuvre to the main course of the Dapha, Mackrell diverted to the village of Tinguan, to enquire about the Mishmi headman who had been so useful to Mackrell, and who had contracted dysentery at the Dapha camp. He was told the man was dead.

It was raining heavily as Mackrell proceeded east.

He arrived at the Dapha camp as the light was fading on Saturday 22 August. There was no reception committee. Black was encamped on the other side of the river, the eastern side, out of sight in the gathering gloom and rain, but Mackrell knew where he was, and Black knew where Mackrell was.

It seemed to Mackrell that even though he had full authorization for another rescue mission, he was being given the cold shoulder, that he was again being required to operate as a freelance. So it was just as well that he had by now made his peace with the mahouts, as it was easier for him to do when all concerned were beyond the reach of officialdom. They had once again become his "boys": "Made tea for all the boys while they were pitching the tent." The mahouts then cooked a meal; Mackrell had a tin of tomato soup and went to bed.

Early the next morning, Mackrell saw Black crossing the river on an elephant. Black dismounted and walked through the rain towards Mackrell. They shook hands with barely a word, and repaired to the wide tarpaulin where tea was brewing. Mackrell held his pipe in his hands, but did not smoke it. He later wrote in his diary,

273

"I asked him as man to man if I was not right in thinking that neither he nor Webster wanted to see me back [at the Dapha camp] — in fact hoped I would not return. I have sensed this all along as I have never had a message from either of them and no reference has been made to my return at all."

Paradoxically, Mackrell was pleased with the reply.

"Black said I was quite correct!"

It was nothing personal, Black explained; it was just that he, Webster and Street felt the baton had been passed to younger men, and they wanted "to put the job through themselves". The two then walked to the long grass of the riverbank, where Black showed Mackrell the grave of Captain Street. It was near the bamboo house that Captain Wilson had built on the point. Mackrell explained his own plans for going forward; Black nodded, and asked what he intended to do about porters. Mackrell said he hoped to recruit some of Black's. Black nodded again, and he mentioned to Mackrell that most of those men had been banking on returning to their villages. Mackrell said he could only ask them.

The next day, a Monday, Black returned to Miao, and Mackrell moved into the house on the point. Here, he called a conference of the men who remained at the Dapha. They were all Indians: the mahouts, most of the forty political porters who'd been forward with Black, Webster and Street, and a unit of Assam Rifles — that is to say, about twenty Gurkha soldiers — commanded by a Havildar called Dharramsing. Mackrell had been given the authority to mount a push towards Rossiter,

274

but this was dependent on manpower. Mackrell put his case to the meeting. The Rossiters and the remainder of the railway party were still stranded; they included a pregnant woman, a baby and people in poor health. It was uncertain whether they could continue to be supplied from the air. Would those present — all of whom had been expecting to return to Miao after the failure of the Black/Webster/Street push — be willing to go forward one more time? Mackrell knew this was much more than a question of money and opium. It was about whether the men would risk their lives again. Mackrell looked towards Dharramsing, the spokesman for the Indians in the hut. But the Gurkhas' faces were impassive. Mackrell would give them time to decide; he stepped out of the house.

Mackrell walked along the banks of the river in the rain. He knew that if the answer was "yes", he would only be able to take about half the forty porters, the others being in no fit state to return to deep jungle. He also knew that even if the answer was "no", he would have to remain at Dapha with the mahouts in case Rossiter tried to come through.

After a while, he lit his pipe.

A Face Like Wood: Dharramsing Decides

Let us divert ourselves while the Indians decide by asking: how do you keep a pipe going in a monsoon? You could just keep your hand over the bowl. Or the man who was going to be doing a *lot* of smoking in the monsoon might own a pipe cap: a steel grill with a spring catch, so it would fit any pipe bowl. You could light the pipe through the holes in the grill, and the tobacco would remain fairly dry as it burned. During the Second World War, a firm called Orlik of Shoeburyness, Essex, began making a pipe with a Bakelite bowl that had a ready fitted grill. The model was called "The Hurricane", and according to the advert it was "Smoked by Shrewd Judges".

Mackrell walked back towards the house on the point, and stood before Dharramsing. Would the men come? Dharramsing had a face like wood. In *The Longest Retreat*, Tim Carew wrote, "the face of the Gurkha, except on the frequent occasions when he is grinning broadly, is expressionless". Slowly, Dharramsing rocked his head from side to side. The answer was "yes".

276

The next day — Tuesday the 25th — Mackrell crossed to the east side of the Dapha, where he began replenishing the camps established by Black and Co. The first of these was at the top of a 200-foot cliff, so a winch was rigged to take the kit up from the river's edge.

The day after, he pressed on east, towards the more forward camps established by Black and his men. At these, the rice had been left on the ground, under tarpaulins, "and so naturally had been damaged by [wild] elephant". Mackrell strung the rice sacks from trees, so they would be ready for Rossiter should he come through, or be available to Mackrell *and* Rossiter on the way back to Dapha in the event of a successful rescue.

Mackrell also began cutting new tracks along the banks of the Noa Dehing, the route used by Sir John having been obliterated by a rise in the water level and more of the landslips Mackrell had seen from the air. One particular headland — newly created by a landslip — could not be avoided. It had to be surmounted then traversed. While prospecting a route in thick jungle, Mackrell and his men saw a wild elephant. They surrounded it in a semi-circle and clapped their hands to frighten it. The elephant cantered up the hill, crashing through branches, so indicating a possible track and opening out that track at the same time.

At the top of this headland, Mackrell and his men used kukris, hoes and pickaxes to cut a path that would be wide enough for elephants, and it had to be a good one since there was a 250-foot drop to the river on the right-hand side of it.

By late evening on Sunday 30 August, Mackrell and his men and his dozen elephants had negotiated this promontory. They struck camp at a lower point, about twenty feet above the water. Too tired to built shelters or erect tents, the men wrapped themselves in tarpaulins or blankets and in some lucky cases lay down on airbeds — lilos — that Mackrell had brought along this time. When he awoke at dawn on his own lilo, Mackrell counted the elephants. One was missing. It had obviously fallen into the river while grazing. Mackrell noted, "Delayed some hours collecting the above elephant." They found it grazing once again, lower down the river, having been carried through one rapid.

Mackrell and his men kept cutting their way forward, negotiating landslips or trying to avoid them by resorting to deep jungle, but here the leeches were "terrific", intolerable. On Friday 4 September, Mackrell and Dharramsing made a long forward reconnaissance on foot but could not find a good elephant track. Mackrell had now been away from the Dapha base for over a week. He had planned to return at this point, having established a route more than halfway to the Tilung Hka, just in case there should be an air-dropped message about what Rossiter was doing. But Mackrell now decided to keep going, before he could be recalled by the men at Margherita. After all, the next message might be telling him to pack up and return to base.

On Saturday 5 September, Mackrell and his men were camped on the left bank of the Noa Dehing. So far, all the action in this story has taken place on its right bank, and the Noa Dehing has been described as uncrossable. That turned out not to be the case in its upper reaches, and Mackrell and his men had first crossed it — by elephant — when looking for the missing elephant. They had discovered that there were fewer landslips on that side and that it might offer a better route. The trouble was that on the left bank they might miss Rossiter should he decide to make a move; because he and his party, having no elephants, would certainly *not* be able to cross the river.

So the plan for Saturday was that men would probe forward on both banks of the river. On that hot and rainy morning, Mackrell, on the left bank, saw one of the accompanying Assam Rifles waving to him from the right bank. He then saw a male European staggering out of the trees towards the soldier. It was Rossiter. Mackrell immediately boarded an elephant and crossed the river. He shook Rossiter's hand. Rossiter said that his wife and baby were coming along a short way behind, together with a dozen others, a mixture of Gurkhas and Rossiter's staff and servants from Putao — in other words, not all of the people who'd been stranded at the Tilung Hka. They had been walking through the jungle for six days, and were very weak. They had ample rice, but much of it was mouldy. Mackrell would later write in a private letter — it was not the sort of declaration he would have made publicly — that Rossiter and his party would have had no

279

chance of reaching Dapha had it not been for running into him. They would all have died.

Rossiter explained to Mackrell that another Gurkha was coming, some way behind. He had been stung several times about both eyes by wasps, and was practically blind. Mackrell crossed Rossiter, Mrs Rossiter and baby and the dozen Indians to the camp on the left bank by elephant. There is footage of Mrs Rossiter (Nang Hmat) crossing on an elephant with three others. She looks very composed and graceful, with baby John in a sling on her back. Mackrell crossed over with the Rossiters, then dispatched them along the left bank to the camp made the night before. Mackrell himself waited at the crossing point, watching for the blinded Gurkha to come through the trees on the opposite bank. Mackrell would have liked to smoke his pipe, but he'd run out of pipe tobacco. He did not approve of Rossiter having left the man so far behind.

It was a brilliant sunny day.

The left-behind Gurkha, wrapped in a blanket, came out of the trees at three o'clock in the afternoon; Mackrell waved and called to him. He then made the international go-to-sleep sign with head on hands. This Gurkha must not have been completely blinded by the wasp stings, because he saw and understood, and after Mackrell had repeated the gesture several times, smiling but insistent, the Gurkha lay down between two rocks and slept. The elephants, or some of them, came back to Mackrell at four o'clock. He crossed the river, woke the Gurkha, made tea for him, then crossed him over the river, riding on the elephant with him, and accompanying him to the camp, where Edward Wrixon Rossiter was drinking tea and eating biscuits with jam on them. It was vegetable marrow jam, obtained by Mackrell from God-knows-where, and carried on the back of an elephant into the jungle. Rossiter's mother had made this jam when he was a boy growing up in Dublin; it had been a particular favourite of his. We know this from a letter he wrote, and which we shall come to shortly.

But first some other letters.

A Delivery of Mail

Rossiter put down the biscuit he was eating and fished a chit out of his shirt pocket. It was a missive from deep in the blue, written by fifty-six-year-old Edward Lovell Manley, formerly the Chief Engineer of the Eastern Bengal Railway, house guest of Sir John, and his number two in the jungle. It was addressed to Pearce, the Refugee Administrator for North Assam based at Margherita, and the man who had put Mackrell in charge at Dapha. (Manley knew of the existence of Pearce because he had sent a note to the Tilung Hka party in the last of the food drops, asking them to stay put.)

Manley put Rossiter's departure from the Tilung Hka camp down to "Mrs Rossiter's pregnancy and the milk shortage"; the Gurkhas and Rossiter's clerks had followed and Manley had been "unable to prevent them in spite of your order to stay put". Manley then wrote of himself in the third person, viz:

There remain here Manley, Burgess-Barnett and Whitehouse with 4 servants. Whitehouse is suffering from Peripheral Neuritis affecting his legs, and has been very ill. He will have to be carried most of the way. Our food situation . . . is very serious [and] it is more so now that we have had to give up much of it to the Rossiter party . . . Do please do your utmost to deliver us from a situation which is becoming desperate.

Was Manley angry at the departure of the Rossiters? It would be hard for any reasonable middle-aged man to quibble about the imperatives of a pregnant woman. He might have advised the couple for their own safety to stay, and it is a mark of their desperation that they did not. Perhaps they had been banking on meeting Mackrell. We do not know their precise plan.

But Mackrell's new project was clear: go and get Manley, Burgess-Barnett, Whitehouse and the four Indian servants, the last of the Chaukan refugees. He had made a promise to the wife and daughter of Dr Burgess-Barnett. He was not to know that at about this time a telegram was being drafted in the quiet, sunlit study of a house in Sudbury, Suffolk. It would be dispatched to the nebulous sounding address, "Railway Board New Delhi": "PLEASE INFORM ME WHERE AND HOW IS MY SON CAPTAIN A O WHITEHOUSE BURMA CHINA RAILWAY LAST NEWS BURMA APRIL". It was signed "Whitehouse" and it is difficult to imagine the father as looking very different from the imperilled son: a slight, wizened, inoffensive-looking man in tortoiseshell glasses.

Minutes after Mackrell read the letter from Manley, two mahouts on elephants came into the camp. These were men whom Mackrell had sent back to Dapha on the morning the elephant had gone missing. One was his personal, and most trusted, mahout, Gohain. The two had been ordered to collect supplies and bring them back. It turned out they had also brought two letters. The first was from G. D. Walker, the man who had taken over from Eric Lambert as Political Officer at Margherita, and it had been dropped by plane on the Dapha camp soon after Mackrell's departure. Mackrell read the letter once, then he read it again. The letter was calling off his mission. Mackrell was to return immediately to base, closing the camps at Dapha, Miao and Simon on his way back, and he was to send all his elephants to the Political Officer at Sadiya, who apparently had need of them.

Mackrell then opened the second letter. It, too, had been dropped on the Dapha camp, but a week after the first. It was from Mr Justice Braund, late of the Rangoon High Court, and now Refugee Administrator for the *whole* of Assam. He was Pearce's boss, and the top civilian in evacuee management. It said the same thing as the first letter, but more tersely. It "confirmed" the earlier letter (the one Mackrell had just opened, and which Braund obviously thought Mackrell had ignored). Mackrell was to "come out" immediately.

What might be the meaning of this? There was no mystery as far as Mackrell was concerned. Just as the other evacuation routes had been wound up, so now the Chaukan Pass was being shut down, not that it had ever been officially established as an evacuation route in the first place. Taking into account the staging posts at

Simon, Miao and Dapha, it was tying up too many soldiers, porters and elephants, all of which were needed for other, military purposes, particularly road building. The majority of those who had entered the pass had now either come through or died. As for the one small party left at Tilung Hka, Mackrell had no doubt that Braund genuinely believed them to be, as he said in his letter, "well stocked and not in immediate danger". Braund must also have envisaged that food drops would resume, and that a rescue would be mounted in the cold weather, when the rivers were down. Of course, the officials must also have envisaged that, assuming everyone at Tilung Hka survived, there would be one extra person to rescue by then, namely the baby that would be born to Mrs Rossiter. They were not to know that, thanks to Mackrell, the Rossiters were now out, and would shortly be sent back towards Dapha by Mackrell. But Manley, Whitehouse, Burgess-Barnett and the four servants remained, and Braund was wrong. They were in immediate danger, as Manley's letter had just confirmed.

Mackrell wanted his reply to look as official as possible, so he unpacked his typewriter — he had indeed brought one but it had got bashed about on the back of an elephant, and the letter "O" came out as an inky blob. His letter was addressed to Braund, and Mackrell stated baldly that in view of Braund's order having been written "in ignorance of the position . . . I am only complying with part of it". He would send orders for Dapha, Miao and Simon to be cleared of personnel, leaving himself no lifeline. But he "must" go

285

on with his rescue. He then wrote a letter to "All my loyal helpers", ordering them to leave the camps. "I will find my own way out."

He gave both these letters to Edward Rossiter to take back with him. He also gave him six elephants, and sent him and his party on to Dapha with all necessary mahouts and porters. Before he departed, Rossiter told something about the food drops. There had been no further drops after 26 July. And the ones that had been made contained not nearly enough food, yet toys by the hundredweight for baby John. There had also been many sackloads of "venereal cures". Clearly these medicaments had been misdirected; there had been enough of them, Mackrell observed, "to cure half the force of our gallant Allies for whom this was no doubt thought necessary", a reference to the Americans.

As Edward Rossiter disappeared into the sun-dappled trees, Mackrell turned and faced the other way: towards the Upper Noa Dehing as it wound away through its great stone canyon.

A Long Wait

As soon as he had dispatched Rossiter, Mackrell and his men crossed the river with the remaining fourteen elephants, taking their camp with them. On the right bank they met up with Havildar Dharramsing who, while Mackrell had been reading and writing letters, had been prospecting forward with a single elephant of his own. This had been a "test" elephant. If it could follow a track towards the Tilung Hka, then so could fourteen others. But there was no suitable track, the ones that might have served being blocked by landslips.

So Mackrell organized what he called a "Striking Party" to go forward on foot, using the track Rossiter had taken. Mackrell did not include himself in this party. As he explained to the others, he was too old. He actually described himself, albeit in Assamese, as "an elderly European". Nor was Havildar Dharramsing in the party. Mackrell would have liked him to lead it, but he was experiencing intermittent fever. Mackrell does name the men of the Striking Party. There were three Gurkhas of the Assam Rifles: Naik Gyanbahadur (Naik meaning corporal), Compounder Havildar Sanam Lama (a compounder is a medical assistant),

Lance-Naik Manichand Rai; and six political porters: Gangabahadur, Tami, Santabir, Chintamani, Dilbahadur and Karnabahadur. They were all, Mackrell notes, "fit and confident of success". The men were dispatched on Monday 7 August. They carried fresh onions, cigarettes, potatoes, sugar, butter, dried apple rings, Klim, Marmite, bully beef, soap, Lysol disinfectant and a lilo for Captain Whitehouse.

At a new camp on the right bank of the Noa Dehing, Mackrell commenced a period of waiting — and fishing. On Thursday 10 August he was assembling his fishing rod on the stony banks of the Noa Dehing when he glanced to the left. He saw a rousing sight: men in boats, and not just that, but men in boats going *against* the current, fighting it, paddling hard, their three long canoes bouncing and swaying in the water. They were boatmen of the Singpho tribe, and they wore circular cane hats. Mackrell was not entirely surprised to see them. Along with the letter ordering him to return to Margherita, another had come, written by one of the Assam Rifles at Dapha. It said that Mackrell's boats had arrived at Dapha. Later that day, Mackrell wrote of the boatmen: "They had been nine days getting up from Dapha. They say the river is terrible." One of them, a man called Chandram, said to Mackrell, "You asked a hard thing of us Sahib but we are here and ready to go further if you say so although the river is like no river we have ever seen." Mackrell wrote, "It is a splendid effort." Boats and tame elephants were unprecedented this high up the river. Mackrell made tea for all the boatmen and handed out cigarettes.

288

Mackrell had realized that for any party of sick people to be brought out of deep jungle, they would need transport; they would need to be carried, in other words, and if elephants couldn't be taken forward, then boats would have to do the job. The boats had been ordered as a back-up, but, now that the way was barred to elephants, they would come into play. Mackrell's plan was to take them as far upriver as possible, then send a Support Party to intersect at right angles with the track taken by the Striking Party. The Support Party would either then go along that track, catching up the Striking Party, or wait on the track for the Striking Party to come back from Tilung Hka. The two parties would then return, together with the rescued men, to the waiting boats.

On the fine morning of Friday 11 August, therefore, Mackrell left some men, and all the elephants, at the camp he had just established. He and the remainder started going upriver by boat. For much of their journey, rock walls towered 150 feet above them on either side; and the further they went, the more rapids they encountered. Seven times they had to unload all their kit and rations in order to drag the boats over shallow rapids. On the Saturday, they "came to a rapid we could do nothing with", so the men built a camp. The Support Party was dispatched, and this one *was* led by Dharramsing. Mackrell embarked on another period of waiting — waiting and smoking cigarettes, since, as we have seen, he had no pipe tobacco left. The men in the government bungalow at Margherita had told him that 35,000 cigarettes had been dropped on

289

the Dapha and Tilung Hka camps, and he was supposed to have been impressed by that. But most of them had been lost in the jungle or destroyed on impact.

Mackrell busied himself by improving the track leading down to the camp. As an added safety measure, he made creeper ropes where the track bordered the river. He and the boatmen collected banana leaves to improve the roofs of the bamboo huts. He also watched the river. The danger was that it would rise, and he would have to move the camp and boats to a higher level. The river was certainly capable of reaching the plateau on which he waited; he could tell that by the grey driftwood lying in the long grass. Meanwhile, the weather was sunny and dry, and the driftwood was good for burning.

Mackrell went fishing.

Saw a fish rise opposite camp and got him on the second cast, a 1½lb Boka, which made excellent fish-cakes and some stew for the boatmen. Number of big horn-bills whose tails seem longer than the plains variety keep going over. The small white flowers on the cliff opposite, resembling white primroses but with orchis stems, are fully out and among them a lot of red Nelsoms and some huge scarlet Chlenodendrons, as well as some Rhododendrons.

He was happy in other words.

We have film footage of this period spent far upriver on the Noa Dehing. The camera shows riverside stones, and you can't tell how big they are. Then a smiling Gurkha walks into view, and you realize that each stone is actually bigger than a house. The camera casually pans past a sheer wall of stone that might be — what? — thirty times taller than a man. Mackrell was never idle, and filming was one way to pass the time. On other occasions, he would set his folding chair and his folding table on a high, flat stone near the river's edge, and type letters to friends. He enjoyed working in this way, close to the white water; it was just a case of watching out for flying tree trunks. The letters were marked "Upper Noa Dehing" and he would apologise for that broken letter "O".

On the Wednesday, he spent over half an hour playing a fish he'd hooked: another boka, this one weighing 4½lb. "It fed the whole camp." But thunder clouds were mustering; the river was changing colour, becoming turbid. A rise was on the way. He had heard nothing from either the Striking Party or the Support Party, "So all must be well or very wrong, one cannot tell which." On the Thursday, he went deep into the jungle to look. He came back in the evening covered in leech bites, and with his shorts torn to shreds.

The next day, he and the boatmen took a walk upriver along the rocks, just in case they could see any sign of anybody or anything. They could not. They made a fire from driftwood, had a cup of tea and one cigarette each and came back to the riverside camp, where they saw Dharramsing and his Support Party. They had seen no sign of the Striking Party, so they had simply left food along what they thought was the right track. Mackrell issued a rum ration to the Support Party, and dressed their sores. It was now twelve days since the Striking Party had left; they were late, and a storm was brewing.

On Sunday the 20th, Dharramsing volunteered to go back into the jungle for another look. Mackrell agreed.

As Mackrell waited, it began to rain heavily. He built a new fire on the margins of the camp, under tree cover. In late morning, he was standing by this fire when a porter from the Support Party returned to the camp. He silently handed Mackrell a chit.

It was written by Manley, and it was the confirmation of success.

They were proceeding slowly because Captain Whitehouse was being carried, but Manley expected to be with Mackrell by about 3.30p.m. Mackrell walked over to his personal kitbag and unwrapped the plum cake. Thanks to the cellophane, it was still good as new. Mackrell then unfolded and erected the canvas bath, and made sure the bed rolls were all laid out in the bamboo hut waiting to receive the refugees.

It was more like 6p.m. when the Striking Party and the Support Party came into the camp together. Captain Whitehouse, still wearing trilby and tortoiseshell glasses, was strung over the shoulders of the political porter called Taja Tami, like a scarf. Tami was not a big man, but nor was Whitehouse — not by now at any rate. Dr Burgess-Barnett ... Manley ... the four servants ... all were filthy, exhausted and ill to varying degrees, but not so ill that they couldn't eat dinner after their hot baths: dall soup, tinned lamb, tinned peas, boiled onions and fresh potatoes. For pudding, tinned peaches and plum cake — and sweet tea, of course, all taken under a wide tarpaulin with the rain sloshing off the edge.

At 7.30p.m., the refugees filed into their bamboo hut. One hour later, Mackrell went over and had a look in. They were all asleep.

Mackrell returned to the fire and broke out the rum. The porters of the Striking Party told Mackrell how, when they came to a precipitous landslip-headland, a place where it was impossible for a man to walk if he happened to be carrying another man on his shoulders, they had simply dropped Whitehouse into the river, and then run around the headland to catch him on the other side.

The next morning, Mackrell took Whitehouse breakfast in bed, since he couldn't stand up: tinned sausages and chipped potatoes. It would be a day of eating. Rabbit curry for tiffin. For dinner, steak and kidney pudding, tinned parsnips, beans and potatoes; apple rings and rice-in-Klim for pudding. Mackrell noted that the rescued men were "all improving visibly", all except Dr Burgess-Barnett, who had a high fever. Also, it was still raining so that Mackrell could not dry the rescued men's clothes, which he had washed.

On the night of Wednesday the 23rd, the Noa Dehing river came to pay a call. Whitehouse and Burgess-Barnett had to be carried to higher ground; and then the boats had to be manhandled up a cliff and out of the way of a whirlpool that had already flung a few tree trunks into the camp, one of them flattening the custom-built refugee hut. Mackrell erected his personal tent on the higher ground, and put Dr Burgess-Barnett into it. He wrapped himself in a bath towel and rain cape, and lay down between two rocks. In the morning, he was pleasantly surprised that his "old enemy", sciatica, had not returned despite such a generous invitation to do so. It had stopped raining. Mackrell noted, "Dr Burgess-Barnett fitter today and Whitehouse looks a little stronger. Manley very weak but looks better. Saw a school of otters in a rapid and some blue sky. Looks hopeful. Took stock of all rations. Not too bad but must be careful. One tea-spoonful of sugar each three times a day is all we must use of that . . . Decided to have a try at getting down."

By a combination of elephants and boats, and with — in the case of the latter — some capsizes, Gyles Mackrell reached the Dapha camp once again on 1 October. He stayed there two days, during which he took white stones from the river so as better to define the grave of Captain Street: "I am afraid it will go out of sight though very quickly."

He reached Miao at five o'clock on Saturday 3 October, and the headman, Mat Ley, told him that a group of Nagas settled nearby had found the cow elephant that Mackrell had lost en route to the Dapha on 9 June. It was perfectly safe and would be restored to him on payment of fifty silver rupees, which they hoped he would agree was a reasonable price. Mackrell "arranged for this".

He arrived at the Margherita golf club on Tuesday 6 October, where he was greeted by the Refugee Administrator for North Assam, Pearce, who congratulated him on disobeying the orders from Political Officer Walker and Mr Justice Braund, which he himself had endorsed. "I take my hat off to you," he said. On 7 October, Mackrell saw one of the rescued men at large on the fairways, not playing golf — that would be too much to expect — but "Whitehouse was walking with a stick!" Mackrell then wired Sir John in Simla to say that all the rest of his people were out, and Sir John wrote to his wife that he was "thumping glad" to hear it.

On 10 October, Mackrell was driving towards the dusty, bustling town of Dibrugarh with Dr Burgess-Barnett in the passenger seat. They were going shopping, and Mackrell wanted to see "Routledge, Superintendent of Police about tyres" (a recondite bit of business that need not detain us). They came to what passed for a traffic jam in that town at that time. They were stationary on a pot-holed road when a lorry came reversing towards them out of a side road. It was carrying long bamboos, sharpened at the projecting ends. These crashed through Mackrell's windscreen, and he and the doctor were about to be impaled when "some Americans in a Jeep" drove directly into the side of the lorry's cab, so as to alert the driver.

On Sunday the 11th the two motored to Shillong, where they both lived. Mackrell drove first to the doctor's house, and waited outside in the car so that the reunion might be a private one. The noise from the doctor's house, Mackrell wrote, "sounded like a football match".

He thought he might have to go in and "rescue him all over again".

Subsequently (Part One)

On arrival in Calcutta, all evacuees were pressed to give their names to the women volunteers of the Evacuee Enquiry Bureau of 12, Wood Street, Calcutta. The women compiled two Registers of Evacuees from Burma, each disarmingly prefaced by "an apologia for the many errors it contains". Volume 1 listed "European, Anglo-Burman, Anglo-Indian and other Non-Indian Evacuees"; Volume 2 listed Indian evacuees, or a small fraction thereof. Most of the evacuees mentioned in this narrative appeared in these volumes, including such Indian railwaymen as were named by Sir John in his diary: C. V. Venkatraman, R. V. Venkatachalam and S. T. Rajan all appear in Volume 2, giving date of arrival in Calcutta as 7 August.

Absent from the register — even though we know he got out safely — is the name of Moses, that enigmatic Dutch wanderer, the International Boy Scout and supposed cheerleader for the Chaukan Pass. It would almost have been disappointing if his name *had* appeared.

In both volumes, there is a category: "Casualties due to enemy action in Burma en route to India and deaths since arrival in India", and there, in Volume 1, appears the name of C. L. Kendall, railway surveyor, whom we last saw being taken by ambulance from Margherita. He died at Panitalo Hospital on 8 July of cerebral malaria, leaving a young wife and a two-year-old son.

For most of the returnees, there was a good deal of form filling, and a good deal of letter writing. Everyone wrote to everyone. (Almost everyone: as far as we know, Mackrell received no communication from Edward Wrixon Rossiter.)

On 15 August, Eric Ivan Milne, the railwayman who'd come out with Sir John, wrote a letter to Mackrell, who did not read it until later, since he was at that point on his way back "into the blue" for a second time. The letter touches all the bases we might expect:

My dear Mackrell,
I write and send you my warmest thanks for all you have done for us blokes through the Chaukan Pass from Burma. There is no doubt we should have been scuppered had it not been for you. We know you will get the rest of the party out.

I flew to Delhi and got to my family at Bombay on 14th where I found everyone in great form. Unfortunately I had a bit of the reaction again and malaria and so I can do nothing much, not even buy clothes. The doctor (Col. Morrison of Rangoon) whom I know very well, said I was to have complete rest for 2 months! Well I doubt whether I'll stick to that without a game of squash or something.

My wife joins me in thanking you again for all the effort you made to get us out.

Cheerio,

Yours sincerely,

E. Milne.

Eric Ivan Milne quickly recovered and was soon, as his wife noted, "eating like six horses". He and his family sailed for England in 1945; he died in 1978, aged seventy-nine, in Uckfield, East Sussex.

After checking into the Grand Hotel, Calcutta, Sir John Rowland had a "real good go" of tertian malaria, but on 30 August he was fit enough to leave Calcutta by train for Delhi; he had an entire carriage to himself, personally reserved for him by the General Manager of the East Indian Railway, the biggest and the grandest of the Calcutta-based networks. It was the least that one top railwayman could do for another. At Delhi, Sir John took the train to the verdant, and cool, hill town of Simla, where he checked into the best hotel, the Hotel Cecil.

The government of Burma — or at least the British version of it — was being run from Simla. The Governor, Sir Reginald Dorman-Smith, was there, writing his Evacuation Report. On 3 September, Sir John had lunch with Dorman-Smith and recounted what probably became, over the years, the mother of all anecdotes. He wrote, "H.E. was most interested in the tale and said, altho' I might not think so, he was most concerned over the fate of my party and myself and exceedingly worried."

From Simla, Sir John wrote a letter to his wife, recounting his own story, and the failure of the Black/Webster/Street expedition to rescue the remainder of "his people": "It is most disappointing and if only I were ten years younger damn it all, I would go myself." But he mentioned that he had high hopes of "another rescue" (Mackrell's). He described in typically pugnacious style the work of the office that had been set up for him in Simla. It was largely concerned with settling claims for compensation from contractors with Burma Railways. A large number of these claims were, Sir John believed, "fictitious, in fact, preposterous". But the decency behind Sir John's bluster was also evident regarding dependants of dead railwaymen: "I am very pleased to say that Government has agreed to give wives and kin (if wholly dependent) pensions; that is, in the case of a widow unless she remarries. This is going to ease the lot of a number of women and children."

Sir John was still not quite over the jungle. He was still having to bandage his "wretched foot" twice a day because of leech bites. And one of the last of the letters that we have from Sir John concludes: "I am penning this in my bedroom at the Cecil and a fairly large sized monkey is peeping in at the side window but he cannot get in as all the windows are covered with wire gauze. I have no doubt he is looking for food. The monkeys here never seem to stop eating."

On 12 October, Sir John Rowland wrote to Mackrell, expressing his thanks for rescuing "my party . . . Well, Mackrell I guess it's just thank you very much over and over again." He wrote of his shock at the suicide of

Street: "He was such a likeable lad, and full of the joie de vivre . . . still, it can be truly said he gave his life for others", and he concluded "Au revoir . . . if it had not been for you, many of us would not be alive today."

Sir John never did return to work in Burma. He retired to South Africa, where he had a long imperial sunset. He was the only one of our evacuees eminent enough to appear in *Who's Who*, but the entry was unvaryingly minimal, Sir John giving his address as c/o The Standard Bank of South Africa, Adderley Street, Cape Town. Career-wise there was no advance on "Chief Railway Commissioner, Burma 1937–41". A marriage is mentioned, but no children . . . and no recreation, thereby frustrating the expectation that he might, in a spirit of irony, have written "walking". Sir John fades from the book, and from life, in 1969, aged eighty-seven.

On 18 October, Edward Lovell Manley, Sir John's number two, who was in Mackrell's last batch of rescuees, wrote a letter to Mackrell beginning as follows: "I am afraid I found it quite impossible, when we parted, to thank you for all you have done for us and even now it seems hopeless to find words adequately to express my gratitude."

He also wrote to the governor of Assam asking Mackrell to be excused for disobeying the order to withdraw, and to various officials expressing his gratefulness to Havildar Dharramsing, and the other men of the Second Battalion, Assam Rifles, and the political porters with whom they worked, including Taja Tami, who had mostly carried Whitehouse. After listing

301

them by name, Manley wrote: "I understand that all these men who have helped us are being suitably rewarded by government and I sincerely trust they will receive the recognition they deserve."

The Havildar and the other Gurkhas of Mackrell's Striking and Support parties were awarded the British Empire Medal.

Edward Lovell Manley sailed for England in 1944, and died on the island of Jersey in 1960, aged seventy-six.

Also in mid-October, Captain A. O. Whitehouse wrote to Mackrell from the United Service Club, Calcutta, thanking him, and saying he was "going into the Tropical School of Medicine this evening", at which precipitous moment he is lost to history.

Subsequently (Part Two)

To summarize in one short paragraph those seismic events that have spawned thousands of books . . .

After the longest campaign of the Second World War, Britain retook Burma in 1945, with the aid of the Americans and the Chinese. The Allies had learnt the dark art of jungle guerrilla warfare, as exemplified by the Chindit campaigns led by General Orde Wingate, an irregular man in more than just the military sense. Britain again ran the country until independence in 1948. India had gained its independence the year before, whereupon the British administrators left more or less immediately. Many commercial people "stayed on" and the British tea planters of Assam continued to enjoy an expansive lifestyle until the 1960s, when they were driven out en masse by the heavy taxation inflicted on them by Mrs Gandhi.

Between Britain and India, and amid all the turmoil of war and sudden independence, some threads of our story have become tangled or got lost. But leaving aside those mentioned in the previous chapter, and two of our principals (whom we will deal with separately), here is an attempt to account for the personnel we encountered roughly in the order in which they appeared.

We start — as we began the book — with Millar and Leyden, who formed the first of what would turn out to be many advance parties making double marches. Guy Millar is still shown as being a manager of the Kacharigaon Tea Company in the 1951 edition of *Thacker's Indian Directory*. He is gone from it by 1956, but the British Library's intervening copies of the directory are missing. We do know that he seems to have gone to Japan on his way home, because he sailed from there to Britain in 1958. He died in Plymouth in 1970, aged sixty-seven. Regarding his servant . . . on 19 December 1942, the Defence Department of the Government of Burma decreed from Simla that "a double-barrelled breech-loading 12 bore shotgun should be presented, suitably inscribed, to Goal Miri". So now Goal would be able to shoot sambhur with his own gun.

Next, to John Lamb Leyden, Millar's partner in that initial breakaway. He died "peacefully" (i.e. not of tropical fever like his poetic eighteenth-century ancestor) in a nursing home in Rhuddlan, Clwyd, North Wales, in 1988, by which time he was John Leyden CBE. There was a *Times* obituary, and Leyden is also mentioned in the *Dictionary of Welsh Biography* in the entry for a man called David Rees-Williams, 1st Baron Ogmore. In 1948, in the last days of British rule in Burma, Rees-Williams — a lawyer and Labour MP — was involved in negotiating independence terms with the Burmese ethnic minorities, the peoples of the Frontier Areas. A committee was established under Rees-Williams, and he was provided with a secretary, a man called Ledwidge, who did not inspire much confidence in Rees-Williams, largely because he always wore "blue shirt, khaki shorts and pink ankle socks". Williams refused to go into the restless Frontier Areas with a man thus attired, and so the Director of the Frontier Areas agreed to accompany him instead. This was John Lamb Leyden, "whose conduct during the war" had, according to the entry, "been heroic".

After Burmese independence, Leyden turned his attention to Africa, and in 1948 he was in the Africa Department of the Colonial Office in London. In the 1950s, he was a director of the Uganda Development Corporation, a consultant to De Beers, and twice a UK Delegate to the United Nations.

His spaniel, Misa, who had, it transpired, fallen into the gorge of the Noa Dehing river, was found, thin but alive and with three puppies, by a Gurkha soldier, one of those crossed over the Dapha by Mackrell. Nobody reading this will be surprised to hear that (a) we do not know the Gurkha's name and (b) that he picked up Misa and the puppies, and, despite being on the edge of starvation himself, carried them all the way to the Margherita camp, where he handed them over to Tom-Tom Thomson, who arranged for them to be delivered to Leyden.

George Rodger, the *Life* magazine correspondent who had observed the red-hot Buddhas in fallen Rangoon, became the first photographer into Belsen concentration camp in 1945. He later said that he felt ashamed of the way he'd tried to make good compositions out of the stacks of bodies, and he gave up war photography, but continued to travel, often in Africa, with camera in hand. He died in 1995 in Ashford, Kent.

Dr Burgess-Barnett died on 9 April 1944 in Dooars, Bengal, aged fifty-six. It is not known of what cause, or whether his condition was a consequence of what he'd been through two years before.

On Easter Sunday in 1958, the maverick botanist Frank Kingdon-Ward was for once at home in London. He was just back from Sweden, where he'd been lecturing on rhododendrons, and was planning a trip to Vietnam. Meanwhile, he was drinking in a pub in Kensington when he felt a tingling in his right foot. It was not the start of that condition of which we've heard so much, beriberi; it was the start of a fatal heart attack. He was buried in the county of his birth, Cambridgeshire, in the churchyard at Grantchester, the village immortalized in verse by the poet Rupert Brooke, who met the fate — death by insect bite — that Kingdon-Ward constantly flirted with. He was seventy-three.

As for the Commandos . . .

Of the Chaukan trek, Ritchie Gardiner, wielder of the silver propelling pencil, had written, "With some weapons training, especially in the use of Tommy guns and hand grenades, I believe I could hold my own with anyone in jungle fighting." Gardiner *would* fight in the jungle, but as it were vicariously. As Lieutenant Colonel

Gardiner, he became the head of the Burmese section of Force 136, the Special Operations unit that succeeded the Oriental Mission. Force 136 was in the same line of business as Wingate's Chindits, albeit a far smaller force and much less well known. Gardiner ran it from Calcutta, planning guerrilla raids on the Japanese from behind their lines, and relaying intelligence from his men on the ground to the RAF for bombing raids. The backbone of the force was men from the Karen peoples, who hated the Burmese.

In 1985, Ritchie Gardiner wrote an article about his war work, which throws light on the fate of one of his fellow Commandos on the Chaukan trek, namely his colleague at MacGregor's timber merchants, Eric McCrindle:

After the 1942 retreat, most of the Karen operatives [British officers liaising with the Karens] had been overrun by the Japanese invaders, but they had been instructed to hide their weapons and await the eventual return of the British. One British officer, Major Hugh Seagrim, deliberately chose to remain behind, and was hidden from the enemy by the Karens. By then the Japs had occupied the country as far North as Myitkyina. During 1943 an attempt was made to contact Seagrim when two officers, Major Nimmo and Captain McCrindle, were dropped by parachute in the hills near Toungoo. It was one of the first operations by 136, and it was a disaster! The Japs soon got news of their arrival and surrounded their camp, Seagrim managed to

307

escape, but both Nimmo and McCrindle were killed, and the Japs started a wide-spread campaign of torture and murder in their efforts to force the loyal Karens to reveal Seagrim's location.

(Seagrim was later executed by the Japanese having given himself up in order to spare the Karens from further persecution.)

In 1945, Gardiner directed Force 136 in skirmishing attacks that were crucial in the defeat of Japan, and he played a decisive political role, too. In early 1943, the Burmese nationalist leader, Aung San, whose Burma National Army had made common cause with the Japanese, decided that he had exchanged one form of imperialism for another, more sinister one. Aung San wanted to switch sides, but Dorman-Smith and the Burma government-in-exile wanted nothing to do with him. Ritchie Gardiner thought differently. He could see the usefulness of Aung San's forces to the operations he was conducting; therefore, he and others "intervened at the highest political level" to have Dorman-Smith overruled. So Force 136 now had two principal — and mutually antagonistic — allies, the Karens and the Nationalist Burmese.

In early 1945, Aung San's Burma National Army revolted against Japanese rule. Aung San then became the favoured British candidate for leader of independent Burma. Dorman-Smith still harboured grudges against him, but Aung San was the coming man and Dorman-Smith was yesterday's man. Accordingly his return to the Governorship in 1946 was shortlived, and while on sick leave in Britain he was replaced by the British Army general Sir Hubert Rance, who was pro-Aung San. (Dorman-Smith would die in Britain in 1977, aged seventy-eight.)

In July 1947, with Aung San poised to take over as the first leader of independent Burma, he was shot dead in Rangoon on the orders of a rival nationalist, U Saw, who regarded Aung San as a British stooge. Aung San's vision of a united and democratic Burma would be bequeathed to his famous daughter, Aung San Suu Kyi, and it is arguable that none of this would have happened without the intervention of Ritchie Gardiner, which in turn means that none of it would have happened without the earlier intervention — in saving Gardiner's life — of Gyles Mackrell.

After the war, Ritchie Gardiner returned to his seat on the Rangoon City Council and his job at MacGregor's. He left Burma after the company was nationalized in 1948. After the war, he and his wife, Mary, had a daughter and three sons, one of whom became an army general. In the 1950s, Gardiner settled down to life as a farmer in Ayrshire. He died in 1990 when he was picking blackberries and a thorn pricked his finger. The wound turned septic, so it might said that the jungle had its revenge, albeit much belated, for Gardiner's having beaten it in 1942.

It should be added that Gardiner had been awarded the George Medal for saving John Fraser (one of the two men who had escaped Japanese custody) from drowning in the Tilung Hka river, and, as a consequence of *that*, Fraser went on to win the Military

Cross for bravery behind the lines in Burma with the Chindits in 1943. He, too, became a farmer in Scotland — a chicken farmer on land near Dalashiels, where he died in 1965, killed in an accident while teaching his son to drive.

Captain Noel Ernest Boyt died in 1985 in Surrey, aged eighty-three.

Of the young Lieutenant William "Bill" Howe, it is possible to say a little more. When walking through the Chaukan Pass, he had been thirty, the youngest of the Commandos. Twelve years before, when he was eighteen and wondering what to do with his life, he'd been picnicking on some long-gone meadow at Denham in Buckinghamshire with some friends of his parents. They had a three-year-old daughter, Nancy, who turned to Bill and said, "When I grow up, I'm going to marry you." Nobody knew quite what to make of that, but in 1948, when Bill was back in Britain, now a major and the holder of the Military Cross for his work in Burma with both the Chindits and Force 136, they met again at another get-together of the families. Nancy — or Nan — Howe, as she became, recalls, "We took the dog for a walk, and that was it." Bill took Nan back to Burma, and they married in Rangoon Cathedral in 1949. He resumed his rice dealership for a couple of years, then the couple returned to Britain, where Bill ran a chain of garden centres.

Bill and Nan Howe had three children, and adopted two others. He died aged ninety-three in 2005, the cause emphysema triggered by a lifetime of smoking. If the inscribed silver cigarette case that sits on the kitchen table in Nan Howe's eighteenth-century house in rural Hertfordshire has gained an unfortunate association as a result of this, you wouldn't know it. She is extremely engaging, and possessed of great vivacity . . . which the present author managed to check for a moment by saying, "It sounds as though you and Bill had a very happy fifty-six years together." "He was everything," she said after a while, "everything . . ." and tears were in her eyes. She has seven grandchildren and four great grandchildren. Age permitting, they know about Gyles Mackrell. Asked whether these children might have reflected that they wouldn't be around but for him, Nan Howe says, "I don't know but I certainly have."

The five-stone Gurkha Mackrell lifted down from an elephant on Wednesday 10 June died on his way back to Miao, and was buried near the Debang river. It is thought that a dozen of the Gurkhas he'd brought across the Dapha died soon after as a result of their ordeal.

. . . And then there is Captain John "Reg" Wilson, who had caused Mackrell to become uncharacteristically testy when he turned up at the Dapha river on 17 June 1942.

In 1943, Wilson returned to the jungle as a lieutenant colonel, later a colonel, in "V" Force, which operated behind the lines in the vicinity of the Assamese border. Wilson was deep into the blue nonetheless, and went six months without seeing a wheel. He was mentioned in dispatches, and actually received a second cigarette case inscribed in gratitude with the names of some other men he'd helped out — this time American soldiers. In 1945, Reg went back to tea planting, managing a garden of 600 acres. In 1947, he was Secretary of the Assam Branch of the ITA, and holder of the OBE "for services to India". He returned to England in 1955, and fulfilled an ambition he'd long harboured: he became the secretary of a golf club, in fact two of them. This suited his sociable nature and his love of sport.

In 1945, Reg had married a childhood sweetheart, Nancy. There are pictures of them dining in what may be Firpo's restaurant in Calcutta: Nancy looks delighted to have landed such a handsome catch, and she never minded that Reg played golf more or less every day after his return from India. They had no children, but Reg's nephew, Brian Wilson, a retired solicitor who lives in Cornwall, remembers him as "a lovely man, the perfect uncle". Wilson eventually returned to Yorkshire, buying a house just off the front in Scarborough.

It was the cigarettes that did for Wilson as they had Bill Howe, and he died of emphysema in 1967.

We know that Edward Wrixon Rossiter was given vegetable marrow jam after being rescued by Mackrell because of a three-page letter he wrote to his mother in Dublin on his arrival in Calcutta. The letter is dated 30 October 1942, and begins "My dear mother". It provides a brisk, lucid account of his trek, which he regards as having been an unnecessary penance. "It had been, as I think I wrote to you, my intention in case of need to go to China and not India. The road to China was comparatively easy, and from various places in China I could have flown to India." But he had been "ordered by Govt" to proceed to India, and by a route he obviously thought ridiculous. He agreed to go that way only because he'd been given to understand that a rescue party was already on its way to meet any Chaukan evacuees. Of the three-week period of near starvation before the first food drop, he informs his mother (a fitting person to receive such a confidence) "my bowels never moved once".

His companion in the jungle, Sir John Rowland, is not mentioned, and the nearest he comes to talking about Mackrell is "we were extremely fortunate to meet a relief party with elephants". Rowland ate the marrow jam "made just as you made it". Of his arrival at Margherita, he says, "I stayed a very comfortable night, had an excellent meal, fish and a bread pudding, the latter so good that I still remember it, also had a warm bath — the first for four months." To read the letter brings a mounting sense of unease at what is not being said. Then, in the penultimate paragraph, "I don't think there is anything else of interest that I can record. We were just over 4 months on the journey ... no Burmans accompanied us ..."

No Burmans, that is, except his pregnant wife and their half-Burmese son, neither of whom is mentioned in the letter. Well, perhaps this is not an outright fib because Rossiter's wife, Nang Hmat, was a Shan. The news that he had lately married a woman, let us say *from* Burma, might have been all too interesting to his mother, because it was not the first time.

The story of Edward Rossiter's first marriage is told in a book published in 1998 called *A World Overturned* by Maureen Baird-Murray, who was the second daughter of that marriage, the first being a girl called Patricia, who *is* mentioned in the closing salutation of Rossiter's letter to his mother: "best love to yourself and Patricia".

A World Overturned reads like a sub-tropical *Jane Eyre*, and begins with Maureen's description of how Rossiter met her Burmese mother, Khin Nyun. It was 1930, before the time of Rossiter's appearance in the above-mentioned book by Maurice Collis, *Lords of the Sunset*. (Whatever Edward Rossiter's flaws, he has twice appeared in fine books.) In 1930, Rossiter was a probationary Assistant Superintendent of the Burma Frontier Service, and moving between various locations. Maureen Baird-Murray writes, "It was while my father was on tour and passing through Taundwingyi that he stopped at a cheroot factory and caught sight of my mother. Struck by her beauty, he made several attempts to engage her in conversation, but it was to no avail as she kept running away to her mother, for she spoke no English and stood in some awe of the foreigner."

But Edward was "not to be deflected". He negotiated a meeting through the headman of Khin Nyun's village, and they were married in April 1930. On the marriage certificate, Rossiter's age was given as "Full" and Khin Nyun's as "Minor". Maureen was born in Mongyai in the Northern Shan States in April 1933. The first daughter, Patricia, had been born in 1931, and Maureen recounts a fleeting family life in Loilem, in the Southern Shan States, where Edward Rossiter was now based. She recalls him as a tall, stern looking man in khaki shorts, with green eyes, and her mother as

> petite and graceful . . . with a close-fitting jacket or blouse called an eingyi. And there are flowers in her hair, always jasmine. As though in a dream there is sometimes a little playmate with me, flitting in and out like a shadow. Together we look for a ball lost in a bed of nasturtiums and come across some caterpillars, huge, hairy and grotesquely coloured which brush our hands. Terrified, we rush to the house where soothing balm is administered to relieve the stinging.

The shadowy playmate was Patricia. For a while, the two girls were known as Big Baby and Little Baby, because Rossiter hadn't got around to naming them. His sister sent two hairbrushes for the girls from Ireland, and the hairbrushes were marked "Patricia" and "Maureen", so that's what the girls were called.

In late 1934, Edward took his wife to Dublin; she was ill, possibly with uterine cancer, and the intention was to find medical treatment. Khin Nyun was disturbed to be turned away from some hospitals because of the colour of her skin — and yet she had been known as Ma Phyu, or "Miss White", in her home village, where a relatively pale skin was prized.

Maureen remained in Burma, cared for by servants. She recalls looking out from the veranda of the house, seeing a hard-baked track covered in snakes: "Short and white, rather like giant maggots, they hold me mesmerised, unable to move, until someone scoops me up and carries me away."

Patricia stayed in Dublin with Rossiter's mother. He himself struck Maureen as still more stern after their return, and her mother was frequently tearful. The marriage was failing, probably over disagreement about Patricia being left in Ireland. The couple drove Maureen to a convent school at Kalaw in the Southern Shan States, where she was entrusted to the Mother Superior: "The impression was that of a crow, a very old black crow . . ." Here she remained until the end of the war. Her mother and father would visit, but separately, and then both faded away. Khin Nyun died in 1943, after a long illness. Before then, as we know — and Maureen didn't — Edward Rossiter married again, and went through the Chaukan Pass with his new, pregnant, wife and their baby son.

In the convent, Maureen was to some extent protected because the nuns were Italian, and Italy was — at first — on the same side as the Japanese, but still she had many frightening times. She had recurring nightmares about her parents. Those concerning her mother featured the nats, the potentially evil jungle spirits that lived in the giant, gnarled banyan trees. In the ones about her father, he was always in a hospital in

Calcutta, and in fact Edward Wrixon Rossiter died on 4 November 1944 at the Presidency General Hospital in Calcutta. Having survived his jungle trek, he had returned to government work as the District Magistrate and Collector in Noakhali District of Bengal. He had then developed peritonitis — a condition unrelated to the vicissitudes of his trek from Burma — and he may have been too far away from good medical care in the early stages of the affliction. His wife, Nang Hmat, had given birth to the baby she'd been pregnant with in the jungle on 12 December 1942. The baby was a girl: Eileen.

The first that Maureen heard of all this was when, aged eleven, she was called into the Mother Superior's room at the convent to hear the reading of her father's will: "Suddenly my ears caught the words '. . . my wife Nang Mat and her two children . . .' which made me leap up shouting, 'That's a mistake. That's not true. My mother was Khin Nyun.'"

The will stipulated that Maureen was to remain in the convent until she was twenty-one, and an amount of money was bequeathed for this. It was not enough, and so Maureen was dependent on the charity of the nuns, some of whom were more charitable towards her than others. Maureen began to find out about her family. Late in the war, a man who had been a friend of her father's showed her a photograph inscribed on the back in her father's hand, "John Rossiter, aged 2". "He was a beautiful little round-faced boy with rather slanted eyes, like a Shan's, and quite irresistible . . ." It

317

was the boy who'd been carried through the jungle by Nang Hmat, and rescued by Gyles Mackrell.

Maureen was finally rescued from the convent by another friend of her father's, a Mr Ogden, a saintly, avuncular official of the Burmese Civil Service, who had himself escaped the Japanese in 1942 via China. When he came to the convent, he put his arm around Maureen and, his eyes brimming with tears, said over and over again, "So this is poor Eddie's little girl." Mr Ogden's wife escorted Maureen to Dublin, where she joined her sister in the care of her grandmother, and her story, or at least her book, ends. Maureen Baird-Murray died in 2005.

In the summer of 2012, seventy-year-old John Rossiter had a dream of his mother, Nang Hmat, who had died aged eighty-three in 2003. In the dream, she was a young woman, and she was dancing with two elephants. The next morning, John Rossiter received an email from the present author and a telephone conversation ensued. John Rossiter speaks as you would expect: intelligently, a light Burmese accent overlain by more gravelly, British-patrician tones. Of course, he has no memory of being taken through the jungle, but his mother would speak about the trek. She told how she would catch small fish with her hands, fry them and mash them up with rice to feed her son. She was grateful to the man with elephants who'd come to the rescue but couldn't recall his name, it being an unfamiliar Western one. She told John that, before climbing onto the elephant that took her over the Noa

Dehing, she knelt down and made obeisance to it, elephants being sacred to Buddhists.

After her husband's death, Nang Hmat stayed in India for a few years with her children, John and Eileen. She received a fairly generous pension from the British government. She then moved back to Burma, where, in 1951, she married for a second time — to a junior officer in the Burmese army. She had a further five children with him. Her daughter with Edward Rossiter, Eileen, lives in Burma and has four sons and a daughter. John Rossiter left Burma for Australia in the late sixties after attending Mandalay University. He is now retired after a varied career. He and his Burmese wife have four daughters.

Asked whether he thought his father had been a difficult man, John Rossiter paused for a moment. "I heard this story," he said. "In Burma, he'd shot two ducks, and he gave them to members of his staff. They then gave the ducks to two Buddhist monks, and my father was not at all happy about that. He said, 'I shot them for you. Why did you give them away?' But the monks are important in Burma. It was natural that the servants would have given them the ducks. Perhaps my father didn't understand." Another pause. "But he was a very clever man. When he came to Burma, he could speak six or seven languages, and that was not normal." John believes that his father made the best provision he could for his children in his will. "But it was Maureen who suffered most."

There is something provocative about the life of Edward Wrixon Rossiter. It forces any chronicler to

319

become a moral judge. In her book, Maureen Baird-Murray wrote, "My father is long dead now and past all criticism . . ." But she comes down on him pretty hard: "Rightly or wrongly, I have always felt that my mother was deprived of her two children and finally abandoned."

It is tempting to write him off as a cad. But he was perhaps a bohemian in the unlikely guise of a colonial administrator; or just an unconventional man who lived by his own rules. He did marry Khin Nyun and Nang Hmat whereas, as Maureen Baird-Murray writes, "many Europeans did not always legitimise their Burmese or Shan offspring". Maureen's impression was of remoteness rather than cruelty, and there were spasms of kindness. He would give her generous presents, and once caused a sensation in the convent by sending her a near-life-size Shirley Temple doll. It also turned out that he had left her a hundred acres of beautiful countryside in the Shan States.

Would a truly villainous man have counted the apparently saintly Mr Ogden among his close friends? Rossiter also inspired affection in Maurice Collis, author of *Lords of the Sunset*. The hallmark of his behaviour on the jungle trek seems to have been impatience to get out — surely forgivable in the case of a man accompanied by a pregnant wife and a baby son. As we have noted, he hadn't wanted to be "left in the lurch" with his wife and child.

You could say that, in making his own escape from the Tilung Hka camp, Sir John Rowland had done just that. Even without these complications, Rossiter the intellectual and sybarite (the taste for beautiful women, for marrow jam, for curry cooked in the jungle) would not have been Sir John Rowland's idea of "a dashed stout fellow". Put next to each other at a club dinner, they'd have turned aside pretty quickly. In the camp at the Tilung Hka, they had cooperated to the extent of jointly writing the memo to Mackrell, and Sir John had stressed the importance of having powdered milk for baby John. But the plight of the Rossiters ought to have brought out the Sir Galahad in Sir John to a much greater extent than it actually did. At some point, the pair fell out, and in the letter Sir John sent to Mackrell thanking him for rescuing the remainder of his party, he asked, "I wonder what you thought of the Rossiter outfit? No I suppose it isn't fair to ask . . ."

If Mackrell gave an opinion, we don't know what it was. We do know that he wrote to a friend saying that Sir John ought to have "settled all differences" and brought the whole of his party out at once. But that would have been impossible, given the condition of some of the party, at which point it might be as well to vacate the judgement seat.

Late Period Mackrell

Thacker's Indian Directory shows Gyles Mackrell as a director of the firm of Octavius Steel in the volume for 1947–8, where he is listed as the holder of the George Medal as well as the Distinguished Flying Cross. He does not appear in the volume for 1948–9.

In 1946, he had married for the second time — to one Rosalind Agnes Slaughter, daughter of a major in the Royal Army Medical Corps. As a match for Mackrell she sounds about right. The two settled down in the village of Bruisyard in Suffolk, which also seems right for Mackrell. It is a beautiful village, with a Saxon church and pretty houses widely separated by trees and woods, and facing away from one another, as though politely agreeing to differ. The village thereby gives a hint of the ranginess of India, and it is only about fifteen miles from the coast, and the air that the returning planters often sought.

It seems that Rosalind liked India, which Mackrell's first wife possibly did not, and the newly-weds sailed back and forth between Liverpool and Bombay a few times in the late 1940s. This was Mackrell taking his last sips from the cup.

Rosalind may be the attractive, dark-haired woman who appears in some of the as yet uncurated films he shot in India after the war. The woman is often seen fishing in wide rivers, occasionally turning to smile shyly at the camera, but clearly much more interested in catching a fish than posing for the lens. These later films are in colour, and they're gentler than the pre-war films, with fewer dead tigers (there were fewer tigers left to kill) and more meditative studies of flowing rivers, or butterflies on leaves. Mackrell would sometimes show his Indian films, including the footage of his rescues, in the dark and dusty village halls of Suffolk. This might seem egotistical, but he himself hardly ever appears in these films. When he does appear he is on the move, talking to Indian servants, organizing, with his pipe or a pair of glasses in his right hand. He looks like a film director, in fact, creating the jungle scenes — an impression reinforced by the invariable prevalence of canvas-back chairs in the various camps.

In the final pages of *Green Gold*, their analysis of the tea industry and wartime Assam, the Macfarlanes wrote:

When the medals were handed out at the end of the war did it never occur to anyone to ask who had actually won the war? Or why tea garden labourers and Nagas, Abors, Mishmis and others did not dangle MBEs from their chests? Without them and their work, both in the construction of

the road [Tamu-Imphal-Dimapur] and in supply-
ing the troops ... the Japanese would have
reached India.

Mackrell took much the same line about the rescue
he led. He was slightly embarrassed about receiving
the George Medal for gallantry. A number of British
newspapers reported the award: "To the 200 people
whose lives he saved, he will always be known as the
Elephant Man ... to the Company which employs him
he is 'a darned good fellow who has done a magnificent
job'." There are no quotes from Mackrell. One of the
articles features a photograph of him; it is blurred, he
looks overdressed in a suit and tie, and he wears a
wide-brimmed hat pulled low over his face. He had
written to a friend that he was worried people would
think he had gone back into the jungle a second time
specifically in order to earn the medal.

His diary of the rescues concludes with the
following:

I close this diary with the statement that I have
already made to everyone: that too much credit
has been given to me, too little to Millar and
Leyden, not nearly enough to the Rifles, Porters,
Mahouts and Boatmen and that without all the
latter splendid fellows, little or nothing could have
been done in time to save the bulk of this party.

When he showed his films, there was always a closing
caption to the same effect.

324

About three hundred people tried to come through the Chaukan Pass, of whom about forty died in the attempt or as a direct result of it. The dead were mainly Gurkha soldiers or lone Indians whose movements it is impossible at this date to chronicle. All those who survived the trek did so directly or indirectly because of Mackrell. In addition to those mentioned in this book as having been saved by him, he also saved other lone Indians, including a young boy, and a couple of further Europeans, but they were not with the main parties, and it is therefore hard to say exactly where and *how* he rescued them.

Gyles Mackrell died at his house in Bruisyard of a coronary thrombosis on 20 February 1959. He was seventy-one. His wife, Rosalind, died in Ipswich in 1987.

A river runs along the bottom of the garden behind the cottage they had lived in. It is the River Alde. The water is green, and green-shaded with bushes and trees; it is about ten feet wide, and fairly close observation suggests that it *remains* about ten feet even after a week of heavy English rain. As rivers go, the Alde is nothing compared to the Dapha; but it runs on to the sea, as they all do.

ACKNOWLEDGEMENTS

As mentioned at the outset, this book is largely based on the diaries of Gyles Mackrell, Sir John Rowland, Guy Millar, Bill Howe, Ritchie Gardiner and Eric Ivan Milne. I read the latter two at the Asian and African Studies reading room of the British Library, and the Imperial War Museum study room respectively, and I am grateful to the ever-helpful staff in both rooms. The other diaries I read at the Centre of South Asian Studies, at Cambridge University. Much of their Mackrell archive was compiled by Denis Segal, and without his help and encouragement this book could not have been written. I am also grateful to Dr Kevin Greenbank and Dr Annamaria Motrescu of the CSAS.

I am grateful to the following descendants of the "Chaukan Club": Scott Rossiter, John Rossiter, Brian Wilson, Nan Howe. I would like to thank Lynne Thompson of Woburn Safari Park for putting me in touch with Dr Khyne U Mar of the Department of Animal and Plant Sciences at the University of Sheffield, who answered my questions about elephants, and Professor Thomas Dormundy, for speaking to me about opium. Steve Kippax and Ron Bridge were also most helpful about military matters in Upper Burma. Stephen Brown, Caroline Findlay and her family told me about the life of a tea planter in Assam, and Dr Rachel Isba of Liverpool University talked me through some tropical diseases.

I am indebted to the staff of the Norfolk and Suffolk Aviation Museum at Flixton; to Andrew Dennis at the Royal Air Force Museum and Alan Scadding, historian of Epsom College.

I travelled to Kolkata, Assam and Arunachal Pradesh with Travel the Unknown, whose guide in Arunachal, Nyaken Riba Munna, never wearied of my constant questions.

All errors in the text are entirely my responsibility.